THE RISE OF MUSIC
IN THE ANCIENT WORLD
East and West

CURT SACHS

The
RISE of MUSIC
in the
ANCIENT WORLD
East and West

W · W · NORTON & COMPANY · INC · New York

PRINTED IN THE UNITED STATES OF AMERICA
FOR THE PUBLISHERS BY THE VAIL-BALLOU PRESS

9

TO

THE NEW YORK PUBLIC LIBRARY

CONTENTS

LIST OF PLATES

PREFACE

VISIBLE RELICS of the ancient world in East and West are more deeply imprinted on our imagination—the Bible excepted—than the other remnants of antiquity. Our visions crystallize around the pyramids emerging from the yellow sands, the phantastic outlines of stupas and pagodas, the festive porticos of Greek and Roman temples against the sunny sky.

But they are dumb visions.

We do not hear Pharaoh's court musicians, so livingly depicted on the inner walls of tombs and pyramids; we do not know how "they beat the sounding stone and swept the *Ch'in* and *Shê*" in ancient China so the ancestors "came down and visited"; nor can we listen to the singing youths who solemnly ascended to the Parthenon for sacrifice and worship. Music, immaterial and transitory, was scarcely ever recorded in antiquity; and even the handful of notations preserved give hardly an adequate idea of its living sound.

The music of the ancient world has faded away.

But one thing can and shall be kept alive: the narrative of man's titanic struggle to rid music of the limitation that it has in primitive society; to establish its laws firmly on nature; to give it the power and subtlety to express what human beings feel, despair and triumph, love and awe and hope.

This struggle has been much more than just a matter of music. It is the battle that mankind has fought for its rise from primitive conditions, the battle against the inertia of deep-rooted habit and narrow-minded contentment. Individualism has been the outcome, but individualism kept from anarchy by the rigid norms that scholars built on laws of nature.

It is an exciting story, how music has for thousands of years been held in balance between the basic facts that, on the one hand, sound is vibration of matter ruled by mathematical ratios and that, on the other hand, musical art works are immaterial, indeed, irrational. And a still greater fascination is it to see in how many different ways the two counterpoises have been kept equal, and how, with all these differences, races living far apart went similar ways and met in strange, unwitting teams: Greeks and Japanese, Hindus and Arabs, Europeans and North American Indians.

This story has never been told. It is true that an incalculable quantity of incompetent, and a less imposing number of competent, describers have dealt with primitive, Oriental, and Hellenic music. But they have only covered certain musical aspects of single countries, of China or India or Greece. With the exception of the excellent, though short, survey in the one hundred small pages of Robert Lachmann's *Musik des Orients* (Breslau, 1929), not a single book has covered all the different and yet so closely related styles of the Eastern world and the manifold problems they involve. Still less has the music of ancient Greece been organically connected with the Orient—not to speak of the integration of both of them in the universal history of music.

In studying this first attempt at a synthesis, the reader should not forget that this book treats the rise of music in the ancient world and consequently is little concerned with the practice, the conceptions, and the misconceptions of medieval and modern Oriental music, except in so far as they throw light on antiquity. Nor should he forget at what disadvantage such an attempt is placed by the incompleteness of our sources, both musical and extramusical.

Despite its shortcomings, I trust that my endeavor is justified by its results: the more distinct outlines given to primitive styles; the reinterpretation of Oriental systems; answers to a great many open questions in the theory and practice of the Greeks; and an exposure of the roots from which the music of the West has grown.

À vrai dire, toute perception est déjà mémoire. Nous ne percevons, pratiquement, que le passé, le présent pur étant l'insaisissable progrès du passé rongeant l'avenir.

All perception, indeed, already is memory. We perceive nothing, actually, but the past, since the true present is the unseizable progress of the past which gnaws at the future.

HENRI BERGSON, *Matière et Mémoire*

Section One

THE ORIGINS OF MUSIC

1

MUSIC IN EARLY SOCIETY

SCIENCE has not yet dissipated the fog in which earlier centuries saw uncertain shadows of gods or heroes who in a supreme act of creation had "invented" music. Scores of philosophers, economists, and scientists have in the last two hundred years attempted to get to the truth, and yet have not been able to present as much as one acceptable theory, indeed, one uncontested fact.

"Imitation of the animals" was one of them. True, some birds sing; but zoologists, unfortunately, do not classify them as ancestors of man. The mammals, his close relatives, may whine and whistle, bark and roar; the ape, his nearest cousin, grunts and coughs. There is no singing among the next of man's kin.

With deeper insight into nature, Charles Darwin later tried to trace music to mating and alluring the opposite sex; but he was easily contradicted by those who knew how insignificant a role mating played in mankind's early songs. And when Karl Bücher's notorious book, *Arbeit und Rhythmus* (first edition 1896), described music as a means of facilitating teamwork, critics justly objected that rhythmical teamwork did not exist among the most primitive tribes.

A third suggestion has been more widespread and tenacious: music, it reads, descended from spoken language; it was intensified speech. Philosophers developed this theory—Jean Jacques Rousseau in France, Herbert Spencer in England, and numberless others in various countries; and musicians, from the Italian masters of the *stile rappresentativo e recitativo* in 1600 to Richard Wagner, clung to it with remarkable enthusiasm. It would be sterile to repeat and analyze these hundreds of opinions pro and contra.[1] But it matters that all of them, pros as well as contras, were failures because they started from two erroneous presuppositions. In the first place, they took for granted that so complicated a thing as music had grown from one root, which of itself is more than improbable. Music, bound to the motor impulse of our bodies, to the vague images of our minds, and

---

[1] Cf. Carl Stumpf, "Musikpsychologie in England," in *Vierteljahrsschrift für Musikwissenschaft* I (1885), pp. 261–349; Carlos Vega, "Teorias del origen de la música," in *Sintesis* II (1929), pp. 179–90.

to our emotion in all its depth and width, eludes whatever attempt may be made to find any simple formula.

The second mistake was to think of the music and the language familiar to ourselves. Thus, the reader, anxious to learn about the origin of music, was presented with references to Beethoven's Seventh Symphony and Schubert's *Du bist die Ruh* and with samples taken from modern English and French speech melody; indeed, in one edifying case the writer unconsciously betrayed that his conclusions on primeval developments were based on the accent of Leipzig. It is strange and almost unintelligible that men used to scientific methods rested satisfied with guessing and speculating where music was concerned.

Critics have found fault with this theory, less for this reason than because it neglected what they considered the fundamental contrast: that music required well-defined intervals, while the pitches and steps of speech were irrational. But knowledge of the simplest facts in East Asiatic music would have cut short this argument: the melodic style of the Japanese *nō* dramas depends on irrational distances.

This remark is not a confession of faith in Rousseau's and Spencer's theories. It proves, on the contrary, that theories are futile unless solidly based on facts and their historical connection.

Theory, therefore, will be postponed until we have drawn as near as possible to the origin of music. Instead of guessing how things could have happened, we go back to their earliest preserved form. I feel embarrassed to write down such a truism; but unfortunately it is necessary to lay stress on the plain truth that the singsong of Pygmies and Pygmoids stands infinitely closer to the beginnings of music than Beethoven's symphonies and Schubert's lieder.

❈   ❈   ❈

HOWEVER FAR BACK we trace mankind, we fail to see the springing up of music. Even the most primitive tribes are musically beyond the first attempts. To be sure, travelers relate that certain peoples of low civilization, the Brazilian Guaraní, for example, still lead too worried a life to think of music, games, and dances. But such tales are little convincing. The lack of music would more likely be due to cultural shrinkage than to music having not yet been arrived at. In most cases, however, the relater was misled by the silence he found: primitive men are shy with white visitors and often would rather pretend that they do not sing or dance at all than exhibit their rituals and entertainments to untried foreigners; or else music and dances are confined to a few special ceremonies and forbidden for the rest of the year lest they might interfere with the normal course of the people's lives.

Since witnessing the very origin of music is denied to us, we must turn to its earliest observable stage. No prejudice or 'plausibility' will do in seeking it out—the only working hypothesis admissible is that the earliest music must be found among the most primitive peoples, in contradistinction to their languages, which have been lost and replaced by the more highly developed languages of civilized neighbors.[2]

Indeed, all the world's tribes, peoples, and races have lived in continuous intercourse since the very beginning of history; they have met in marriage, trade, and war. In this process of exchange and merger, they discard their weapons, tools, and implements for better ones. But they preserve their ancient songs; for singing, an expression of man's soul and motor impulse, has little to do with the mutable surface of life, and nothing with the struggle for existence. This is why music is one of the steadiest elements in the evolution of mankind. It is so steady that races of a relatively high cultural level—Polynesians and Micronesians, for example—and many groups of European peasants hold onto musical styles of an astonishingly archaic character; indeed, of the most primitive character we know. The general culture of a people, therefore, cannot be judged by its music. But there is hope, inversely, that the music of the most primitive peoples has preserved a very early stage of evolution without the interference of higher civilizations.

❋   ❋   ❋

"THE MOST PRIMITIVE PEOPLES," however, is not quite the correct term. We are fully aware that among the races living today there is no group of men for which a previous lower level of evolution could not be supposed. Nevertheless, some of them represent a stage of social development that we are allowed to call a minimum—especially those who live in the open air without any shelter save a cavern or a quickly made *abri*. As far as music is concerned, such peoples sing but have no instrument of their own.

Music began with singing.

However rudimentary this singing may be, it flows all through primitive man's life. It conveys his poetry, and in rest and peaceful work diverts,

[2] Cf. Curt Sachs, *The History of Musical Instruments,* New York, 1940, pp. 60–2.

elates, and lulls; it gives hypnotic trance to those who heal the sick and strive for luck and life in magic incantation; it keeps awake the dancers' yielding muscles, intoxicates the fighting men, and leads the squaw to ecstasy.

The most primitive tribe I came across were the Kānikas. . . . They told me, "we live among tigers and elephants. We are not afraid. We say 'shoo' to a tiger, and he goes away. . . . The headman of the village picked up his *kokkara* [scraped iron tube], bowed his head over it, and murmured a prayer. Another, likewise, and another followed, scraping them up and down with growing excitement. The leader recited a list of twenty or thirty divinities, in no particular order, repeating some more than others. After five minutes or so one of the men began to tremble violently, and holding his kokkara with both hands straight out in front of him tapped it rhythmically on the ground. The leader was the next to tremble, and his access was more violent. He flung himself about, his *pagrī* fell off and his hair fell down. A third leapt, when the fit was on him, from his sitting posture about three feet into the air, and dropped again into his original cross-legged position. The whole service was interspersed with shouts and yells from individual performers. When it was over the *mantizomenoi* bent forward sobbing vehemently, and took a minute to recover. One felt ashamed to have been merely an interested spectator amongst so much sincerity.[3]

Of this kind are the typical songs that shamans perform when they try to heal their tribesmen. A medicine man's song from the Taulipang in North Brazil may serve as an example. The tiny motif, a rapid triplet on the lower note and a sustained note a semitone higher, is steadily repeated.

Ex. 1. TAULIPANG   *after Hornbostel*

The triplets are breathless; the tempo increases; the notes grow irregular and inexact, and at last the melody, losing its curve and rhythmic organization, trickles away and sinks to a slightly lower level; here, it fades away in a final note which in our example lasts eighteen seconds.[4]

❊   ❊   ❊

[3] A. H. Fox Strangways, *The Music of Hindostan*, Oxford, 1914, pp. 44–5.
[4] Transcribed by Erich M. von Hornbostel, "Musik der Makuschí, Taulipáng und Yekuaná," in Theodor Koch-Grünberg, *Vom Roroima zum Orinoco*, vol. III, Berlin, 1916, p. 436. Cf. also Curt Sachs, *The History of Musical Instruments, op. cit.*, pp. 27 f.

A PRIMITIVE SINGER behaves in different ways. He often refrains from utmost pitch and power; but when frenzy pushes him to extremes, his singing is strained: it is, and is meant to be, unlike the performer's speech voice; it is expected to be superhuman; indeed, supernatural. He ventriloquizes, sings through the nose, cries and yodels,[5] yells and squawks, but is never what modern singers strive to be: at liberty and natural.

Primitive singers even have used special devices to veil their inborn voices —*voice masks* might be an appropriate term. With the Chukchi in Northeastern Siberia, "the shaman uses his drum for modifying his voice, now placing it directly before his mouth, now turning it at an oblique angle." [6] The earliest trumpets were megaphones cut from hollow branches or large canes, into which the player sang; [7] and in one of the most primitive tribes of New Guinea the chieftain always held "a trumpet shell before his mouth when speaking to his people, so his voice had a very hollow sound." [8] The so-called *mirliton,*[9] a small and tightly stretched membrane, never had any other purpose than to give the singer's voice a buzzing nasal timbre.

This is a strong argument against deriving music from speech.

＊　＊　＊

THE MANNER OF SINGING, its timbre, force, and specific animation are often more suggestive and essential than the melodies; cultural and anthropological traits depend on the way things are done rather than on the things themselves. Musicology should be more interested in technique, if this not entirely appropriate word is admitted. Only one style of singing and its anthropological area have been outlined so far: American Indians are

easily to be recognized by a peculiar "emphatic" manner of singing which results from such factors as a certain voice-quality, strong accents on every time-unit, pulsation, slow and constant time. . . . This style prevails among the Indians of both Americas, including the Eskimo (also in Greenland), and among Siberian tribes who are related to the Indians, both somatically and culturally as, e.g., the "Palaeo-Asiatic" Chukchei and the Keto (Ostyak) on the Jenissei River, and among the semi-Tungus Orotchee on the lower Amur River, and in Korean folksongs.[10]

[5] Erich M. von Hornbostel, "Die Entstehung des Jodelns," in *Bericht über den Musikwissenschaftlichen Kongress in Basel 1924,* Leipzig, 1925, pp. 203–10.
[6] Curt Sachs, *The History of Musical Instruments, op. cit.,* p. 34.
[7] *Ibid.,* p. 47.
[8] *Ibid.,* p. 48.
[9] Curt Sachs, *Geist und Werden der Musikinstrumente,* Berlin, 1929, p. 106.
[10] Erich M. von Hornbostel, "Fuegian Songs," in *American Anthropologist,* n.s., vol. 38 (1936), p. 363. Cf. also: George Herzog, "Musical Styles in North America," in *Proceedings*

The anthropological and historical importance of such statements is obvious; and it is a great pity that we have not yet a deeper insight into the physiological aspects of singing styles.

But then the primitive branch of musicology is very recent.

of the Twenty-third International Congress of Americanists, 1928, pp. 455–8; A. O. Väisänen, "Wogulische und Ostjakische Melodien," in *Suomalais-Ugrilaisen Seuran Toimituksia,* LXXIII, Helsinki, 1937.

2

COMPARATIVE MUSICOLOGY AND ITS METHODS

NO SERIOUS RESEARCH work in the field of primitive music was done before the end of the nineteenth century. Occasionally, to be sure, travelers in remote countries had printed native melodies in their books; but the usefulness of such examples was rather limited. The traveler's ear and even more his training in musical dictation were doubtful factors. When I asked Georg Schweinfurth, the first explorer to cross the African continent, how he had found the only song printed in his famous work, he naïvely told me that he had heard the melody somewhere in Africa and, having neither a musical ear nor the training to write notes, he had whistled the few bars to himself every day until, several months later, he had met his brother and made him write down the song he whistled. It is easy to imagine how authentic the script was. Besides, Schweinfurth had bad luck: the song he whistled, far from being native, was a well-known European 'hit' melody handed over to Negroes by some white sailor or factory clerk.

Hence the first rule in studying primitive music: European and other foreign influences must be eliminated beforehand. Music from cosmopolitan seaports, and melodies sung by natives who have lived among white men or done military service, should be left untouched or at least approached with special care. Every song collected should be accompanied by a detailed text, indicating sex, age, and living conditions of the singer.

It is often rather difficult to distinguish between native style and recent importation. In early civilizations certain songs look suspiciously European, but this impression is most often misleading; against the rash assumption of European influence, a careful examination will show that the traits in question are primitive and as such have also survived in European music. Hence a second rule: our critical sense should never be guided by a seeming similarity, nor by any other prejudice. Primitive music must not be compared with the music of white men.

❈   ❈   ❈

THE WHITE MUSICIAN must set aside not only his music but his very self, with all his tradition and prejudice. However mechanically and hence objectively our ear records impressions, our brain reads and interprets them quite subjectively. Western man is never free from adapting foreign melodies to his own musical language; he perforce hears the equal-sized six-fifth tones of Javanese orchestras as alternating seconds and thirds, and he unconsciously squeezes the intricate rhythms of India into the few rhythmic patterns of his own music. In the same spirit, painters of the eighteenth and early nineteenth centuries delineated Indians and Negroes with the classical Greek bodies and gestures that academic training had forced upon them.

To check this weakness, we need an objective, incorruptible control both of other writers' musical transcriptions and of our own attempts to understand and render the music of foreign races. The first device of this kind was the *phonograph* with wax cylinders that Thomas A. Edison invented in 1877. A dozen years later, about 1890, another American, Dr. Walter Fewkes, introduced the new invention into musicology by recording selected songs of the Passamaquoddy and the Zuñi Indians. Dr. Benjamin Gilman of Harvard University marked the very beginning of scientific study in primitive music when he published transcriptions of these records.[11]

As a consequence, archives of phonograph records have been founded in the United States [12] and other countries. They provide suggestions, equipment, and instruction to missionaries and anthropological field workers; they keep and duplicate the recordings and hold them ready for students. These latter, again, are encouraged to transcribe and edit the melodies recorded.

Transcription into Western notation depends not merely on gifted and well-trained ears, but also on a special technique of symbolizing the peculiarities of primitive and Oriental music. After all, our musical notation is in the same position as our alphabet: it serves those familiar with the language, but fails when it tries to convey the pronunciation and speech melody of any other language. Our musical script, exclusively created for modern Occidental music, is unable to record distances different from standardized tones and semitones, or the timbre or the peculiar technique

[11] Benjamin Ives Gilman, "Zuñi Melodies," in *Journal of American Ethnology and Archaeology* I (1891), pp. 63–92. Jesse W. Fewkes, "A Contribution to Passamaquoddy Folklore," in *Journal of American Folklore* III (1890), pp. 257–80. Carl Stumpf, "Phonographierte Indianermelodien," in *Vierteljahrsschrift für Musikwissenschaft* VIII (1892), pp. 127–44; the same in *Sammelbände für Vergleichende Musikwissenschaft* I (1922), pp. 113–26.
[12] George Herzog, "Research in Primitive and Folk Music in the United States," in *American Council of Learned Societies*, bulletin no. 24, April, 1936, pp. 1–96.

of singing which in primitive and Oriental music are often more important than the notes themselves. With this in mind, Dr. Otto Abraham and Dr. Erich M. von Hornbostel attempted in 1909 to develop a method for a more accurate transcription of exotic melodies, with the means of our usual musical script, to be sure, but with certain modifications and additional symbols for vague pitches, phrasing, timbre, grace notes, tempo, etc.[13] Most of these suggestions have become obligatory, notwithstanding some alterations made by later authors.

For instance, we feel today that a series of separate eighth or sixteenth notes confuses the reader, and therefore join the crooks of two, three, or four of them in accordance with the melodic accents, even if the individual notes convey different syllables of the text.

Another system, on the contrary, favored in this country by B. I. Gilman and Frances Densmore, consists in replacing notes and staff lines by curves, round or angular, to represent the general trend of a melody. But this system, useful in certain cases, is neither accurate nor graphic enough to be accepted.[14]

Transcription of exotic melodies by means of Occidental notes and staves is, however—at least psychologically—misleading. It takes our musical system for granted and marks by special signs what then are made to appear as deviations, so that the reader falls victim to the suggestion that exotic scales swerve from the absolute norm. This is a real danger.

❋　❋　❋

THE EQUIPMENT of students in primitive and Oriental music was completed in 1890 by Alexander J. Ellis's system of Cents.

This system has left intact the definition of any individual note as the result of a certain number of vibrations per second: $a = 220$ v., $a' = 440$ v. It cares only for describing distances between two such notes.

The earlier method ignored the conception of distance. While we clearly feel that the distance from B to C is shorter than the distance from A to B, science had no means of adequately defining them and circumvented the difficulty by the complicated process of comparing ratios: if a' has 440 v., b' 495 v., and c'' 528 v., the distance from a' to b' is to the distance from b' to c'' as $\frac{495}{440} : \frac{528}{495}$. Nobody can see from this ratio of ratios that the two

---

[13] Otto Abraham und E. M. von Hornbostel, "Vorschläge für die Transkription exotischer Melodien," in *Sammelbände der Internationalen Musikgesellschaft* XI (1909), pp. 1–25.

[14] Cf. B. I. Gilman, "Hopi Songs," in *Journal of American Ethnology and Archaeology* V (1908).

distances are as 2:1. Still, this is a comparatively simple case. It is more impressive to be presented with the ratio 524288:51441; but who understands that this means the distance called the Pythagorean comma, which amounts to exactly 12 per cent of a tone? It is hardly necessary to give more examples, as, say, that the series 352:404½:464½:534:613:694:809 stands for a scale of seven equal steps, each of which measures seven-eighths of a normal whole tone.

The ingenious system of Cents, on the contrary, describes any distance by one simple number.[15] A Cent is the one-hundredth part of an equal-tempered (piano) semitone: the distance between two notes a semitone apart comes to one hundred, and the octave, consequently, to twelve hundred Cents. The essential standard distances are:

Semitone	100 C.	Fifth	700 C.
Second	200 C.	Minor sixth	800 C.
Minor third	300 C.	Major sixth	900 C.
Major third	400 C.	Minor seventh	1000 C.
Fourth	500 C.	Major seventh	1100 C.
Tritone	600 C.	Octave	1200 C.

Single distances as well as complicated scales become simple and intuitively evident: a second of, say, 180 C. means a distance by 10 per cent smaller than an equal-tempered second; a distance of 220 C. is by 10 per cent larger than a second; and so on.

Cents, it is true, cannot be gathered directly from a voice or a measuring device; they must be calculated from the vibration numbers. This can be done by a simple logarithmic operation.[16] Another method can be substituted if no table of logarithms is available: multiply the difference of the two vibration numbers by 3477 and divide the product by their sum. In case the triple of the larger vibration number exceeds the quadruple of the smaller one, multiply the greater number by three and the smaller number by four before starting the operation indicated above, and you finally add 498 (the perfect, not the equal-tempered fourth) to the result. If, on the contrary, the proportion of the two vibration numbers is greater than two to three, multiply the greater number by two, and the

[15] Alexander J. Ellis, "On the Musical Scales of Various Nations," in *Journal of the Society of Arts*, 1885, March 27 and October 30. In music libraries it will be easier to find its German translation by Erich M. von Hornbostel, in *Sammelbände für Vergleichende Musikwissenschaft* I (1922), pp. 1–75.

[16] Indicated, e.g., in Grove, *Dictionary of Music and Musicians*, II, p. 718 s.v. "Interval."

smaller number by three, before starting the operation indicated above, and you finally add 702 (the perfect fifth) to the result.

❀   ❀   ❀

THE PHONOGRAPH and the Ellis system have added a new branch to the complex of musical sciences. Its German name *Vergleichende Musikwissenschaft* was translated into "Comparative Musicology" and has in this form made its way through Anglo-Saxon countries. But this term is inappropriate and misleading. Music *history,* too, compares national, epochal, and personal styles; indeed, no science can dispense with comparative methods. So-called comparative musicology, furthermore, has left the initial stage of mere comparing, in which its students, thrown back on chance information, tried to outline the stylistic similarities and differences of whatever they were able to pick up—a few songs from one Indian tribe, a melody from Bantu Negroes, a little Japanese collection. In the meantime, systematic research into all continents and archipelagos has piled up so much material that we have become conscious of a gigantic evolution from the embryonic rudiments of early singing to the sophisticated intricacies of Oriental art music. With such vision, comparative musicology has passed into the primitive and Oriental branch of music history.

As late as 1900, the French writer, Judith Gautier, reporting on the primitive and Oriental music at the World's Fair in Paris, had called her book *Les musiques bizarres.* The scientific and historical approach has fostered a new conception of these styles, and the interest in "exotic" music has more and more glided from futile curiosity and snobbish sensation of things strange, remote, and picturesque into realizing how deeply they concern ourselves and our past. The songs of Patagonians, Pygmies, and Bushmen bring home the singing of our own prehistoric ancestors, and primitive tribes all over the world still use types of instruments that the digger's spade has excavated from the tombs of our neolithic forefathers. The Orient has kept alive melodic styles that medieval Europe choked to death under the hold of harmony, and the Middle East still plays the instruments that it gave to the West a thousand years ago.

The primitive and Oriental branch of musicology has become the opening section in the history of our own music.

3

MELODIC STYLES

PRIMITIVE LIFE is almost uniform; despite all differences in temperament, character, and intelligence, every act, be it practical or artistic, is
understood by the fellow tribesmen, much as an animal's act is understood by its fellow creatures. Nor is primitive music the personal idiom,
the individual expression of lonely masters. It says what everyone could
say; it sings the life of a whole tribe; its soul is everyone's soul.

On the Andaman Island in the Gulf of Bengal—to single out a good
example—all natives invent songs

and even the children are instructed in this art. While carving a boat or a bow,
or while rowing, the Andamanese sings his song quietly to himself until he is
satisfied with it and then introduces it at the next dance. His female relatives
must first practice it with the women's chorus; the inventor himself, as song
leader, sings it at the dance, and the women join in the refrain. If the piece is
successful, it is added to his repertory; if not, it is discarded.[17]

The texts themselves are unpretentious and within the reach of everybody in the tribe: "Poio, the son of Mam Golat, wants to know when my
boat will be finished; so I must be as quick about it as possible." No
obvious relation would be required between a text and the occasion on
which it is sung. The Andamanese quite unconcernedly sing hunting or
boatbuilding texts at mourning dances, while they prefer turtle texts for
boys' initiations. The Sakai of Malacca even recite series of river and mountain names instead of connected texts. Indeed, the singers would even use
obscure and disfigured words of some language long forgotten.

❋   ❋   ❋

SINGING in ancient civilizations cannot exist without words, meaningless
as they may be; nor can poetry exist without singing.

It has been a grave error to take this primeval unity of singing and
poetry for the more recent and quite different—indeed opposite—modeling

---

[17] Curt Sachs, *World History of the Dance*, New York, W. W. Norton, 1937, p. 182, after
A. R. Brown, *The Andaman Islanders*, Cambridge, 1922.

of melodies on the natural speech tones of the words.[18] The reverse is true; poetry, in its broadest sense, leads both melody and words away from conversational speech.

Poets disfigure and level the logical accents obligatory to making ourselves understood in talk between man and man; they replace the free, expressive rhythm of spoken phrases by stereotype patterns of long and short or strong and light; they supplant the natural flow of speech by artificial arrangements of words that often wrong the rules of grammar and syntax; they even replace common by uncommon words that none would use in ordinary speech. Art denaturalizes nature in order to raise it to a higher, or at least a different, plane.

And the singers follow: they forcibly avoid the vague, irrational tones of the spoken word. As far as we can look back, the melody of speech, so free and fluent when we talk, has in singing turned into a series of uniform steps between two or three notes on a medium level, if not into a monotonous scansion on one note.

"If not into a monotonous scansion on one note." The conditional form of this sentence is due to the problematic position of one-tone melodies in the evolution of music. Everyone knows such psalmodies. They are at home in the liturgies of most religions all over the world; plain people use them for reciting poems; and they may be heard in schools of the East and the West as vehicles to memorize texts and rules, though nowhere do they reach the magic power they have in the hypnotic trances of Polynesian sitting dancers.

For all that, pure one-tone melodies as independent structures are comparatively rare. Most of them are short sections within more elaborate melodies, either strictly on one note or with cadences falling off or rising on the last syllable. The most fascinating examples of this style are to be found in Celebes and the western Carolina Islands: [19]

Ex. 2. CAROLINA ISLANDS   *after Herzog*

To the evolutionist, one-tone melodies as a first step before the rise of two- and three-tone melodies would almost be too good to be true. But

---

[18] This latter subject has been discussed in G. Herzog, "Speech-Melody and Primitive Music," in *The Musical Quarterly* XX (1934), no. 4.

[19] George Herzog, "Die Musik der Karolinen-Inseln," in *Ergebnisse der Südsee-Expedition 1908–1910*, II B, *Band 9, II. Halbband,* Hamburg, 1936, nos. 21, 32, 34–6, 70, 73, 83, 85, 86, 89, 93, 94, 96, and p. 340.

the question whether a primeval one-tone melody existed in pure form cannot yet be answered; too many primitive peoples are musically unexplored, and even where they have been explored, the recording anthropologist might be suspected of having failed to record one-tone recitations because he did not consider them to be musical performances.

The earliest melodies traceable have two tones.

❀   ❀   ❀

THE TWO-TONE STYLE, in its narrowest form, comprises melodies pendulating between two notes of a medium level, the distance of which is a second or less. And the melodic span is narrow: the themes, or rather motifs, are extremely short and often consist merely in a single step up or downward. There is not always a center of gravity; often, the two notes have equal importance, and if one predominates, it is rather the upper one, while the lower seems to peter out like an accessory note, so that the cadential trend unexpectedly leads to the higher note.

In such a case, we may be allowed to speak of a 'negative melody,' as in geometry we speak of a 'negative curve,' which in the main runs below the zero or 'reference line.' In a melody in which the first and the last notes are approximately at the same pitch, the imaginary connecting line indicates the 'reference'; a melody is *positive* if it runs essentially above this line, and *negative* in the contrary case.

❀   ❀   ❀

ALL RECENT PUBLICATIONS on primitive music have started from the Vedda, a Pygmoid people of primeval hunters in the interior of Ceylon. Still the melodies of these men, though simple, are not rudimentary enough to mark a real beginning. A much simpler style has been found among the Boto-

EX. 3. BOTOCUDOS   *after Strelnikov*

cudos in East Brazil,[20] who again and again repeat the poor group, and among the Pygmoids of the Dèm tribe in Central New Guinea, who per-

---

[20] J. D. Strelnikov, in *Proceedings of the Congress of Americanists 1928*, New York, 1930, p. 801. Unfortunately, the Botocudo songs printed in this paper have not been phonographically recorded.

sistently repeat two notes a fourth apart,[21] an example we mention here despite its larger interval.

Though rudimentary, these melodicles are not orderless. As they are indefinitely repeated, they follow the same principle of co-ordination that children use when they annoy their parents with endless reiterations of a tiny scrap of melody; performers of national epics, in Finland, in Yugoslavia, in Egypt, and probably in Homeric Greece, follow the same principle, and so do modern composers of *bassi ostinati, ciaconnas* and *passacaglias*.[22] Most of these patterns are vehicles for words, not autonomous pieces; they are expected to be heard, not to be listened to.

Primitive poetry, too, is based on repetition—modified repetition, to be sure, since words appeal to the intellect, and no intellect can stand stagnation. A Vedda would solve the problem by verses like these:

> Where the talagoya was roasted and eaten,
>   there blew a wind.
> Where the meminna was roasted and eaten,
>   there blew a wind.
> Where the deer was roasted and eaten,
>   there blew a wind.

The lines are strictly repeated except for the change in the animal's name, so that interest cannot weaken.

As late as the Assyrian civilization, variations were imbedded in otherwise identical lines. One Assyrian prayer begins:

> Father Nannar, lord Anshar, chief of the Gods;
> Father Nannar, lord great Anu, chief of the Gods;
> Father Nannar, lord Sin, chief of the Gods;
> Father Nannar, lord of Ur, chief of the Gods;
> Father Nannar, lord of Egishirgal, chief of the Gods; etc.[23]

Dr. George Herzog quotes a similar poem of the Navaho:

> The first man—you are his child, he is your child;
> The first woman—you are her child, she is your child;
> The water-monster—you are his child, he is your child;
> The black-water horse—you are his child, he is your child

[21] Jaap Kunst, *A Study on Papuan Music*, Weltevreden, 1931, Plate II.

[22] Cf. also Robert Lach, "Das Konstruktionsprinzip der Wiederholung in Musik, Sprache und Literatur," in *Akademie der Wissenschaften in Wien, Phil. Hist. Klasse, Sitzungsberichte*, 201–2, Wien, 1925.

[23] Charles Gordon Cumming, *The Assyrian and Hebrew Hymns of Praise*, New York, 1934, p. 73.

and so on with the Big Black Snake, the Big Blue Snake, the White Corn, the Yellow Corn, the Corn Pollen, the Corn Bug, the Sacred Word. And still another one, in which the line *Where is it going to be hidden?* is sung six times before the strophe ends:

> Big turkey
> His wattle goes up and down.[24]

The Vedda sing such poems at an almost constant absolute pitch and keep the notes clearly apart without any *portamento*. The notes *a* and *b* are a whole tone or somewhat less distant from one another and follow each other in nearly equal beats; the final notes, however, are sustained. Thus the melody pendulates between the two notes in even beats. The time, mostly 4/4, is less strict when the number of syllables changes. Such irregularity seldom embarrasses the singer. If he faces too many additional syllables, he splits some of his notes in order to maintain the rhythmic flow. Falling ligatures of two eighth notes are frequent, but never appear at the end, which is either rising or level. As a rule, the two notes alternate; but once in a while *a* is repeated again and again as in chanting. The poetical, and therefore also the musical, phrases have become longer than those in the melodies of the Botocudos; the thread is spun over eight or ten quarter notes before repetition sets in:

Ex. 4. VEDDA   *after Wertheimer*

A REVOLUTIONARY INNOVATION interfered with mere reiteration on the very level of Veddoid and Patagonian music. The original motif and its first repetition were tied together to form a complex unit by varying the final notes: the first time, the voice rested on a level that kept the listener in suspense; the second time, it shifted to the other level to give a satisfactory ending. To put it technically: the first phrase ended on a semicadence, and the second, on a full cadence. Or, to use the more characteristic terms that the French coined in the Middle Ages: the first ended in an *overt*, the second in a *close*.

24 George Herzog, "Speech-Melody and Primitive Music," *loc. cit.*, pp. 460, 464.

Ex. 5. FUEGIANS   *after Hornbostel*

All these words are more than mere figures of speech. A. H. Fox Strang-ways relates that at Poona in India

the water was drawn from a well by a cattle which marched slowly down an incline, pulling on the ropes, and, as soon as the contents of the skin had been emptied into the trough which carried the water out over a neighboring field, backed again up the incline a little slower still. When the well-man started them down he sang (A) and when, after a minute's interval, he backed them up again, he sang (B). This process went on to my knowledge for three hours, and probably many more.[25]

Ex. 6. POONA, INDIA *after Fox Strangways*

The cadential contrast, reflecting the antithesis of the unfinished and the finished act, finds no better illustration, except in the dance. In many dances all over the world, the performers take a few steps forward, then return to the starting point; they do "a 'static' swinging, which nullifies every movement and every tension, as the contracted muscle is released, or the lung which breathes in the air sends it out again, as in all human ac-tivities and processes the harmonious, satisfying, restful norm is sought"; [26] and the accompanying song as a rule ends on a semicadence with the forward movement, is repeated with the backward movement, and ends on a full cadence when the dancers are in place again.

By uniting two phrases with cadential distinction to form what musical theory calls a *period,* primitive peoples at a very low level of civilization had created the most fertile of musical structure schemes, the *lied* form.

One of the immediate consequences was the discrimination between the two tones: the full-cadential note, being the goal of the melodic trend, took the ascendancy over the half-cadential note, and the later conception of a *final* (to avoid the misleading word tonic) was prepared.

❊   ❊   ❊

[25] A. H. Fox Strangways, *The Music of Hindostan, op. cit.,* pp. 20–1.
[26] Curt Sachs, *World History of the Dance, op. cit.,* pp. 168 f.

TWO-TONE MELODIES often exceed the distance of a second to reach a third or even a fourth. It is hardly necessary to emphasize that the word "third" includes all sizes of this interval, from short minor thirds to full-grown major thirds.

EX. 7. THOMPSON INDIANS   *after Abraham and*
                                 Hornbostel

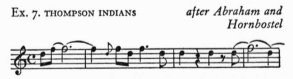

Until recently, students were inclined to presuppose an evolution from smaller to larger distances; primitive man, so they said, is narrow-minded; therefore his melodies are narrow as well and widen only on higher levels of civilization. This is not quite true. Some of the most primitive peoples prefer two-tone melodies with distances larger than a second, and small children in modern Europe, as we shall see, seem to improvise in thirds even before they sing in seconds.

The problem is certainly not a question of development. Were there any evolution, some trace of transition would be found—an occasional third replacing a second, or, inversely, a second replacing a third. The two types are definitely distinct.

Distances in early music depend on motor impulse rather than mentality. It is not without good reason that we speak of steps and strides and leaps, both in melody and in dance; they are similar responses to the same impulse in man and consequently depend on it in a similar way.

In the history of the dance, two elementary motor types stand out with impressive clarity, though they often ran into each other: *closed movement* and *expanded movement*.[27] The expanded dance is characterized by a stronger motor reaction, by wider strides, and even by leaps. The chief characteristic of the closed dance is the fixed center of motion to which the limbs come back again and again.

Roughly speaking, peoples whose dances are somewhat expanded use larger melodic steps than those whose dances are more or less closed.

Singing is indeed an activity of our bodies, or rather, of the totality of our being. It requires almost all the muscles from the stomach to the head and, with the primitive, even the arms and the hands; a native is often not capable of singing if forced to keep his hands still. So narrow is the connection between singing and arm motion that the ancient Egyptians expressed the meaning 'to sing' by the paraphrase 'to play with the hand.'

[27] Curt Sachs, *ibid.*, pp. 24–48.

As an activity of our body, music is inseparable from motor impulse and motor type. It expresses the performer's temperament as gesture, dance, and walking do.

If this holds true for individuals, it also holds true for tribes, peoples, and races, especially under primitive conditions; for the lower the level of animals and men, the less an individual emerges from the general standard.

This is why peoples of the same cultural level have melodies that differ only in their widths.

❋   ❋   ❋

A FIRST EVOLUTION carried the number of tones from two to three. Such growth did not at once produce actual three-tone melodies. For a long time, musical imagination clung to simple two-tone melodies even after the recognition of a third tone and kept the original nucleus intact and easily perceptible. Tradition has been amazingly persistent. The new tone generally ventures to appear only toward the end of the phrase, when the nucleus has been well established; it is rarely introduced at the start in some initial stress of temperament, and in such cases disappears almost immediately for the benefit of tradition. Conforming to the terminology of grammar, we call the additional tone an *affix* if it joins the nucleus outside and, if necessary, more specifically a *suprafix* if it is added above, and an *infrafix* if it is added below. A filler within a third, a fourth, or a fifth, is called an *infix*.

Simple additions may be classified in the following way:

1) *Second plus second* appears in the very earliest styles of the Vedda and the Fuegian Yamana. Our example is a song of the Colombian Uitoto Indians:

Ex. 8. UITOTO INDIANS, COLOMBIA   *after Bose*

2) *Second plus third*. Again, an example of the Uitoto:

Ex. 9. UITOTO INDIANS   *after Bose*

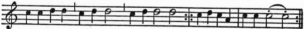

3) *Second plus fourth*. Song from Buka, Solomon Archipelago:

Ex. 10. SOLOMON ISLANDS   *after Frizzi*

4) *Third plus second*. Song from East New Guinea:

Ex. 11. EAST NEW GUINEA   *after Marius Schneider*

5) *Third plus third*. Bakongo Negroes:

Ex. 12. BAKONGO NEGROES

after Marius Schneider

6) *Third plus fourth*. No example.

7) *Third plus* filling note (*infix*). Example from North New Guinea:

Ex. 13. NEW GUINEA   *after Marius Schneider*

8) *Fourth plus second*. Song from Buka, Solomon Archipelago:

Ex. 14. SOLOMON ISLANDS

9) *Fourth plus third*. Playing song of the Bellacula Indians:

Ex. 15. BELLACULA INDIANS   *after Stumpf*

10) *Fourth plus fourth*. Men's duet from Tibet:

Ex. 16. TIBET
transcribed by Curt Sachs

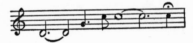

11) *Fourth plus infix.* Brazilian Yecuaná Indians:

Ex. 17. YECUANÁ INDIANS   *after Hornbostel*

✻   ✻   ✻

FOUR-TONE MELODIES almost eschew classification. Infixes, suprafixes, infra-fixes in all possible arrangements and sizes result in a kaleidoscopic infinity of variations and permutations.

Only what we might call *chains* captivate our interest: the conjunction of either thirds or fourths. A chain of thirds is the following song of a Papuan in Northwest New Guinea:[28]

Ex. 18. PAPUA   *after Jaap Kunst*

A truly extraordinary chain of no less than five consecutive thirds occurs in the music of the Zuñi Indians:[29]

Ex. 19. ZUÑI INDIANS   *after Stumpf*

The Hopi sometimes sing in chains of fourths:[30]

Ex. 20. HOPI INDIANS   *after Stumpf*

Although such melodies attain an imposing range and emotional power, they lack organization. The singer jumps from note to note without sub-ordinating his notes to higher units. He is not able to pass from addition to integration.

It is seldom possible to decide whether the amplification of the original two-tone nucleus has been brought about by the natural evolution of either

[28] Jaap Kunst, *A Study on Papuan Music, op. cit.*, p. 63*a*.
[29] Carl Stumpf, "Phonographierte Indianermelodien," *loc. cit.*, p. 123.
[30] Benjamin Ives Gilman, "Hopi Songs," *loc. cit.*

the individual or the tribe, or else by special influences, sexual or foreign. If singing is indeed an activity of all our being, *sex,* the strongest difference between human beings, must have a decisive influence on musical styles.

Once more, a reference to dancing may be helpful. Dancers as well as athletes know the fundamental fact that, as a rule, men strive for release, for strong motion forward and upward; women, particularly in lower civilizations, keep to the ground and move inward rather than away from their torsos. Compared with masculine motion, a woman's movements are diminutive; the bold leap shrinks to a standing on tiptoe, and the large stride degenerates to timid tripping. Even where theme and occasion call for departing from the usual restriction, a woman's dance will almost certainly relapse to a closed form.

In the same way, the sexes also form opposite singing styles. Boat songs of the Eskimo rest on the third; when women row, they sing the same melodies with infixes to avoid the masculine stride.

Woman's influence was particularly strong in shaping the structure of melody. Robert Lachmann drew attention to the symmetry in those forms of singing in which women, whatever their cultural level, accompany their work or lull their babies, and he compared German children's songs with lullabies of Vedda mothers and with melodies trilled by Indian women while rasping roots. His juxtaposition is so striking that we reiterate it here; [31] only, we give the German song the slightly different form in which we ourselves have known it:

Ex. 21. MACUSÍ INDIANS *after Hornbostel, first line*
LATERNE, LATERNE, *second line*

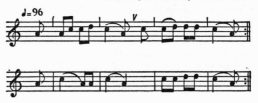

Out of innumerable examples, the Northwest Siberian Voguls may be cited; the men do almost all the singing, and their melodies are free in rhythm and structure; the women, confined to the so-called Songs of Fate, arrange their melodies in simple and regular verses: [32]

[31] Robert Lachmann, "Musik der aussereuropäischen Natur- und Kulturvölker," p. 8, in Ernst Bücken, *Handbuch der Musikwissenschaft* (1929).
[32] Cf. A. O. Väisänen, "Wogulische und Ostjakische Melodien," *loc. cit.,* p. 3.

Ex. 22. VOGULS, SIBERIA   *after Väisänen*

Both examples confirm an innate tendency in women to neatly regulate the songs of domestic life also, in doing which they—and their daughters —have faithfully preserved archaic traits that the men have lost.

❀   ❀   ❀

THE MUSIC CONSIDERED SO FAR is *logogenic* or word-born. Men who sing on two notes actually use the melody as a mere vehicle for words and keep it in a medium pitch and a medium power of voice without emotional stress.

But this is only one side of primitive music. For music is often due to an irresistible stimulus that releases the singer's utmost possibilities. Not yet able to shape such *pathogenic* music in premeditated longer patterns with the climax in the middle or at the end, he lends all his force and passion to the beginning of his song and lets the melody drop as his vocal cords slacken, often passing to a scarcely audible pianissimo. For 'loud' and 'high-pitched' 'soft' and 'low-pitched' are closely associated—so closely that the Romance languages have only one word for either couple of qualities: *alta vox* and *bassa vox*.

In their most emotional and least musical form, descending melodies recall savage shouts of joy or rage, and may have come from such unbridled outbursts. Spasmodically, the voice sets in as high as possible with its maximum strength and tension, or leaps up, from a medium note as a springboard, and then comes down by steps or jumps, until it fades away in its lowest register. The details differ; the Kubu in Sumatra glide almost as along a ramp, the Indians rumble down a flight of stairs, the Negroes nimbly walk from step to step. The crudest form of this kind of melody, midway between brutish shouts and human singing, seems to be preserved on the islands of Torres Straits between Australia and New Guinea. On phonograph records from Central and South Australia, the same style appears less stirring, tamer, more musical, less like shouting; the range is an octave, and the intervals of the fourth and fifth begin to stand out as landings; the melody is often definitely pentatonic without semitones.[33]

[33] E. Harold Davies, "Aboriginal Songs of Central and Southern Australia," in *Oceania* II (1932), pp. 454–67.

Describing these Australian songs (which I have not heard), E. H. Davies uses the words "frenzy" and "spasm," and speaks of "ecstatic leaps to the upper octave," of "steadily growing excitement," and of "a good deal of passion." This is fully confirmed by the few records from Australia that I have been able to study. In Africa, again, the jerking, nervous character is almost lost; the melody is generally reduced to the range of a sixth, and its steps are well graduated.

The most impressive stair melodies are sung by North American Indians (cf. Ex. 19). Some of them are of an overwhelming power, full of pathos and passion, and still reserved and solemn. Many of them rush down in thirds; in others, the fourth is the structural interval.

❀   ❀   ❀

MELOGENIC MUSIC represents the wide middle area between the extremes of logogenic and pathogenic music. Here, cantillation of words has sufficiently increased in range to reflect the pathos of the words themselves in a flexible melodic line; and the unbridled outbursts of the pathogenic style have so much settled down that the words become distinguishable and important; with the greater range, too, the level trend of the logogenic style yields to the same drift downward that characterizes the pathogenic style. This tendency appears as early as the stage of three-tone melodies: the author tested several hundreds of them and found that only 8 per cent ended on the upper note, 39 per cent on the middle note, and 53 per cent on the lower note. Later on, with four-tone melodies, the level trend has become a rare exception.

On this melogenic level, both the logogenic and the pathogenic styles are submitted to *structural intervals* as a second principle of organization.

The logogenic melodies of two tones, and even of three tones, discussed in the first part of this section, were still beyond the notion of rational intervals. The singer, starting from an initial note, arbitrarily proceeded to the following one, much as a walker takes his steps without conforming to any rule except his ease. The space in between is a *distance,* which, though measurable in terms of Cents, does not obey any law of nature.

Most melodies exceeding the range of a third, on the contrary, tend to crystallize in certain *intervals;* that is, spaces determined by simple proportions of vibration numbers: the ratio 2:1, which we call the octave; 3:2, the fifth; 4:3, the fourth. The strongest magnetic power emanates from the fourth—for physiological reasons it is here best to accept without attempting discretionary explanations.

Such magnetic attraction appears in two forms. In the first, notes approximately and unintentionally a fourth or a fifth apart spontaneously adjust themselves (with more or less success): four notes in a series of irrational seconds submit to the law of the fourth and become a *tetrachord;* a melody of two consecutive thirds, the outer notes of which originally refer only to their common middle note but not to one another, turns into a *pentachord,* shaped to the size of a perfect fifth.

The other form of magnetic attraction is the continual return to either boundary note, which leads as a natural consequence to the organization of melody in main and accessory notes. And here the way opens into the complex structures of more highly civilized peoples.

Yet despite crossing and interbreeding, the original dualism of the two opposite principles still shows even in the complexity of higher musical styles. Their innate traits appear as in Mendel's hares and dandelions— in the logogenic tidiness of Chinese music and the fiery pathos of Balinese orchestras, in the strictness of Indian dance songs and the unbridled freedom of Mongolian laments. They are even more apparent in the characteristically European alternation between static, 'classical,' styles, which have the accent on form and balance, and dynamic styles with 'endless melody' and unbound passion.

❋ ❋
❋

IT IS AN EXCITING EXPERIENCE to learn that the earliest known stage of music reappears in the babble songs of small children in European countries. For once the ontogenetic law is fully confirmed: the individual summarizes the evolution of mankind. We owe to Dr. Heinz Werner, the psychologist formerly of Vienna, a methodical series of phonograph recordings [34] that clearly reflect the results of our own research.

The earliest attempts of children less than three years old resulted in one-tone litanies and in melodies of two notes a narrow minor third apart, the lower of which was stressed and frequently repeated. At the age of three, children produced melodies of two notes a second apart, and even three-tone melodies. Children three and a half years old sang in descending tetrachords. Continual repetition was the only form.

[34] Heinz Werner, "Die melodische Erfindung im frühen Kindesalter," in *Akademie der Wissenschaften,* Vienna, *Philol.-Historische Klasse, Sitzungsberichte* CLXXXII (1917), no. 4.

Ex. 23. EUROPEAN CHILDREN'S BABBLE   *after Heinz Werner*

These children could not be suspected to have been influenced by a single trait of our own music. Thus we cannot but accept their babbling as an ontogenetic reiteration of man's earliest music and, inversely, conclude that the music of today's most primitive peoples is indeed the first music that ever existed.

4

RHYTHM AND INSTRUMENTAL MUSIC

RHYTHM, both as meter and as time, is still undeveloped in two- and three-tone cantillation. The unit is a verse, or a small melodic phrase; and what we should call a piece is merely an arbitrary, unorganized series of such verses. Attention does not carry beyond the individual verse; it ends with the verse and reawakens only after a few irrational moments of respite. If the following verse has either more or fewer syllables than the preceding one, the singer would conform his rhythm to the new situation, again without much regard for the whole, which actually does not exist as an organism.

When a Western musician transcribes such songs into his own notation, he has the unpleasant choice between two ways. One is to be inaccurate and fake a tidy one-two one-two where irregularity is typical. The other way is pedantically to count beats not destined to be counted, to change dizzily from five-four to seven-eight and six-eight (beats), suggesting a Stravinskylike exuberance—or chaos. And all this is against the naïve spirit of primitive cantillation, which is neither regular nor sophisticated nor anarchic.

The best way is to avoid any indication of time and, in general, bar lines also; to neglect infinitesimal vacillations; and to represent irrational rests by fermatas rather than by precise symbols.

❀ ❀ ❀

CO-ORDINATION OF SINGING and bodily rhythm is weak on the level of the Vedda and certain Patagonian tribes. But in the next higher stratum, most singing submits to the imperious rhythmic impulse of our body, which in its simplest form is an endless unorganized sequence of equal beats. Once man has become fully conscious of the comfort and stimulus that regular pulsation gives he seldom sings without clapping his hands, stamping the ground, or slapping his abdomen, chest, legs or buttocks.[35]

[35] Cf. Curt Sachs, *World History of the Dance, op. cit.,* p. 25, and *The History of Musical Instruments, op. cit.,* p. 26.

In order to intensify the effect, primitive singers reached for extrabodily devices—rattles, clappers, stamping tubes, and drums—and therewith created instrumental music.

There can be no doubt that a species of rhythmic intoxication is the natural consequence of this vigorous clashing; and many cases have been experienced by the writer where an unwillingness to sing on the part of the native has been overcome by beating together a couple of boomerangs. In every case it acts as a stimulant to greater enthusiasm.[36]

Man does not listen to the seconds of his watch or the jolts of his railway car without decomposing the endless sequence of uniform beats into an alternation of accented and unaccented beats. He organizes the monotonous *tick-tick* into a sequence of *tick-tock* periods and would even unite every two of these periods to form a higher unit: *tick-a tock-a.*

Tick-a tock-a is more than just strong-weak/strong-weak. It is also light-weak/dark-weak, or bright-weak/dull-weak. Two new elements have entered rhythmic organization: timbre and pitch.

Instruments meet this end. Stamping tubes appear in pairs of different length, width, and pitch; and drums are alternately struck with a stick or with the bare hand, or on the skin and the solid rim, or on two differently pitched heads. In Samoa, to give this one concrete example, "the beating of the mats sounds like the trotting of a horse, the first tone struck with both sticks, the second with only one—a trochaic pattern." [37]

The resulting rhythmic pattern is in the first place due to the player's personal motor impulse under the special conditions of mood and ability, age and sex, race and profession. But the shape and playing position of the instrument are important factors, too; the player acts in a different way according as his drum is big or small, vertical or horizontal, suspended or in hobby-horse position; or as from a drum he passes to a xylophone or any other instrument. All of them deflect the personal motor impulse into a special technique that determines the realization of musical ideas. Musicians know this principle from modern Occidental practice: an organist improvises in another style than a flutist or a violinist; every instrument creates its own style.[38]

❊   ❊   ❊

---

[36] E. Harold Davies, "Aboriginal Songs of Central and Southern Australia," *loc. cit.*, p. 459.
[37] Curt Sachs, *World History of the Dance, op. cit.*, p. 38.
[38] Cf. Curt Sachs, "Prolegomena zu einer Geschichte der Instrumentalmusik," in *Zeitschrift für Vergleichende Musikwissenschaft* I (1933), pp. 55–8; *The History of Musical Instruments, op. cit.*, pp. 26, 37, 52.

VOCAL AND INSTRUMENTAL styles never mix and seldom converge in early music. Melody is not an abstract conception to be indiscriminately realized either on instruments or with human voices. Indeed, no instrument was expected to play cantabile, as in the modern West. Playing some instrument and singing poetic texts were separate acts which did not melt into one; nor had any primitive language a word for our collective term 'music' which comprises both of them.[39]

So it happened that the voice, detached from the rigid beats of the drum, would soar above in unrestricted freedom; even that voice and drum would without any inconvenience follow two entirely different rhythms—a remarkable lack of conformity which might or might not prove a particularly strong feeling. Such feeling certainly is very strong with some of the aboriginal tribes in India, where cross rhythm develops into actual polyrhythmy: Fox Strangways heard a couple of natives of the Pānan tribe of India alternately singing in a four-beat meter while a frame drum and a triangle divided the beats respectively as 3–2–3 and 2–2–4 eighths:

Ex. 24. INDIA
after Fox Strangways

In another Pānan tune, the four beats of the voices were met by the clapping hands on the second, third, and fourth beat, and by a drum on the second, fourth, fifth, seventh, and eighth eighths, the second being syncopated.[40]

Apparent syncopation (though not the example just described) is often explained by the fact that some peoples [41] understand the lifting phase in drum beating as accented tension, and the beating, that is, dropping, phase as unaccented relaxation. This results in lifting the arm on the first and third beats and striking on the second and fourth beats—an interesting syncopation in Western terminology but a quite straight and natural rhythm to North American Indians and other races. Such a conception, however, is only possible in countries where drums as a rule are struck with sticks so that the arms are lifted with a certain emphasis. With hand-beaten drums, and even in a rapid succession of beats with a light stick, the lifting phase is practically insignificant and the sound appears on what we call the down beat.

[39] Robert Lachmann, "Zur aussereuropäischen Mehrstimmigkeit," in *Kongressbericht der Beethoven-Zentenarfeier*, Wien, 1927, p. 324.
[40] A. H. Fox Strangways, *The Music of Hindostan, op. cit.*, p. 34.
[41] Curt Sachs, *The History of Musical Instruments, op. cit.*, p. 215.

5

POLYPHONY

THE DEEP-ROOTED PREJUDICE that harmony and polyphony have been a prerogative of the medieval and modern West does not hold water. Not one of the continents, not one of the archipelagos between them lacks rudimentary forms of polyphony.

When in musical ensembles several singers or players perform the same melody, either successively or simultaneously, they actually claim the freedom of varying in minor details. Repetition of a melody seldom agrees with its first form, nor do the voices of a chorus or the parts of an accompanied song agree with each other. Each participant realizes the melodic idea according to personal taste and ability and to the special conditions of voices and instruments. Nobody minds the chance collisions that result from such discrepancies, nor is anybody concerned about their consonant, or at least pregnant, character. An agile singer would dissolve his partner's slower third steps into faster seconds; a less-well-trained voice might replace excessively high or low notes by some bend or break; a premature need for breath would cause an unseasonable cadence among the parts.

Such *heterophony* is certainly a rather negative form of co-operation—neither polyphonic nor harmonic, and seemingly anarchic. But the willful maladjustment often has a particular charm, and nobody who has heard the rich and colorful symphonies of Balinese and Javanese orchestras can deny that, once more, freedom is a good root of organization in art.

❀ ❀ ❀

PARALLEL OCTAVES are the unavoidable result of any vocal co-operation of the two sexes and therefore practiced by peoples on the lowest level of civilization. Unnoticed at first, they later became intentional. On the same level, for instance in the Tierra del Fuego and on the Andaman Islands, the difference in pitch, either of the two sexes or else of higher and lower voices of the same sex, causes parallel fourths and fifths, which occur even in our own civilization against the singers' will.

Still, the difference in pitch of human voices does not—or at least not exclusively—account for parallels: in parallel thirds and seconds the two voices have practically the same range; neither do they occur spontaneously nor unintentionally; nor is it permissible to speak of European influence.

Parallel thirds, particularly frequent in Bantu Africa, have often been ascribed to the influence of white settlers. But this will not do: certain ancient stringed instruments of Africa are tuned in consecutive thirds.[42] An even more important argument is the fact that parallel thirds occur in the western Carolina Islands as a frequent feature of one of man's earliest musical styles. The following example was sung on the island of Mogemoc by a chorus of eleven boys and girls. It consists of only three notes a second

Ex. 25. CAROLINA ISLANDS   *after Herzog*

apart, both in the upper and in the accompanying part, so that there is practically no difference in natural ranges. Similar as the two parts are, they differ in one point: while the upper part comprises two whole tones, the lower consists of a tone and a semitone. The resulting parallel has alternately major and minor thirds—just as in Africa and Europe.

Is there, on a very low level, a root of our harmonic feeling, however embryonic and doomed to stunt?

The most startling kind of parallel is the seconds of the western Carolina and Admiralty archipelagos.[43] The melodies submitted to this continuous

Ex. 26. CAROLINA ISLANDS   *after Herzog*

friction are themselves confined to two or three notes. This probably explains why the accompanying voice follows at such close distance; here as elsewhere, the greater or lesser closeness of the melody appears frequently to determine the space between the two voice parts.

A strange counterpart is the singing of parallel seconds in Istria at the

---

[42] Curt Sachs, *Les Instruments de Musique de Madagascar,* Paris, 1938, p. 53.
[43] George Herzog, "Die Musik der Karolinen-Inseln," *loc. cit.,* p. 274.

northern end of the Adriatic Sea,[44] which once more shows how little difference there is between primitive and European folk music.

❊   ❊   ❊

DRONES, that is, sustained notes above or below the melody, have comparatively little importance in primitive music. A Kubu woman will keep up a high note while a man sings a simple melody on two notes,[45] but such continuous drones are rare. In most cases drones are intermittent, as a regular or as an irregular feature. On a phonograph record from the island Lifou in the Loyalty Archipelago, made for the Archives de la Parole in Paris, the author found a short motif of three eighth notes, leading to a sustained *f'*, repeated some twenty times by a chorus of women, while either a single woman or a second chorus seconded by setting a *g'*

Ex. 27. LIFOU, LOYALTY ISLANDS
transcribed by Curt Sachs

against the *f'*. Irregular drones are more frequent; a solo or a chorus accompanying the melody will repeat some note while the other part ascends or descends, or it may rest on a kind of pause. In such instances the drone technique seems not fully out of the stage in which accident is becoming intent. It is definitely a case of heterophony.

Antiphony resulted from both forms of repetition, from seriation and from symmetry. It was almost unavoidable when in working crews or dance groups two singing choruses, or two soloists, or a soloist and a chorus, alternated, either to escape from exhaustion or to stress the dualism in some pantomime—combat, wooing, the struggle of the light and the dark moon.[46]

Whenever continual antiphony without the regulating force of dance movements becomes too wearisome, impatient singers start repeating be-

[44] Ludwig Kuba, "Einiges über das istro-dalmatinische Lied," in *III. Kongress der Internationalen Musikgesellschaft 1909, Bericht*, pp. 271–6. Cf. also: Ernst Th. Ferand, "The 'Howling in Seconds' of the Lombards," in *The Musical Quarterly* XXV (1939), pp. 313–24.

[45] Cf. Erich M. von Hornbostel, "Ueber die Musik der Kubu," in B. Hagen, *Die Orang-Kubu auf Sumatra*, Frankfurt a.M. 1908, no. 25, and in *Sammelbände für Vergleichende Musikwissenschaft* I (1922), p. 374.

[46] Curt Sachs, *World History of the Dance, op. cit.*, pp. 155 ff. Nguyen Van Huyen, *Les Chants alternés des garçons et des filles en Annam*, Paris, 1934.

fore the others have properly finished their section. The result is a *canon*
in unison.

It was one of the greatest among the numerous surprises of modern
musicology to find that the Samoans, indeed the primitive Semang in the
jungles of Malaka and certain Pygmies in the swampy forests between
the sources of the Nile and the Congo, had developed overlapping antiphony into regular canon singing:

Ex. 28. MONI, MALACCA   *after Kolinski*

The Malayan island of Flores has even developed an elaborate combination of a canon, sung by women, on a double drone of tonic and fifth that
the men sustain. A more impressive warning against the prejudice of a
'plausible' evolution from simple to complicated forms could hardly be
given.

Ex. 29. FLORES   *after Jaap Kunst*

[6]

CONCLUSION

DESPITE SUCH ACHIEVEMENTS, primitive music depends on routine and instinct rather than on knowledge. This is its weakness that nothing can overcome—not even the erroneous claim that from lack of intellectual rules primitive singers will express themselves with greater emotional intensity than educated musicians who filter their inspiration through the tightly knitted cloth of rules and technique. The claim is unfounded, because in primitive society the inertia of tradition, more inexorable than any well-devised system could be, dooms every spontaneous gesture.

Notwithstanding this narrowness, one fact has safeguarded development and perfection: the primordial dualism of two different, indeed opposed, singing styles.

One of these, derived from cantillation, was *logogenic* or 'word-born.' Its melodies started with only two notes—which imposed a *level* course —and were spun out in the continual repetition of a tiny motif. Evolution was *additive;* more and more notes at certain *distances* crystallized around the nucleus of two notes. But even before this evolution set in, primitives on the lowest level of civilization developed endless repetition to the symmetry of answering phrases, anticipated the tonic, invented the sequence, and progressed to part singing and even to strictly canonic imitation.

The other style, derived from passion and motor impulse, was *pathogenic.* Its melodies started from orderless cataracts, which imposed a *downward* trend. Evolution was *divisive:* octaves were marked out, and after them, fifths and fourths, which, instead of a nucleus, formed a solid skeleton.

All higher, *melogenic,* forms arose from mingling and mixing the two basic styles; and this process, again, was inevitable, since intermarriage, trade, and warfare counteracted tribal seclusion and omnipotent tradition. It stimulated comparison and, with comparison, discrimination of features common and divergent, acceptable and inacceptable. In this continual readjustment, insight, knowledge, and scientific method had to counterbalance the evil powers of inertia and imitation.

But the mental process necessary to pass from imitative reproduction to conscious creation was beyond the capacity of primitive men. It eventually developed when the conflux of tribes, somewhere in Asia, had produced the phenomenon that we call 'high civilization.' Due to science, which was the essential achievement of high civilization, music progressed to an art. It needed mathematicians to express in numbers and ratios what seemed to exist in an imaginary, unmeasurable space of its own. And since analysis and synthesis were functions of logic, it needed philosophy to disintegrate melody into single notes and intervals and to rearrange the elements in ever new configurations.

Section Two

THE WESTERN ORIENT

1

HIGH CIVILIZATION AND MUSIC

N AÏVE THINKING, prone to personalize evolutions that never depended on single persons, and more interested in scenic acts of creation than in slow and simple developments, has ascribed the art of music to gods and deified mortals. The Bible makes Adah's son Jubal "the father of all such as handle the lyre and pipe." The Egyptian god of wisdom, Thot, was credited with having written forty-two books, including treatises on astronomy, acoustics, and music, and was also said to have invented the lyre; Apollo, the Greek god of wisdom, light, and order, played the kithara; while the Indian inventor of the harp, Narada, borne by the goddess of learning, speech, and eloquence, was a lawgiver and astronomer.

Only the Chinese make an exception; the origins of music, they say, lie far back, nor did one single generation create it.[1]

One fact stands out clearly, for all this mythical vagueness: the high civilizations carried music from the stage of carefree instinct and narrow-minded tradition to the level of law and logic, of measure and reckoning. Music was called to rank with the liberal arts long before Alexandrine scholars linked it into the classical quadrivium with arithmetic, geometry, and astronomy, and the trivium of grammar, rhetoric, and dialectic.

Science, indeed, based the theory and practice of music on numbers and ratios, on analysis and synthesis, to help in building and tuning instruments, in defining consonance and dissonance, in systematizing melody and rhythm, in devising musical scripts.

Subject to numbers, ratios, and measure, music was given a place among the phenomena of nature and shared the various forms of interest that they aroused in man. It was submitted to the speculations of astrology and mysticism, but also to sober experimentation and reckoning; it was claimed by magicians, by philosophers, by physicists. And in this manysidedness, music permeated science, medicine, education, and even politics, for good and evil.

Law and logic, measure and reckoning are features of "high civilization," not of primitive life. They require thought beyond the nearest needs of

---

[1] Lü Pu-we, *Shi Ch'un Ts'iu* (3rd century B.C.), ed. Richard Wilhelm, p. 66.

existence, and the aptitude for subsuming particular notions under general conceptions.

A mental evolution of this kind coincided with, and probably was conditioned by, the organized society typical of high civilizations: by division of labor and, hence, of classes and even castes, in which a trade passed from father to son. Artisans, peasants, and workmen retained what later was to be called folksong, that is, the heritage of the past with additions in a traditional style and in any case naïve. The upper class, on the contrary, which paid for its musical entertainments, fostered the gradual formation of a class of well-trained professional singers and players able to provide both amusement and splendor and anxious to outdo their competitors. Still higher was the standing of musicians attached to the temples where they were in contact with priests trained in mathematics, astronomy, and philosophy, who assisted them in establishing a sound theoretical basis of music.

The typical gradation according to knowledge and ignorance, to art and folk music, is particularly well reflected by the old social order of Japanese musicians.

In this order, the highly respected first class comprised educated musicians who read notation and specialized in spiritual music. The second class, formed by players of secular music who were uneducated and, the koto players excepted, ignorant of notation, was on the social level of the merchants. The third class embraced the blind singers for folk music. Women were, as a rule, confined to the lowest style of music, and this was true also for girls of society who performed music as a part of their education. The better classes of musicians insisted on their privilege of playing music of a higher style; certain pieces were the property of a certain guild and must not be played by other people. The guild masters were entitled to confer honors on the members—on koto players, for instance, the curious right of tuning their first string an octave lower.[2]

* * *

THE OLDEST RECORDS of organized and systematized music are Sumerian and Egyptian. Sumerian texts written in the third millennium B.C. frequently speak of ecclesiastic music; in the great temple of Ningirsu at Lagash, a special officer was responsible for the choir, and another for the training of

---

[2] Mueller, "Einige Notizen über die japanische Musik," in *Mittheilungen der Deutschen Gesellschaft für die Natur- und Völkerkunde Ostasiens* I (1876), Heft 6, pp. 13, 14.

several classes of singers and players, both male and female. The guilds of temple singers at last became a

learned community, a kind of college, which studied and edited the official liturgical literature. They appear to have interested themselves in astronomy also. We have . . . a considerable liturgical literature of the learned college attached to the temple of Bel in Babylon. . . . We may also suppose that great centers like the temple of Shamash in Sippar, of Enlil in Nippur, of Innini at Erech, each possessed its musical school.[8]

Folk music, on the contrary, had little to do with the scenes depicted by official painters and sculptors; still, it appears now and then on Babylonian plaques and seals of the second and third millenniums B.C., with shepherds piping or strumming the long-necked lute to the great pleasure of their dogs and sheep.

In its unique continuity, Jewish history gives the best picture of typical evolution in the field of music. The times of the patriarchs and the judges represent a primitive stage in which emotion and free effusion shaped the patterns of melody and rhythm. Everyone in Israel sang, and playing the lyre and the timbrel was a common achievement, at least among women. When the children of Israel had walked upon dry land in the midst of the sea and were saved out of the hand of the Egyptians, Moses himself struck up the holy tune to glorify the Lord, and all men joined the leader's voice, while the women responded antiphonally; and Saul and David, on their return from the victorious battle against the Philistines, were welcomed by women singing, playing, and dancing. Music exulted and wailed; it was both whipped up and soothing; it caused ecstasy to take possession of the seers, and it drove the demons from Saul's soul, when David the shepherd played for him. No mention is ever made of professional musicians.

Musical life changed in the days of David and Solomon (c. 1000 B.C.). Foreign instruments appeared all of a sudden, just as they had appeared in Egypt after 1500 B.C.: harps, zithers, oboes, cymbals, sistra; and Pharaoh's daughter, whom King Solomon took to wife, is, in the Talmudic tractate *Shabbat 56b,* said to have had "a thousand kinds of musical instruments" in her dowry (which in view of the 329 female musicians that Alexander the Great's general captured in the retinue of King Darius of Persia is not necessarily exaggerated).

Israel began at that time to develop professional musicians and even a musical organization. The kings and queens supported court musicians of both sexes, and the 42,360 persons, who after the Babylonian Exile re-

[8] Stephen Langdon, *Babylonian Liturgies,* Paris, 1913, pp. xii, xix

turned to the Holy Land, had with them some seven thousand servants and some two hundred "singing men and singing women," doubtless attached to the households of rich people.[4]

King David founded the earliest official body of musicians when he bade Chenaniah, the chief of the Levites, "to appoint their brethren the singers, with instruments of music, harps and lyres and cymbals of both forms. So the Levites appointed Heman the son of Joel; and of his brethren, Asaph the son of Berechiah" and others. Three singers struck the cymbals; eight played harps; and six, lyres. "And Chenaniah, chief of the Levites, was over the song; he was master in the song, because he was skilful." [5] When they had brought in the ark of the covenant "and set it in the midst of the tent that David had pitched for it, he appointed certain of the Levites to minister before the ark of the Lord, the God of Israel: Asaph the chief" with cymbals, nine Levites with lyres and harps, and two priests with trumpets.[6]

This number was greatly increased when King David made preparations for the Temple before his death. "David and the captains of the host separated for the service certain of the sons of Asaph, and of Heman, and of Jeduthun, who should prophesy with harps, with lyres, and with cymbals; and the number of them that did the work according to their service was . . . two hundred fourscore and eight," divided into twenty-four classes "under the hands of their fathers." [7]

When at last King Solomon was able to consecrate the Temple, "the Levites who were the singers, all of them, even Asaph, Heman, Jeduthun, and their sons and their brethren, arrayed in fine linen, with cymbals and harps and lyres, stood at the east of the altar, and with them a hundred and twenty priests sounding with trumpets—it came even to pass, when the trumpeters and singers were as one, to make one sound to be heard in praising and thanking the Lord; and when they lifted up their voice with the trumpets and cymbals and stringed instruments, and praised the Lord: 'for He is good, for His mercy endureth for ever'; that then the house was filled with a cloud, even the house of the Lord, so that the priests could not stand to minister by reason of the cloud; for the glory of the Lord filled the house of God." [8]

❀ ❀ ❀

[4] 200: Ezra 2: 65; 245: Neh. 7: 67.
[5] I Chron. 15:16–22.
[6] *Ibid.*, 16: 4–6.
[7] *Ibid.*, 25.
[8] II Chron. 5:12–14.

DAILY TEMPLE MUSIC at the beginning of the Common Era is well described in the Talmudian tractate *Tamid* 7: 3–4. We learn how the priests spent the night, got up early in the morning, washed, and followed their various duties, such as baking cakes, cleaning the altar, bringing up faggots, setting the altar fire in order, and slaughtering the victim. This done, they pronounced benedictions and recited the "Hearken Israel," the Ten Commandments, and two passages from the Pentateuch—Deut. 11: 13–21 and Numbers 15: 37–41. Lastly the high priest, solemnly received by the priests, came in to give the blessing and to burn the offerings.

They gave him the wine for the drink-offering, and the Prefect stood by each horn of the Altar with a towel in his hand, and two priests stood at the table of the fat pieces with two silver trumpets in their hands. They blew a prolonged, a quavering, and a prolonged blast. Then they came and stood by Ben Arza, the one on his right and the other on his left. When he stooped and poured out the drink-offering the Prefect waved the towel and Ben Arza clashed the cymbal and the Levites broke forth into singing. When they reached a break in the singing they blew upon the trumpets and the people prostrated themselves; at every break there was a blowing of the trumpet and at every blowing of the trumpet a prostration. This was the rite of the Daily Whole-offering in the service of the House of our God. May it be his will that it shall be built up again, speedily, in our days. Amen.

This was the singing which the Levites used to sing in the Temple. On the first day they sang Psalm 24; on the second day they sang Psalm 48; on the third day they sang Psalm 82; on the fourth day they sang Psalm 94; on the fifth day they sang Psalm 81; on the sixth day they sang Psalm 93; on Sabbath they sang Psalm 92, a Psalm, a song for the day that shall be all Sabbath and rest in the life everlasting.

The chorus had a minimum of twelve singers, all men between thirty and fifty years of age, who, according to a none too clear passage in the Talmudian Gmara Hullin, apparently had spent five years of training. Boys of the Levites were allowed to join the choir in order "to add sweetness to the singing." In the last time of the Temple, Hygros ben Levi was "over the singing." [9] He had a great name as a brilliant virtuoso; but his memory "was kept in dishonor" because he would not teach his special art to any other.[10]

The orchestra at that time consisted of harps from two to six in number; lyres, nine or more; oboes, from two to twelve; and one pair of cymbals.[11]

[9] Talmudian tractate *Shekalim* 5:1.
[10] Tractate *Yoma* 3:11.
[11] Tractate *Arakhin* 2: 3.

The First Temple, which was destroyed in 586 B.C., had no oboes in its service.

❊   ❊   ❊

LIKE ISRAEL, EGYPT had experienced a sudden importation of foreign instruments and musicians. When she had conquered the southwest of Asia in the eighteenth century B.C., the subjugated kings had sent tributes of dancing and singing girls with their strange instruments. In one of the paintings in King Amenophis the Fourth's residence at Amarna they can be seen busy practicing in a special harem that the painter has left unroofed like a doll's house.

At that time, Egyptian music (to quote my *History of Musical Instruments*) "underwent a decisive change. Nearly all the ancient instruments were discarded. The standing harp became larger and abounded in strings; several new types of harps were introduced; shrill oboes replaced the softer flutes; lyres, lutes, and crackling drums were introduced from Asia. A new kind of noisy, stimulating music seems to have taken possession of the Egyptians."

Indeed, in no higher civilization is music self-supporting; its very life depends on a sound balance of constancy and variation, of tradition and receptivity. Constancy is safeguarded by the inertia of folksong and the conscious conservatism of liturgical music. Variation is due to the claims of less naïve circles of society. Easily palled by artists who steadfastly "harp on the same string," they foster variation and innovation, for good and for evil.

The manure of novelty, both decomposing and fertilizing, has been conveyed in the cultivation of music chiefly by foreigners.

The importance of alien musicians will appear in every chapter of this book. Historians of medieval and modern music would have to stress the creative role of monastic monks from Ireland in Carlovingian Germany; of Burgundian masters in the Italian Renaissance; of Italian composers all over Europe in the seventeenth century; of the Florentine Lully as creator of the French national opera; of Handel's music in England; and of German music all over the world in the nineteenth century.

Not *all* over the world; to be more exact, only over the world of Western civilization. Wide as this internationalism may be, it is confined to a certain type of mental atmosphere, an atmosphere that does not depend on 'race,' with skull indexes and pigments, but on a cultural assimilation through agelong intercourse in warfare, trade, and intermarriage.

This shows with particular impressiveness in the region discussed in this section as the Western Orient. The Egyptians borrowed from Mesopotamia and Syria; the Jews from the Phoenicians; the Greeks from Crete and Asia Minor and again Phoenicia; the harp, the lyre, the double oboe, the hand-beaten frame drum were played in Egypt, Palestine, Phoenicia, Syria, Babylonia, Asia Minor, Greece, and Italy. The Egyptians called lyres and drums by their Semitic names, and the harp by a term related to the Sumerian word for bow; the Greeks used the same Sumerian noun to designate the long-necked lute and adopted a Phoenician word for the harp; they gave the epithets Lydian, Phrygian, Phoenician to the various types of pipes; indeed, they had not a single Hellenic term for their instruments and repeatedly attributed them to either Crete or Asia. The Phoenician and Egyptian instruments in Israel have already been mentioned.

Instruments imply music: hand-beaten drums attest refined rhythm; double oboes, drone technique; fretted lutes, autonomous instrumental melody. Moreover, instruments have traveled with their music or, to put it more concretely, a Javanese would play European pieces, not native gamelan parts, on a Dutch trombone; nor would a Cameroon Negro pluck the Marseillaise on his little *zanza*.

As to melodies, Herodotus relates that among other curious songs the Egyptians have one that is also sung in Phoenicia, Cyprus, and elsewhere. "It is much similar to the one that the Greeks sing as the Linos song. I wonder whence they got the Linos song, just as I am surprised at a great many things in Egypt." [12]

This cosmopolitan reciprocity, however, is confined to the eastern Mediterranean, Arabia, Mesopotamia, and Iran. For three or four thousand years of ancient history these countries formed a musical province in which agelong intercourse had created that mutual understanding that admitted musical exchange. When antiquity had come to an end, this same area, united under the sway of Islam, continued to form a well-defined province. Even the loss of Greece failed to make any actual change in its frontiers, since the Mohammedans built their music on the fundamentals of Greek theory.

[12] Herodotus, *Historiarum Liber* II, ch. 79.

2

MUSICAL SYSTEMS IN GENERAL

NO DIRECT SOURCE betrays the nature of Hebrew melodies; nor do we know how the temple singers of Egypt and Babylonia regulated their chants. But one thing is certain: wherever a higher class of musicians was distinguished from a lower class, wherever the official standard of an educational center was respected, there must have been law and logic, measure and reckoning. Heman, Asaph, Jeduthun, and their brethren in Mesopotamia and Egypt had the concepts 'correct' and 'faulty' music; they had a *system*.

A system, generally speaking, is the specific organization of the musical space taken up by a certain national or epochal style.

All such systems are based on one presystematic trend: to make, as Herbert A. Popley nicely puts it, "a bold plunge for the nearest consonant note." In other words, to crystallize in one or more of the three consonant intervals innate in man: the fourth, the fifth, and the octave. They give the melodic range a solid skeleton, they stress certain notes for rest or suspension and, in short, prevent the melody from getting lost in anarchy.

Where the fourth acts as the shaping force, the melody settles down in a *tetrachord* (from Greek *tetra* "four"), that is, a melodic organism spanning a fourth, usually with one or two filling notes of minor importance. Wider melodies with the fourth as regulating force crystallize in two such tetrachords linked together, or 'conjunct,' so that the note of contact belongs to either tetrachord and acts as the center and main note of the heptad (series of seven).

Where, on the other hand, the fifth acts as the shaping force, the melody settles down in a *pentachord* (from *pente* "five"), that is, a melodic organism spanning a fifth, usually with one, two, or three filling notes of minor importance and the main stress on the lower terminal note.

A pentachordal melody, wide enough in range, settles down almost never in two pentachords but, under the imperious sway of the octave, in the conjunction of a pentachord and a tetrachord. This most perfect form of organized scale unites the three innate intervals: octave, fifth, and fourth.

A pentachord and a tetrachord can be combined in two ways, which

PLATE I. Egyptian players with double oboe, lute, and harp. Mural from the tomb of Nakht near Thebes, 15th century B.C. After Davies.

PLATE 2A. Egyptian flutist, clarinettist, harpist, and four singers. Relief from a tomb of the Fifth Dynasty, c. 2700 B.C. After Maspero.

PLATE 2B. Egyptian flutist, harpist, and singer. Relief from a tomb of the Twelfth Dynasty, 2000–1800 B.C. After Blackman.

imply different, indeed opposite, kinds of equilibrium: modern musicians, trained to the dualism of medieval church modes in their contrapuntal studies, know them as *authentic* and *plagal*. In the so-called authentic combination, the tetrachord is above; the lowest note of the octave becomes *finalis* or tonic, and the fifth, in the middle of the octave, *confinalis* or dominant. In the plagal combination, the pentachord is above; the final or tonic shifts to the middle, a fourth from the lower end, which becomes a kind of confinal or dominant. Medieval Dorian, for example, has the two combinations:

Authentic: *D E F G A B C D*
Plagal: *A B C D E F G A*

But this terminology is misleading and should be avoided. It suggests that the authentic condition is primary, and the plagal condition secondary. Actually, it is the other way around. In India, the 'plagal' *sa-grāma* is the standard form; the 'authentic' *ma-grāma* was less important and even disappeared in the sixteenth century. In Greece, the primary scales Dorian, Phrygian, Lydian had the 'plagal,' and the *hypo* scales the 'authentic' form.

Instead, I propose two terms which, though not Greek and impressive, denote the actual difference in the simplest way without conflicting with any specific traits that the scales might have in various countries and systems:

Fifth on top for 'plagal'
Fourth on top for 'authentic'

All notes ever used are supposed to find a definite place within these two basic forms of skeletons. This, however, turns out to be both impossible and undesirable. It is impossible because singers, following their changing whim and motor impulse, fill the fourth and the fifth with practically an infinite number of different steps that nobody could or would codify. It is undesirable because the usefulness of most instruments depends on the greatest possible versatility of few notes; that is, on selection and standardization.

To achieve these two goals, the organization devolving on any system is threefold: as to *pitch,* to *genus,* and to *mode.*

The pitches may here be left out as self-evident and irrelevant.

A genus roughly denotes the (essentially) indivisible sizes of steps used. The *diatonic* or *heptatonic* genus rests on whole tones and semitones; the recent *twelve-tone* genus, on semitones; the *pentatonic* genus, on minor thirds and whole tones, or major thirds and semitones or similar combinations. The exact sizes of these steps were fixed in what the Greeks called "shades"; the Western *diatonic* genus, for example, has existed both in numberless forms of unequal temperament and in the equal temperament of modern keyboards.

❁   ❁   ❁

A GENUS yields, not yet an actual scale, but at least a steady circle of steps without a definite pitch, without a start, and without an end. The seemingly great number of possibilities in arranging, say, the two minor thirds and three whole tones in a pentatonic octave is practically limited to two: no more than a single third finds room in a tetrachord—either above the whole tone or below it. Both possibilities are obviously latent in any set of tones that—like the black keys of our piano—separates two minor thirds by alternately two and three whole tones:

$$\cdots \; C\sharp \; \overline{D\sharp \; F\sharp} \; \overline{G\sharp \; A\sharp} \; \underbrace{C\sharp \; D\sharp} \cdots$$

The upper brackets indicate the tetrachords with the third below the whole tone, and the lower brackets those with the third above it.

Even if the tetrachords are conjunct instead of disjunct, the resulting heptads appear in the given set of tones:

$$\cdots \; \overline{C\sharp \; D\sharp \; F\sharp} \; \underbrace{G\sharp \; B} \cdots$$

In a similar way, the simple case of the diatonic or heptatonic genus on disjunct tetrachords implies one semitone in each tetrachord, either at the upper end, or in the middle, or at the lower end. In each of these three cases, the semitones are alternately a fourth and a fifth apart, so that the two semitones (as they are on the white keys of our piano) are alternately separated by two and three seconds. This is another set without a definite pitch, without a start, and without an end, which again may appropriately be represented by a circle.

❁   ❁   ❁

MODE originates when, as mathematicians would say, the circle is made a 'cycle' and a 'clock.' The cycle—a circle with an arrow on it—denotes the direction in which the circle devolves, clockwise or counterclockwise: a mode is either ascending or descending, at least in its prevalent trend. The clock is a circle on which one point is emphasized as the initial one: a mode is brought about by selecting one note of the endless set as a starter or tonic. All modes of a genus, though following the same sequence of notes, differ in the tonal relations within the octave, since their tonics differ: each mode implies a structure and tension of its own.

This is best illustrated by the *church tones,* familiar to all musicians from their contrapuntal studies. The white keys of the piano provide the endless set of the diatonic genus; the so-called *Dorian tone* starts on *D* and has a tone (*T*) as the first step and a semitone (*s*) as the second step; the so-called *Phrygian tone* starts on *E* and has a semitone as the first step and a whole tone as the second step; the *Lydian tone* starts on *F* and begins with three whole tones; the *Mixolydian tone* starts on *G* and begins with two whole tones:

Dorian   T s T T T s T
Phrygian   s T T T s T T
Lydian   T T T s T T s
Mixolydian   T T s T T s T

In other words, the various modes of a genus appear as a series of octaves (sometimes heptads) in which the lowest note of each in turn is removed, to be readded at the head of the next, or vice versa. For the sake of concise terminology, we shall call these transformations *toptail inversions.*

It is almost needless to emphasize that such shifting and inverting is a theoretical expedient rather than of the essence of mode. Mode did not come from any dead abstraction but from living melodies which under the stress of varying emotion and varying tradition crystallized, now in major now in minor intervals.

From this standpoint, it is much better to project all modes of a genus into the same octave (or octave and a half, when authentic and plagal modes have to be demonstrated), so that they are all on the same pitch and have the same tonic. At any rate, modal juxtaposition has been accomplished in most cases through such projection, particularly by players, who because of the limited number of notes available on most instruments were forced to co-ordinate all usual scales on the basis of as many common notes as possible.

❀   ❀   ❀

MODAL INTERPRETATION is generally easy. A melody that reaches or even exceeds the range of an octave will clearly show whether the pentachord is above or below the tetrachord. When the structure has been determined as either plagal or authentic, mode becomes evident in the tetrachord.

The three modal tetrachords are usually given the Greek names Dorian, Phrygian, and Lydian. But this is not commendable: since they were mistakenly confused in the Middle Ages, we are never certain whether "Dorian" is meant to denote a tetrachord with the semitone at the bottom, as in Greece, or with the semitone in the middle, as in medieval music. In this book, we consistently eliminate the medieval misnomers, but for safety's sake add the epithet "Greek" whenever we use the terms Dorian, Phrygian, or Lydian.

It is more desirable, however, to do without the Greek terms and, instead, to project the modal tetrachords and octaves on the white keys of the piano, and define them by the English or else the Italian names of the notes, which in non-Latin countries have a connotation of relative rather than of absolute position in the scale. Lydian, both Greek and medieval, and major are Do modes, since the semitone is at the top, no matter whether Do starts an ascending tetrachord Do Re Mi Fa or a descending tetrachord Do Si La Sol; similarly, Greek Phrygian and medieval Dorian are Re modes; Greek Dorian and medieval Phrygian are Mi modes.

The remaining four symbols, Fa, Sol, La, Si, do not link similar tetrachords and therefore cannot denote tetrachords without danger of mistake. Instead, they well denote the terminals of species of octaves: Greek Hypolydian and medieval Lydian are Fa modes; Greek Hypophrygian and medieval Mixolydian, Sol modes; Greek Hypodorian and medieval Aeolian, La modes; Greek Mixolydian is a Si mode.

If the melody does not reach the range of an octave, analysis is often more difficult though for the most part feasible. The main point is to distinguish well between tetrachordal and pentachordal melodies. In pentachordal structures, the third is more stressed than the fourth.

*   *   *

SCALES, indispensable in demonstrating systems, align step by step the notes used in a certain mode at a certain pitch. In a narrower sense, they extend from the ground tone of a mode to its octave and include all fully qualified notes, but leave out those due to casual alteration or modulation.

Modern musicians take the scale for granted. They have gone through the analytical process of mincing live melodies into dead notes, out of which any desired number of new melodies can be put together. And they accept as self-evident that these notes are held ready to be seen and used in a graduated arrangement from low to high. They do not realize how abstract and sophisticated such arrangement is unless, doing research work in exotic or folk music, they try to make the person they are testing sing or play the scale on which, according to Occidental inference, his melodies are based. A man untouched by Western civilization will take a good time to understand what he is asked for, and even so he will be at a loss to construct a scale. "It is curious," writes Fox Strangways of a Kadar musician that he met in India, "how hard it was to arrive at the scale of this instrument. The player had no notion of playing a single note by itself, he invariably played a grace with it, showing how inseparable grace is from even the simplest phrase. It was achieved at last by my holding down his fingers in succession." [13]

To the naïve player, a note cut from its melodic context has no more reality than a hair pulled out of an animal's pelt.

❀   ❀   ❀

HIGH AND LOW, on the contrary, have been common metaphors all over the world. For they stem from motor impulse and reflex. To this day, the Hindus who learn to chant the Vedas closely adapt the position of the head to the three tones of cantillation; they give it a normal position for the middle tone *udātta*, incline it for the lower note *anudātta*, and raise it for the higher note *svarita*.[14]

The association of the spacial categories "high" and "low" with qualities of sound has nevertheless not been consistent.

The West calls sounds with more vibrations per second *higher*: sopranos are "high" voices and bases, "low" voices, and the vowel *i* is "higher" than *u*.

The ancient Greeks did just the opposite: the lowest note of the scale was *hypatē*, "high," and the highest note, *nētē*, "low."

The Semitic Orient has exactly the same terminology as the Greeks. The Jewish grammarians called *o* and *u*, the darkest vowels, *hagbāhāh*, from *gavoah* "high"; in Hebrew script, a dot *below* a consonant means that it is followed by the vowel *i*, a dot above, that it is followed by *o*. In a similar way, the Arabs write a short, slanting dash below the consonant to indicate that it is followed by *i*, and above it, to indicate that it is followed by *a*; they call the *i* group of vowels *hafḏ* or "sinking," and a man's voice

13 A. H. Fox Strangways, *op. cit.*, p. 32.
14 Martin Haug, "Ueber das Wesen und den Werth des wedischen Accents," in *Abhandlungen der k. Bayrischen Akademie der Wissenschaften* (1873), p. 20.

"high," while a woman's voice is low.[15] Accordingly, they 'jump up' to a lower note and call the lowest lute string *bamm*, the "highest."

The original meaning of "higher" in the Semitic Orient was not, as with us, "at a greater altitude," but "taller," just as the tallest organ pipes produce the lowest notes.

[16] Eberhard Hommel, *Untersuchungen zur hebräischen Lautlehre*, Leipzig, 1917, p. 47.

3

MUSIC IN THE ANCIENT WESTERN ORIENT

ON EGYPTIAN RELIEFS and wall paintings, music is mostly connected with those scenes from the lives of the great that the artists depicted in order to facilitate, indeed to enforce, bliss and pleasure in a future existence of the dead. Banquets with singers, players, and dancers are much more frequent than temple ceremonies. (Pl. 2, p. 65)

Kneeling players are plucking harps or blowing pipes while singers face them, the better to keep in time. Many of these ensembles are actual orchestras; there are seven harps and seven flutes on one relief. This is an important evidence, since it suggests that in many scenes the artists might have reduced the number of participants merely for lack of space. Instrumental orchestras without singers were obviously not yet considered.[16]

The chief instruments were the often beautifully adorned harps. We would not know how they were tuned but for a single word hidden in an unexpected source: the *Jewish Antiquities* of Flavius Josephus, the Jewish historian and general, written in the first century A.D., defines the Egyptian harp as an *órganon trígonon enarmónion* used by temple harpists (*hieropsaltai*). The Egyptian harp was enharmonic.

There cannot be any mistake about this evidence. The enharmonic tetrachord, as the Greeks understood it, was composed of a *major* third and a semitone; the term also applied to a heptad of two such tetrachords conjunct, or to an octave of two such tetrachords disjunct. The later Greeks split the semitone into two microtones; but this 'modern' variety is not to be considered in Egyptian temples with their tradition of thousands of years. The scale, consequently, was approximately $A\ F\ E\ C\ B$, with as much repetition through higher and lower octaves as the number of strings permitted.

This means that the Egyptians had the same archaic scale that the Greeks honored as their earliest genus and that the Japanese have preserved to this day.

Lyres, which appeared in Egypt in the fifteenth century B.C., that is,

---

[16] Cf. the illustrations in Curt Sachs, *Die Musikinstrumente des alten Aegyptens*, Berlin, 1921, Figs. 73, 76, 109, 109a, 112.

about twelve or thirteen hundred years later than harps first appeared on reliefs, can hardly be supposed to have followed the same genus of major third pentatonics. Josephus expressly called the harps enharmonic, but not all Egyptian music. And then, all lyres of which we know the tuning, in ancient Greece as well as in modern Nubia and Ethiopia, have been submitted to the usual pentatonic genus with minor thirds, that is, *E G A B D,* continued upward and downward according to the number of strings.

We can hardly be mistaken in assuming that the ancient harpists and lyre players had to rely on their ears just as modern harp, piano, and organ tuners do; and the ear applies three innate standards: the intervals of the octave, the fifth, and the fourth. Starting from a medium note that fitted the singer's voice, the ancient players must have tuned another string to its fifth; a fourth backward from this provided the second above the starting tone. Or else the other way around: a fourth up and a fifth back would provide the second below the starting tone. This is not just a circle or cycle of fifths, as it is generally called, but a continual, indeed cyclic, rising and falling, as $_c{}^g{}_d{}^a$. The *cyclic principle* might be an appropriate short name for it, or, less formally, the *up-and-down principle.*

❊ ❊ ❊

Pipes followed a different law. Their scales depended on the relative position of fingerholes; and this arrangement was determined by measures of length, that is, by feet and inches, not by any musical conception. I have discussed the general principle in my *History of Musical Instruments* [17] and need not repeat its details except for the main point: "Most pipes, both primitive and highly developed, have equidistant fingerholes. But this equidistance absolutely precludes the production of any musical scale unless the notes are corrected by the size of the holes, the breath, the fingering, or some special device."

Unfortunately, the many pipes depicted on Egyptian and Sumerian art works are not distinct enough to yield exact measurements. But a sufficient number of real pipes have been excavated in both countries to give us this information:

Of two Egyptian flutes from a tomb of the Middle Kingdom (c. 2000 B.C.) [18] one, though cut without much care, 95 cm. long, has fingerholes

---

[17] *Op. cit.,* pp. 181 f.
[18] J. Garstang, *The Burial Customs of Ancient Egypt,* London, 1907, pp. 154 ff.

at ten, eleven, and thirteen fifteenths of its entire length; and the other, only 90 cm. long, at eight, nine, and ten twelfths. The scale of the first flute was *theoretically* 15:13, 13:11, 11:10, or 248–289–165 Cents; of the second flute, 12:10, 10:9, 9:8, or 316–182–204 Cents. Each had the range of a fifth (702 Cents), and the smaller one was correctly subdivided to form a pentatonic pentachord. Actually, the insufficient width of the holes and the interference of the pipe below the hole flattened the notes beyond control—the higher notes more than the lower ones, since a longer part of the pipe interfered with the theoretical pitch. I repeat: the theoretical pitch.

From early Sumeria (c. 2700 B.C.) we possess two slender oboes in the University Museum at Philadelphia. One, with four fingerholes, is broken and must be disregarded; the other, with only three holes, is arranged in the ratios 10:9:8:7, that is, approximately in whole tones (182–204–231 Cents).

Egyptian pipes of the last two thousand years B.C. were not essentially different. Despite their variability and the shrinkage unavoidable with so delicate a material, the principle of equipartition is unmistakable. The steps from hole to hole approximate whole tones and semitones, and the position of the highest hole, in the middle of the lower half of the pipe, indicates that these oboes, too slender to yield the ground tones, normally produced the higher octave and, by overblowing, the fifth above.[19]

❊　❊　❊

EQUIPARTITION, the obvious principle in arranging the fingerholes of pipes despite much carelessness and also much intentional variation, needed all kinds of compensation to be musically acceptable. With strings, on the contrary, equipartition became a sound basis of tone generation that rightly might be called both natural and scientific.

Division of strings, meaningless with harps, which for every note had an individual, 'open' string, was imperative where all notes had to be produced on one or two strings by instantaneous changes of the vibrating lengths. This was done by stretching the string for a short distance along a stick or board, against which it was pressed by one of the left-hand fingers, thus bounding the vibrating length of the string. In stopping—as this is called— the hand was guided by *frets,* which in Western antiquity were loops tied about the fingerboard at the given points.

[19] In the museums at Leyden, the oboes nos. 475 and 477—12:9:8:7:6 twelfths; Torino no. 8 and Berlin no. 20667—12:11:10:9:8 twelfths; Torino no. 12—14:12:11:10:9:8:7 fourteenths; Torino no. 11—11:10:9:8:7:6 elevenths.

Stopped instruments first reached Egypt in the fifteenth century B.C. on their way from Asia—together with oboes. They belonged in the family of *long lutes,* in which the stick was much longer than the tiny body.

The earliest serviceable evidence of a fingerboard is the mural painting, in Nakht's tomb at Thebes in Egypt (fifteenth century B.C.), of a lutanist who plays a West Asiatic lute with nine frets on its long neck. The distinctly drawn frets were tempting enough to stimulate imagination; so my late friend Dr. Erich M. von Hornbostel endeavored to measure the distances between the ligatures and to translate them into musical Cents.[20] The eminent scholar seems, however, to have gone too far in interpreting and even emending the data of that painting; Egyptian art works, though fairly accurate, cannot be expected to stand a complicated mathematical test. Besides, Hornbostel's scale rested on an obvious mistake. The first and highest ligature means a stopping place only on instruments with a pegbox that meets the fingerboard at a certain angle, such as the modern violin, on which the little ebony ridge at the upper end of the fingerboard determines the beginning of the vibrating section of the string. The Egyptian lute had neither pegs nor a separate headpiece. Consequently, the strings, which were simply attached by cords tied around the upper end of the stick, needed one first ligature to raise them from the fingerboard and secure free vibration; the sounding length of the string began only with this first ligature, and it was the *second* ligature that marked the first stopping place.

This gives a different picture. The string is divided into two halves; the upper half is again divided into thirds and quarters; the first quarter is split in two, and a fifth quarter is fretted beyond the middle of the string. Thus the frets follow two superimposed arithmetic progressions, one in sixths and the other in eighths of the whole, providing a scale in which at least the lowest tetrachord is chromatic. Any more detailed discussion would be guesswork, the more so as on fretted instruments pitch does not vary in quite exact proportion to the sounding length. Essential here, however, is the general principle that not the ear but *equipartition* of a string decides the scale (Pl. 1, p. 64)

Equipartition on lutes was not unparalleled. A pre-Islamic long lute from Bagdad had its strings divided into forty equal parts,[21] of which only the upper five were used and marked by frets. Since the sections were

---

[20] E. M. von Hornbostel, "Musikalische Tonsysteme," in H. Geiger und Karl Scheel, *Handbuch der Physik* VIII, Berlin, 1927, p. 435.

[21] For the number 40, cf. Wilhelm Heinrich Roscher, "Die Zahl 40 im Glauben, Brauch und Schrifttum der Semiten," in *Abhandlungen der philologisch-historischen Klasse der Kgl. Sächsischen Akademie der Wissenschaften* XXVII (1909), pp. 91–138.

but tiny in comparison with the full length, the tonal distances were practically equal quarter tones.

Later examples of equipartition into twelve in the Near East were based on the fact that twelve is the common denominator of the fractions that designate the three intervals innate in man: the octave 1:2, the fifth 2:3, the fourth 3:4. Pythagoras, according to Gaudentios' *Isagoge,* divided his *kanón* or monochord into twelve parts. In the second century A.D., the Greco-Egyptian Ptolemy followed him, when he recommended his tetra-chord *diatonikòn homalón,* produced by the frets zero, one, two, and three of a lute string divided into twelve equal parts: eleven twelfths resulted in a three-quarter tone, ten twelfths in a minor third, and nine twelfths in a fourth. The Arabian theorist, Safi al-Din, described exactly the same principle as being consonant and much used.[22] It still is at the bottom of most Islamic scales.

❀ ❀ ❀

DIVIDING A STRING by equipartition was not the only, and not even the most usual, system. True, twelve equal parts were in some measure satisfactory since they allowed for just octaves (12:6), fifths (12:8), fourths (12:9), and minor thirds (12:10). But the other stops, such as 12:11 or 12:7, were musically unsatisfactory.

As a consequence, lutanists did what pipers did not dare to do: they replaced the inappropriate arithmetic progression of frets, with its equal distances between tones, by a geometric progression, with its proportionately increasing distances. Struck by the fact that stopping at one half, one third, and one quarter of the entire length resulted respectively in the three principal intervals, they logically went a step further and accepted the stopping at one fifth of the string as producing the major third and that at one sixth as producing the minor third.

We call this victorious principle *divisive.*

Both the divisive principle and the up-and-down principle, already discussed, being natural themselves, yielded 'natural' scales. But only their octaves, fifths, fourths, and certain whole tones agreed; in divisive scales, the major third was smaller and the semitone larger, while the whole tone came in two different sizes.

A few fractions will easily show the reason. The first whole tone, say from *C* to *D,* is found (just as in following the up-and-down principle)

[22] Carra de Vaux, *Le traité des rapports musicaux par Safi ed-Din,* Paris, 1891, pp. 308–17.

by deducting a fourth from a fifth, that is, *C–D* is *C–G* minus *D–G*. This is done by *dividing* the ratio of the fifth, 3:2, by the ratio of the fourth, 4:3, the result (according to the rule of crosswise multiplication of fractions) being 9:8 for the whole tone.

The following whole tone *D–E*, however, is the difference between the major third *C–E* (5:4) and the whole tone just found (9:8), or, dividing the ratios as above, 40:36, or, reduced, 10:9. It is smaller than the whole tone *C–D*.

This distinction between whole tones is impossible where the scale is provided by a cycle of fifths and fourths, for there every whole tone results from a rising fifth (*C–G, D–A,* etc.) and a falling fourth (*G–D, A–E,* etc.) and is therefore invariably 9:8.

In the cycle of fifths and fourths, consequently, the major third follows not the ratio 5:4, as in the divisive system, but (adding two equal whole tones) that of 9:8 *multiplied* by 9:8, or 81:64, which exceeds the divisive ratio 5:4 (or 80:64) by the so-called Didymian (or syntonic) comma.

Finally, the difference in size between the two major thirds involves also a difference in size between the two semitones of the two systems, the semitone being the difference between the fourth (*C–F*) and the major third (*C–E*). Since the divisive third is smaller, the semitone left over when it is deducted from a fourth must be larger:

Up-and-down	Major tone	Major tone	Semitone
Divisive	Major tone	Minor tone	Semitone

The equivalents in Cents for the intervals derived from the two systems are:

One perfect fifth:		702
One perfect fourth:		498
Two major thirds:	Cyclic	408
	Divisive	386
Two minor thirds:	Cyclic	316
	Divisive	294
Two whole tones:	Cyclic and Divisive	204
	Divisive	182
Two semitones:	Divisive	112
	Cyclic	90

❊ ❊ ❊

A REMARKABLE and somewhat unexpected evidence of this contrast between the divisive and the up-and-down principles is the slight divergence in an otherwise analogous musicocosmological conception in Babylonia—of which Plutarch speaks about 100 A.D.[23]—and in China. Both civilizations connaturalized the intervals between the four seasons of the year and the simplest musical intervals. The connotation (starting, say, from C) reads (upward) in

CHINA		BABYLONIA
	C′	Summer
Winter	G	Winter
Autumn	F	Autumn
Summer	D	
Spring	C	Spring

There is agreement except for the position of the summer. Why? Here, I think, is the reason: the Chinese arrangement follows a cycle of fifths or fourths (F, C, G, D or D, G, C, F) and the Babylonian, the division of a string into ground tone (1:1), octave (1:2), fifth (2:3), and fourth (3:4). Thus the same philosophical idea materializes, with a difference that is characteristic of each system, in the up-and-down principle in China, the typical country of the cycle of fifths and fourths, and in the divisive principle in Babylonia, earliest home of the fretted long lute.

❊   ❊   ❊

PARTIALS OR 'OVERTONES' as the natural route markers, a pet idea of some writers who try to offer a 'plausible' theory of scale formation, should be entirely eliminated from our order of thought. To the extent that they appear as the overblown notes of wind instruments, they would indeed be poor standards; wild-grown animal horns and reed pipes yield sensibly false octaves and fifths, and even instruments of higher workmanship depend on their wider or narrower bores. *Partials,* in the proper sense of the word, that is, covibrations of a note played or sung, are difficult to hear and were hardly considered before the later Middle Ages. Even in India, the theoretician Śārngadeva discovered the second partial, that is, the harmonic octave, as late as the thirteenth century, and three hundred more years elapsed before Rāmāmātya heard higher harmonics and used them

---

[23] Plutarch, "De anim. procr.," in *Timaeus* 31.

in arranging the frets of his vīṇā.[24] The idea that musicians of antiquity, indeed of primitive epochs, would have taken their notions of octaves, fifths, and fourths from the short vibrations of plucked harp or lyre strings is truly inadmissible.

To be sure, these 'harmonics' were perfect and represented the ideal intervals of all systems, at least down to the fourth. But they did so only for the simple reason that they originated from exactly the same vibrations of the half, the third, the fourth parts of the string as the notes produced in following the divisive principle. They were a parallel, not a creative, phenomenon.

* * *

THE SINGERS represented on Egyptian pictures bring their left hands to their left ears in a gesture familiar to many Oriental singers of ancient and modern times; the wrinkles, particularly between the eyebrows, indicate nasal singing from a compressed throat and probably at a high pitch.

The right arms are even more fascinating: the singers communicate with their accompanists by stretching out the right forearms and performing a few stereotype gestures; they turn the palm upward [25] or the thumb upward,[26] bend the thumb against the forefinger [27] or turn the palm downward.[28] (Pl. 2b, p. 65)

Exactly the same thing has been done in India: Hindu singers silently beat time by lifting the forearm, turning the palm either up or down, and stretching or doubling up the fingers.

Audible time beating was known in Egypt as well: the tomb of Amenemhêt at Thebes (soon after 1500 B.C.) depicts a conductor, standing before and facing the performers, pounding time with his right heel and snapping both his thumbs and forefingers.[29]

And this, too, is paralleled in India: leaders bring the thumbs against the forefingers and snap, either with the right or the left hand, or even with both.

The singers' melodies, however, cannot be read from murals. In Egypt

[24] N. S. Ramachandran, "The Evolution of the Theory of Music in the Vijayanagara Empire," in Dr. S. Krishnaswami Aiyangar Commemoration Volume (1936), pp. 396 f.
[25] Cf. the illustrations in Curt Sachs, Die Musikinstrumente des alten Aegyptens, op. cit., Fig. 86 from the 5th Dynasty.
[26] Fig. 110 from the 5th Dynasty, and Fig. 109 from the 12th Dynasty.
[27] Fig. 109a from the 5th Dynasty.
[28] Fig. 76.
[29] Fig. 9 from the 18th Dynasty.

and Sumeria vocal music was just as little concerned with rigid systems as it was elsewhere; the freedom granted to unaccompanied singers eliminated the question of shade, if not of mode. No deduction from instruments gives the remotest idea of vocal styles in the ancient Western Orient. But there are several indirect means of approach that do.

❀ ❀ ❀

JEWISH MUSIC is the best gateway to the vocal style of the ancient Western Orient, since in spite of unavoidable variation it has lived for four thousand years without any interruption.

No Jewish music was recorded in ancient times, to be sure; the melodies were orally transmitted from generation to generation. Still, the late Abraham Z. Idelsohn, Professor at the Hebrew Union College in Cincinnati, has opened an indirect way to the old music of Israel: he found the exact counterparts of several Gregorian melodies in remote Jewish congregations, in Yemen, Babylonia, and Persia, which were separated from Palestine and the further development of Jewish ritual music after the destruction of the First Temple (597 B.C.) and the Babylonian Exile. Consequently, these melodies must have existed in the homeland before 600 B.C.

We are less fortunate with other melodies. The Jewish people has been dispersed for twenty-five hundred years and has crystallized in three groups: Orientals in the Middle East, Sephardim in the Mediterranean, Ashkenazim in the rest of Europe. Their liturgical melodies are quite different; not even the most essential parts of the musical service agree (just as in the Ambrosian and Gregorian versions of the Catholic Church music). And yet the basic style is the same and therefore must be an old heritage from times before the dispersion.

❀ ❀ ❀

THE OLD HERITAGE is best preserved in the liturgy of the Oriental Jews, who have lived uninterruptedly in the Near and Middle East, and who have never allowed worldly music to enter the synagogue, nor let their cantors improvise. To be sure, such stagnation implies the risk of decadence. But the Jews of Yemen, Mesopotamia, Persia, and Buchara seem to have escaped degeneration. Otherwise their cantillation could not be so strikingly similar to the melodies of the Sephardim many thousand miles away.

Thus we turn to the Oriental Jews in order to have our questions answered.

In one important point, however, even the Oriental Jews behave differently, not only from their forefathers, but from most archaic singers: their cantillation is unaccompanied. (However, Dr. Joshua Bloch has kindly drawn my attention to the fact that the synagogue in Bagdad had, in the thirteenth century, instrumental music on the Middle Days of Passover and Tabernacles.) [30]

The Bible gives many evidences of the inseparableness of singing and playing. By the rivers of Babylon upon the willows the exiles hung their lyres—how should they sing the Lord's song in a foreign land? And several times, in Chronicles and Kings, lyre and harp are called *klē shîr*, the "tools of singing," or *lsharîm*, "for the singers." [31]

In ancient Egypt, all solo singers depicted in paintings or reliefs either accompany themselves or are sitting opposite an accompanist whom they direct with expressive gestures. Sumerian singers are scarcely ever mentioned without instruments; [32] and, leaving our Western area for an instant, we might think of the Chinese Tsai Yü's words: "The ancients did not sing without accompanying the words on the strings, nor played a stringed instrument without singing." [33]

It is hard to say why such an obligatory connection existed and why it was discontinued by the Oriental Jews. Was it the general evolution, all over the world, from complex execution, including words, singing, playing, dancing, acting, to specialized expression?

How did the ancient Jews sing? Did they actually cry at the top of their voices? Some students have tried to make us believe that such was the case, and they particularly refer to several psalms that allegedly bear witness to praying in fortissimo. But I suspect them of drawing from translations rather than from the Hebrew original: even the soul that in Psalm 42 according to Luther *schreiet* after God as the hart *schreiet* after the water brooks does in the original actually *pant*. At best, the verb *zā'aq* in Psalm 22:5 might actually mean "crying."

True, forceful singing is the normal expression of fervor and agrees with the primitive idea that God's attention follows impetuosity more easily than reserve. When Samuel's mother, Hannah, went to Shiloh to

[30] Leopold Zunz, *Die Ritus,* Berlin, 1859, p. 57.
[31] Ps. 137; I Chron. 16:42, II Chron. 9:11, and I Kings 10:12.
[32] Stephen Langdon, *Babylonian Liturgies, op. cit.,* Introduction.
[33] R. H. van Gulik, *The Lore of the Chinese Lute,* Tokyo, 1940, p. 66.

pray for a child in the Lord's temple, "only her lips moved, but her voice could not be heard; therefore Eli thought she had been drunken." Silent prayer was not yet practiced. As late as the second century B.C. the Book of the Maccabbees twice described Jews as crying aloud to God.

Christianism has its examples as well. Abbot Pambo, who lived in Egypt in the fourth century A.D., stormed at the "monk who, whether situated in the church or in his cell, lifted up his voice like a bull," and even today the Christian priests of Ethiopia sing in a loud voice until they reach the highest point of ecstasy and are completely exhausted.[34]

The drastic and anthropomorphic idea that God's ear was widest open to the loudest crier was counter to the uplifted Judaism of the Prophets. When on Mount Carmel the heathen priests cried to Baal, the Prophet Elijah scoffed and shouted to them: "Cry aloud: for he is a god; either he is talking, or he is pursuing, or he is in a journey, or peradventure he sleepeth, and must be awaked." [35]

There is no more evidence in the archaic liturgies of today. Yemenite congregations give a forte only to certain Amens, the Qdusha (Sanctus), and the Great Blessing. But the chanter is supposed to have a sweet, expressive voice, rather than a strong one, and to sing from the chest. Tenors are preferred.[36]

Nevertheless it is true that Yemenite as well as Persian Jews sharpen the notes the more their frenzy increases.[37]

Choral discipline is excellent in Yemenite congregations; all men and children (but no women) join in the congregational songs, all are well versed in the melodies of the synagogue and actually sing in unison; rhythm—not beat—is strict, and nobody happens to be fast or slow.

The melodic style is quite simple. The Yemenites sing the Book of Esther prestissimo on two notes a small whole tone (191 Cents) apart, while they give three notes to the lyrical poems in the Pentateuch, the Book of Job, and the six Mishna tractates of the Talmud. Idelsohn's tests have yielded 469, 533, and 566 vibrations for these three notes, of which the middle one, c', acts as the final, the other two lying respectively a too-large whole tone below and a normal semitone above.

Even in more elaborate melodies the range never exceeds a sixth; pentatonic tunes do not occur. Thus, Jewish music in its most archaic form is definitely 'additive' in the sense outlined on pages 37-43.

[34] Gustave Reese, *Music in the Middle Ages,* New York, 1940, pp. 66, 94.
[35] I Kings 18:27.
[36] A. Z. Idelsohn, *Hebräisch-Orientalischer Melodienschatz* I, Leipzig, 1914, p. 17.
[37] *Ibid.* III, p. 37.

A melody, reaching or exceeding the range of a fourth, settles down in a tetrachord of one of the three diatonic kinds. (Greek) Lydian has been used for plaintive themes, such as the Lamentations, the Book of Job, and the Confession of Sins, while Phrygian is passionate. The Dorian tetrachord is lyrical and solemn; Clemens Alexandrinus, the Church Father, who lived in Palestine from 202 on, quotes Aristoxenos as having said that King David's psalms were similar to the Dorian *harmonia*.[38]

Ex. 30. BABYLONIAN JEWS   *after Idelsohn*

Way-yo-sha   a-do-nay

❋   ❋   ❋

THE TALMUD SCORNS those who read the Scripture without melody and study the words without singing. Service, based on reading the Holy Books, was musical throughout, alternating between the cantor's chant and the tunes of the congregation. In both forms it was what we call cantillation, though not in the stagnant monotone of a Christian lesson, but rather in the noble fluency of Gregorian melodies. Keeping a middle line between boring recitation and independent melogenic tunes, it was the ideal means of conveying the divine word in all its shades, from the dry enumeration of pedigrees—"Now these are the generations of the sons of Noah"—to the exalted pathos of the Psalms—"Save me, O God; for the waters are come in even unto the soul." The Jewish liturgy had the 'endless melody' of the Catholic rite and of the musical drama, not the contrast of Gospel and choral in the Protestant service or the 'numbers' of the usual opera, alternating between recitativo and aria. True, the so-called songs of the Pentateuch, such as Lamech's Confession, the Prophets, the Song of Songs, or the Psalms, had special melodic patterns; but to our minds they are cantillation just as much as the epic parts of the Scriptures.

Ex. 31. PERSIAN JEWS   *after Idelsohn*

How did all these melodies originate?

All Jewish melodies are in the proper sense of the word *composed* out of ready-made melodicles.

---

[38] Clemens Alexandrinus, *Stromata* 6:11.

In two of the most archaic liturgies, the Yemenite and the Persian, the various parts of the Scriptures—Pentateuch, Prophets, Psalms, Esther, Lamentations, and so on—have their own melodic patterns composed of two motifs—a starter and a final cadence—or of three and even four motifs which, alternately given to the half lines of the text, are flexible enough either to expand or to shrink according to the varying number of syllables. As an example, we print the beginning of the "Song of the Red Sea" (Ex. 14: 30) in the Yemenite version.

Ex. 32. YEMENITE JEWS   *after Idelsohn*

There are two patterns, one semicadential and another, cadential, in strict alternation, though shorter or longer as required.

It is probable that the psalms originally used a greater stock of melodies and even folk tunes of a similar kind before they were assigned definite places in a rigidly organized liturgy. A great number of them are preceded by a special heading that indicates how the psalm should be performed. Earlier writers misunderstood these directions; they thought that the enigmatic title words such as *nginot,* or *gittit,* or *hanchilot* referred to some unknown instruments and advised the players how to accompany the song. I was able to refute this interpretation and to show that the headings very probably indicated the appropriate melody.[39]

However, no ready-made melody invited the poet to compose some poem fitting it in meter and length—as indicated in modern hymnbooks—for the simple reason that the psalms were different in length and had no equal meter. "Melody," in the Orient, has always meant one of those flexible patterns that the Arabs finally classified as *maqamât* and the Hindu as *rāgas,* which imposed upon the singer their specific genera, scales, pitches, accents, tempos, and moods, but granted him full personal freedom for their elaboration.

❊   ❊   ❊

THE LATER CANTILLATION receded from line patterns to word motifs: ready-made motifs, of two or more notes each and altogether some twenty in number, change from word to word, not from line to line. In the first line

[39] Curt Sachs, *The History of Musical Instruments, op. cit.,* pp. 124-7.

of the Bible, for example—*Brēshít* in the beginning *bārâ* created *Elohím* God *ét hashāmayim* the heaven *weêt hââreṣ* and the earth—each of the seven words has its own motif (although *weêt* shares its motif with the corresponding accusative prefix *êt*, and *hashāmayim* repeats the motif of *brēshít*). These *tropes* or *accents* are to the initiated known under technical terms such as 'hand's breadth,' 'resting,' 'end of verse,' and many others.

Such procedure seems mechanical at first sight and calls to mind certain composing automatons devised in Europe around 1800, in which ready-made groups of notes joined kaleidoscopically to form ever new melodies. However much these machines and kindred games caricatured the act of composing, they expressed the truth that even in modern times melodic invention was 'composition'—in the exact sense of the word—more than we dare realize. In all folksongs, in the art of the German *Meistersinger*, in Luther's chorales, in Calvin's Psalter, and way back in the Gregorian chant, the mosaic is quite obvious.

The essential difference between the ancient and the modern Western principle consists in the conception of what constitutes the melodic unit. The modern unit is the inert single note; the ancient unit was the step; that is, the Jews understood melodic movement as composed of motor elements or 'motives,' in the true sense of the word, which is both philosophically and musically more correct. The reader will excuse a historian of the dance for comparing the contrast to the similar alternative in choreography, where a dance can be characterized either by its transitory positions, or by the sequence of its steps.

The following is the cantillation of Exodus 12:21—"Then Moses called for all the elders of Israel"—sung by a Babylonian cantor:

Ex. 33. BABYLONIAN JEWS   *after Idelsohn*

Each word in this line has its own ready-made motif: *wayiqrā* 'called' is sung on *qadma* 'preceding'; *mośe*, 'Moses,' on *tvír* 'broken'; *lchol-ziqnē*, 'for all the elders,' on *paśṭā* 'stretcher'; *ísrāēl*, on *ṭarchā* 'burden' or *tipchā* 'hand's breadth.'

The result is an amazingly natural, fluent, and convincing melody: the composer of cantillations, far from being a patcher, might better be compared to an ingenious gardener who arranges his two dozen of motley flowers in ever new bunches. Or, to put it more specifically, he might be compared to a dancing master of the Renaissance who, out of the more than limited stock of *pas simples, pas doubles, reprises,* and *branles,* created an infinite number of *basses danses, saltarelli,* and *balli.*

    ❋   ❋   ❋

To SAVE TRADITION in the critical times of the first thousand years A.D., Jewish scholars in Babylonia and Palestine devised not only the well-known dots and dashes that, added above or below the consonants, indicated the previously unwritten vowels to follow, but also special symbols for correct melodizing. Tradition itself was called *Masora;* the scholars, who played the role that the Alexandrian grammarians had in the Greek world, were known as *Masoretes,* and the signs, as *Masoretic.*

The melodic symbols of the Babylonian Jews were the initials of those names under which the tropes were known: the letter *taw* denoted the trope *tvir;* the letter *yod* stood for the 'staying' *yetiv;* the letter *zaīn* for the 'raising' *zāqaf;* and so on. They were written above the corresponding vowel signs, which, in contradiction to the usual practice, were written above their consonants.

This Babylonian notation by letters, however, was abandoned and generally replaced by the later Palestinian or 'Tiberian' symbols, which were hooks, dots, and dashes, some written above and some below the corresponding syllables.

The older, alphabetical Babylonian accents draw our attention to another Babylonian script, though a thousand or more years earlier, the musical character of which was doubtful. Some sixty cuneiform letters or, better, syllables appeared as marginals on clay plaques on which the Babylonian myth of the world's creation was written in two languages, hieratic Sumerian and vernacular Semitic. They were arranged in lines of three, four, or five to each line of the text:

me me kur kur
a a a a a
ku ku lu lu
etc.

The texts ended with the solemn formula: "Secret. The initiated may show it to the initiated."

In 1923 I made a tentative attempt to interpret the marginals as a musical notation but failed, since I thought of single notes at definite pitches. Dr. Francis W. Galpin failed in a similar way fourteen years later.[40] I resumed the question from a new angle in 1939,[41] dropping the assumption of single notes at definite pitches and correlating the Babylonian script with musical group notations of Ethiopia and India.

Villoteau, the excellent musicologist in the French scientific expedition that explored Egypt during the Napoleonic conquest (1798–1801), had learned from Ethiopian priests in Cairo that Abyssinian church singers used a secret—again secret!—notation of syllables written above the sacred verses. The forty-seven syllables that he was taught were either single, like *he, le, ma,* or else double, like *lama* or *raha,* or even contracted, like *hal,* just as in the Babylonian script.

Some decades later, the French Orientalist, Hermann Zotenberg,[42] found no less than 168 symbols of the same kind in a liturgical book in the Bibliothèque Nationale, of which he published a complete list in his catalogue of Ethiopian manuscripts. Unfortunately their meaning is unknown; our knowledge does not go beyond the forty-seven definitions that Villoteau was able to give. But these suffice to make clear that the Ethiopian notation indicated groups of notes, including grace notes, not single notes. The syllable *se,* to give a few examples, indicates a descending semitone; *ḳa,* an ascending whole tone; *wā,* a whole tone up with a trill on the higher note; *wa,* a minor third with an infix; *we,* a fourth up, either in a leap or with infixes; *zēze,* the same, a fifth up; *re,* a final cadence.

This is obviously the principle of the Judeo-Babylonian accents: the syllables (Abyssinian has no single letters) mean groups of notes, melodicles, and tropes. Ethiopian priests write *zēze* for a fifth ascending in one leap, and such is the *mūnāh* of the Sephardic Jews. They call *si* a fifth descending stepwise with a slight rest on the last note: it is the *zarqā* of Ashkenazic Lamentations. *Se* is a fourth stepwise descending in a rapid fall—exactly like *rvīaʿ* in the recitation of the Prophets by Babylonian cantors.

Eastward from Babylonia, in South India, chanters of the Veda use a

---

[40] Francis W. Galpin, *The Music of the Sumerians,* Cambridge, 1937, pp. 38–50, 99–104.
[41] Curt Sachs, "The Mystery of the Babylonian Notation," in *The Musical Quarterly* XXVII (1941), pp. 62–9.
[42] Hermann Zotenberg, *Catalogue des Manuscrits Ethiopiens de la Bibliothèque Nationale,* Paris, 1877, p. 76.

similar script: syllables, like *ka, ki, ko* and other consonant-vowel combinations, indicating groups of notes, not single notes, are inserted in the text or, as in Babylonia, written by the side of the verses. Not only is the Veda cantillation very old, but this form of syllabic script is expressly called the oldest Veda notation.

The Ethiopian, Indian, and Jewish accents favor a musical interpretation of the ancient Babylonian script, although the lack of dates is a serious handicap. If it actually was a notation, it would push the 'accents' back by more than a thousand years.

❀   ❀   ❀

THE TITLES of books and papers discussing Hebrew and non-Hebrew accents would fill a portly volume of bibliography. Readers interested in the various ramifications of this complicated matter may look to the special literature.[43]

Our own interest is limited to those dealing with the relation of melody and language. The fact that grammarians were interested in adding musical neumes; that the earliest accents of which we know were the Greek acute, grave, and circumflex, which belonged to both orthograph and pitch; that in some systems of cantillation, like the Armenian, symbols similar to the Jewish accents indicate commas, colons, periods—all these facts and many others point to a common root of certain linguistic and musical phenomena.

An illuminating, though late, testimony comes from a Judeo-Syrian authority, Bar Hebraeus, who lived in the thirteenth century A.D. In his Book of Splendors he writes:

> Since in all languages a sentence changes its meaning by mere intonations, without adding or removing nouns, verbs, or particles, the Syrian scholars who laid the fundament of correct language discovered a way out by devising accents . . . and since these accents are a form of musical modulation, there is no possibility of learning them except by hearing and through tradition from the master's tongue to the pupil's ear.[44]

It follows from Bar Hebraeus' statement that the main concern was to secure an unadulterated and unadulterable version of the text. This required (*a*) correct vocalization and (*b*) correct intonation. The necessity for adding vowels needs no comment: an English sentence with the letters *bt* written without vowel in the Hebrew manner would allow for several

---

[43] Cf. Peter Wagner, *Neumenkunde*, 2nd ed., Leipzig, 1912; Carsten Höeg, *La Notation ecphonétique*, Copenhague, 1935.

[44] Carsten Höeg, *La Notation ecphonétique, op. cit.*, p. 142.

interpretations according as *bt* is read *bat, bet, bit, bot,* or *but*. The full meaning of intonation, however, can hardly be exemplified in modern English and still less in American English. But even in so leveled a speech melody, a person is exposed to being misunderstood if he fails to lift and drop the voice in time. Thus it is probable and almost certain that in areas of highly developed speech melody the accents were created by grammarians in the interest of an unmistakable text.

Several ways opened from such original creation, and all of them were followed. Where no holy text was read in solemn cantillation—in ancient Greece, for example—the accents developed into punctuation marks and phonetic symbols. In Jewish and Christian countries the opposite was true: since the Bible was chanted and illicit changes of melody endangered the meaning and power of its verses, the accents were multiplied and converted into neumes in order to denote all possible steps and melismatic groups.

Unfortunately, the very thing happened that the accents were expected to prevent: the notation, faithfully preserved in all branches of Jewry and identically applied to the holy texts, stands for quite different melodies. A *mūnāh,* indicating a bold jump upward by a fifth in all Oriental liturgies, means a narrow, creeping melisma in Ashkenazic countries, while a *pashṭā* is answered by a step downward in the Babylonian, and a step upward in the Sephardic reading of the Prophets.

Ex. 34. JEWISH ACCENTS

We are not yet in a position to explain these discrepancies.

❊   ❊   ❊

IN VIRGIL's AENEID, the hero says:

In-fan / dum Re- / gi-na ju- / bes re-no- / va-re do- / lo-rem

A translation, in poor English but faithful to the original syllables and their metrical characters, would be:

Un-speak- / able, my / La-dy, you / bid to re- / mem-ber af- / flic-tion where the natural meter of *unspeakable* is being violated, as the meter of *infandum* is in the Latin verse.

Hebrew poetry never puts the words in a ready-made frame. Every word, indeed every sentence, keeps its meter. In consequence, there is no regular sequence of dactyls or iambs, nor is there a constant number of feet in a verse. Hebrew poetry is a poetical prose. "Hebrew prosody differs fundamentally from classical prosody. No poem is written according to a repeating meter scheme. The rhythm of Hebrew poetry depends, not on the relative position of the prominent syllable with respect to the surrounding syllables, but on a certain relative position of the important syllable in the verse. Classical verse, comparatively, is mechanical; Hebrew verse is dynamic." [45]

The number of unstressed syllables that preceded the accents was one, or two, or three, or even four, and the poet was free to shape his verses in accordance with the greater or lesser dynamic tension of his phrase. But the verses were always 'rising'; they began either in iambic form with one unaccented syllable or, oftener, in anapaestic form with two unaccented syllables before the first accent. This, for example, is the rhythm of the Song of Songs 1:2-3:

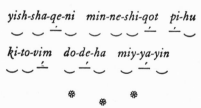

＊　　＊　　＊

THE NUMBERLESS AUTHORS who have dealt with the problems of Hebrew rhythm maintain that the Jews, having no stereotype alternation of long and short syllables, practically ignored the length of syllables and instead stressed a few syllables by a strong accent due to their significance in the text rather than to formal qualities. While the classical meter was qualitative (long-short), Hebrew meter, they say, was accented (heavy-light).

The only exception, as far as I see, has been Elcanon Isaacs' statement that "Hebrew meter employs the combination of the mora [time unit] basis of poetry and the accent. It is based on the number of morae as determined by the accented syllable." [46]

[45] Elcanon Isaacs, "The Metrical Basis of Hebrew Poetry," in *The American Journal of Semitic Languages* XXXV (1918), pp. 29 f.

[46] *Ibid.*, p. 30.

Had any philologist looked at Hebrew music, he would have found this statement confirmed. A 'qualitative' meter leads to musical accents with increased intensity and time beating. But such is not the case here. The unaccented syllable is evenly rendered by a 'brevis' that we might transcribe as an eighth note; rarely is this replaced by a ligature of two sixteenths or reduced to one sixteenth. The accented syllable is rendered by a longa or quarter note. In brief, Hebrew melody follows the quantitative long-short principle. On holidays, some longae are spun out to form melismatic groups, just as in the Gregorian chant.

As a whole, Hebrew rhythm is free; it does not obey any ready-made metric pattern or the measures of beaten time.

❀   ❀   ❀

ARCHAIC HEBREW RHYTHM was less free. Elcanon Isaacs found, in Hebrew poetry, a development "which may be characterized as a movement away from a strict regard to form to the freer movement of prose." Sporadic examples found in the earliest books of the Bible he calls "vigorous folk poetry—often lyrical, with metrical feet of three morae predominating, and great regularity of beat. The verses are short, very distinct, and of uniform length. The accent is for the greater part on the ultima, and the word-foot units are similar in their form."

We select, as an example, the first two verses of the song on the early defeat of Moab (Num. 21:27):

> bo-nu chesh-bon / tib - an - ēh wti-bo-nēn 'ir si-chon
> ḳi-ēsh jāz' - āh / mē-chesh-bon le-hā-vāh mi-qir-jat
> ˘ ′   ˘   ′   ˘ ˘ ′   ˘ ˘ ′   ˘ ˘ ′

In Greek terminology, each verse consists of an iambic dipody and an anapaestic tripody; the only difference is that the Greeks would not allow a long syllable like 'ir to pass unaccented.

In view of an evolution from stricter to freer rhythm in poetry, we come to the unavoidable conclusion that Jewish music in nomadic times before 1000 B.C. was less unrestrained than in the later liturgy. Two reasons seem to confirm this conclusion. Firstly, almost all musical episodes up to the time of the Temple describe choral singing with group dancing and drum beating: the wedding songs of modern Yemenite Jews show how the accompaniment of dancing men and drumming women forces free rhythm into regular two-quarter beats.[47] And secondly, this kind of singing was

---

[47] A. Z. Idelsohn, op. cit., p. 42.

to a great extent women's music; and in all times and countries women have preferred neat and lucid form (see pp. 40–41).

❀ ❀ ❀

JEWISH WOMEN'S SONGS in archaic communities have recently been described by Robert Lachmann.[48] The essential fact is that such a species of music exists and is strictly separated from men's music both in style and performance.

Since Dr. Lachmann has not published the music of any of these songs, it might be proper to follow his own words.

The production of the women's songs is dependent on a small store of typical melodic turns; the various songs reproduce these turns—or some of them—time and again. . . . Their tone relations reveal one of the many kinds of conduct of vocal music before its subjection to the rational scale-system of theory.

The poems all are arranged through alternating rhymes in pairing verses or stanzas. In addition, certain poems have a refrain. . . . Most of the songs consist of a 2–4 part melody and its repetitions. Two singers—or groups of singers —alternate in these repetitions. . . . The lines or pairing lines of the poem are alternately sung by both singers.

The women's songs belong to a species the forms of which are essentially dependent not on the connection with the text but on processes of movement. Thus we find here, in place of the free rhythm of cantillation and its very intricate line of melody, a periodical up and down movement. This type of song —like the recitation of magic or liturgical texts—goes back to prehistoric times. . . .

In the Jewish communities not only Oriental-Sephardic districts but also, for example, in Yemen, the women accompany their songs on frame-drums or cymbals which they beat with their hands. . . . The beats follow at regular intervals; they fall on each period of the melody. They fulfill herewith but one of the various functions of which the drum in the Near East is capable; they only give the length of the unit of line [as obviously the cymbals in the Temple did], but they do not divide the melody into bars, nor do they bring it within the limits of a systematic rhythmic figure. . . . The songs group themselves partly in 4/4 time and partly in 3/4 time—i.e., in the two simplest forms.

This description might come nearest to the picture we should draw of Jephthah's daughter welcoming her father and of the women hailing David after the battle against the Philistines.

❀ ❀ ❀

[48] Robert Lachmann, *Jewish Cantillation and Song in the Isle of Djerba,* Jerusalem, 1940, pp. 67–82 and *passim.*

PARALLELISMUS MEMBRORUM is the philological term to express the leading principle in the structure of Hebrew poems: the half-verse is answered by another half-verse that expresses either an intensification or an antinomy, not in the same meters, but in similar words. Read the initial words of the Book of Joel:

> Hear this, ye old men,
>> And give ear, all ye inhabitants of the land.
>
> Hath this been in your days,
>> Or in the days of your fathers?
>
> Tell your children of it,
>> And let your children tell their children.

Or the earliest poem in the Bible (Gen. 4:23):

> Adah and Zillah, hear my voice;
>> Ye wives of Lamech, hearken unto my speech;
>
> For I have slain a man for wounding me,
>> A young man, for bruising me;
>
> If Cain shall be avenged sevenfold,
>> Truly Lamech seventy and sevenfold.

The Assyrians, too, clung to 'tautological' and other parallelisms. One of the hymns to Sin begins:

> O Lord, who is like thee,
>> Who can be compared to thee?
> Mighty one, who is like thee,
>> Who can be compared to thee? [49]

❊   ❊   ❊

ANTIPHONY is the musical associate of poetical parallelism. This term means, in a narrower sense, the alternate singing of the two parallel lines by two half-choruses and, in a wider sense, the alternate singing of a soloist and an answering chorus, which in the Roman Church has been called responsorial singing.

Antiphony on a gigantic scale is roughly outlined in the Talmudian tractate *Sotah,* which refers to an episode of the Book of Joshua:

[49] Charles Gordon Cumming, *The Assyrian and Hebrew Hymns of Praise,* New York, 1934, p. 97.

When Israel crossed the Jordan and came unto Mount Gerizim and unto Mount Ebal in Samaria . . . six tribes went up to the top of Mount Gerizim and six tribes went up to the top of Mount Ebal. And the priests and the Levites stood below in the midst; and the priests surrounded the Ark and the Levites surrounded the priests, and all Israel were on this side and on that . . . and began with the blessing . . . and both these and these answered, "Amen!" [50]

When Moses, having led his people through the Red Sea, struck up the hymn of praise with his men:

"I will sing unto the Lord, for He is highly exalted: the horse and his rider hath He thrown into the sea . . . " Miriam the prophetess, the sister of Aaron, took a timbrel in her hand; and all the women went out after her with timbrels and with dances. And Miriam sang unto them: "Sing ye to the Lord, for He is highly exalted: the horse and his rider hath He thrown into the sea."

The Jewish philosopher Philo (b. 30–20 B.C.), who in spite of his Greek erudition lived in the atmosphere of Hebrew tradition, interpreted this singing as antiphony: "On the shore," he says in his *Life of Moses*, "the Hebrews formed two choruses out of the men and the women and praised God; Moses struck up the singing of the men, and his sister the singing of the women. They were the leaders of the choruses." [51] But if, notwithstanding the identical texts the men and the women sang, it was not an antiphony in the narrower sense, women against men, it was at least antiphony in the wider sense, the choruses answering their leaders.

Actual antiphony is obvious when on David's return from his victory over the Philistines "the women sang *one to another* in their play, and said: 'Saul hath slain his thousands, and David his ten thousands.' " [52] The verb *'ānāh* means "to answer, respond."

A large-size antiphony, possibly of singers and of players, seems to be described in the Book of Nehemia. When after the return from the Babylonian Exile (538 B.C.) the leaders rebuilt and dedicated the walls of Jerusalem

they sought the Levites out of all their places to keep the dedication with gladness, both with thanksgiving, and with singing, with cymbals, harps, and with lyres. And the sons of the singers gathered themselves together. Then [Nehemia] brought up the princes of Judah upon the wall, and appointed *two* great companies that gave thanks and went in procession: on the right hand half of the princes of Judah and certain of the priests' sons with trumpets, and Judah, Hanani, with the musical instruments of David. And the other company of them that gave thanks went to meet them, and they stood still in the gate of

[50] *Sotah* 7:5.
[51] Philo, *De Vita Moysis* I ¶ 180.
[52] I Sam. 18:7.

the guard. So stood the two companies of them that gave thanks in the house of God. And the singers sang loud, with Jezrahiha their overseer.[53]

The older rabbis of the Talmud, who still had seen the Temple, describe basic forms of responsorial antiphony:

1) The soloist sang the entire melody, and after each half-verse the congregation answered with the same first half-verse as a refrain. This form was used for the *Hallel* (Ps. 113–118) and the Song of the Sea (Ex. 15).

2) The soloist and the congregation alternated half-verse by half-verse. This was the traditional form of the *Shma Israel*.

3) In school, the children repeated the teacher's cantillation half-verse by half-verse.

4) Confirming refrains were prescribed as early as the time of Moses: "And all the people shall say Amen" (Deut. 27:21–26).

The finest evidence of choral antiphony is Philo's description of a congregational supper of the Therapeutic sect:[54]

They all stand up together and . . . two choruses are formed . . . the one of men and the other of women, and for each chorus there is a leader . . . selected, who is the most honourable and most excellent of the band. Then they sing hymns which have been composed in honour of God in many meters and tunes, at one time all singing together, and at another answering one another in a skilful manner. . . . The chorus of male and female worshippers, throughout the singing and the alternation of the melodies, makes . . . a truly musical symphony, the shrill voices of the women mingling with the deep-toned voices of the men.[55]

Responsorial antiphony is still used in all Jewish liturgies. The Yemenites, particularly, sing the *Hallel* in the form (1) the Jerusalemites used in the time of the Temple, and the Babylonians sing it on Passover in form (2).

Choral antiphony exists also, though only outside the synagogue. The Yemenites, for instance, sing all but one form of extrasynagogical poetry in the following arrangement. The chorus (of men) is divided into two half-choruses of at least two singers each. The leader, a member of the first half-chorus, sings the first verse (eight measures) alone in order to call the melody to mind, and the following verses are alternately sung, the first half-verse by the first half-chorus and the second half-verse by the second half-chorus. If there is a coda, it is done by all together. Drums are supposed to beat the rhythm; in case they are not available or, on Sabbaths, not admissible, the onlookers clap their hands. Never are these antiphonies

---

[53] Neh. 12:27–42 (abbreviated).
[54] Philo, *De Vita contemplativa* 11 ¶ 83.
[55] Quoted from Gustave Reese, *Music in the Middle Ages, op. cit.*, p. 60.

sung without one or two couples of men dancing—slowly at first and thereafter in an ever increasing tempo up to a frantic prestissimo.

❋   ❋   ❋

ANTIPHONY IN ASSYRIA should be taken for granted with the close relationship between Assyrian and Hebrew religious poetries. Though there is no direct, irrefutable evidence of this, C. G. Cumming, the monographer of *The Assyrian and Hebrew Hymns of Praise,* had material enough to write a whole chapter on the subject and to state: "The use of the refrain in the Assyrian hymns, as in the case of the Hebrew hymns, indicates antiphonal responses between priest and choir and choir and choir." [56]

Nearer at hand as evidences of non-Jewish antiphony are playful performances of the Nubians in Upper Egypt, who in their archaic civilization have faithfully preserved a number of ancient Egyptian traits. A hundred and fifty years ago, the French musicologist, Villoteau, saw them sing and dance in two fronts of four, six, eight, or even more men each, which faced one another at a distance of two or three feet, exactly as on certain ancient Egyptian reliefs. Villoteau's musical examples show continual alternation of the two choruses, each one singing two measures, or else the second chorus joining in with an overlapping refrain.[57] I myself participated in 1930 in Nubian rowboat parties on the Nile near the First Cataract, where the leader improvised and the crew responded very much in the same way as the cantor and the congregation in a synagogue.

Ex. 35. NUBIANS   *heard by Curt Sachs*

All these evidences are outshone by a letter of one of the Church Fathers, St. Basil (c. 330–379), which defends the singing of the psalms both antiphonally and responsorially, as do "the Egyptians, Libyans, Thebans, Palestinians, Arabians, Phoenicians, Syrians, the dwellers by the Euphrates." [58] This proves that antiphonal and responsorial singing between Libya and Mesopotamia was no less than universal.

❋   ❋   ❋

[56] Charles Gordon Cumming, *The Assyrian and Hebrew Hymns of Praise, op. cit.,* pp. 72–82, 99.

[57] Villoteau, "De l'état actuel de l'art musical en Égypte," in *Description de L'Egypte, Etat moderne,* Paris, 1826, XIV, 254–9.

[58] Cf. Gustave Reese, *op. cit.,* p. 63.

THE CHRISTIAN LITURGY of Syria, nearest to the Jewish liturgy of Palestine, proves that antiphony is by no means the only trait that Israel had in common with the rest of the Eastern world between Libya and Mesopotamia.

Although none of its melodies can actually be traced back to antiquity, scholars are unanimous in assuming that they contain original elements.

Ex. 36. SYRIAN CHRISTIANS   *after Idelsohn*

There is, indeed, the same preference given to tetrachordal structure, the same style of cantillation, and even certain standard melodies closely related to the most archaic Jewish tunes; adaptability of melodic patterns to texts of different length and rhythm; the interpretation of irregular qualitative meters by irregularly alternating short and long notes; accents and neumes; *parallelismus membrorum;* and elaborate antiphony in its two forms as half chorus against half chorus and chorus against soloist.[59]

Northward, Syrian influence shaped the earliest church music of Armenia. We do not know this music, however; the old notation has not yet been deciphered, and the present melodies seem to be of a much more recent date. But even the modern cantillation of Armenia is based on melodic formulas, not on scales, and her most ancient hymns are said to have been in prose, that is, in free rhythm. Both qualities constitute a relation with Jewish music.[60]

In a similar way, the features of Jewish cantillation recur in the chant of Israel's Christian neighbors in the West: the Copts of Egypt.

❊   ❊   ❊

THE COPTS, native Christians of Egypt, have preserved the racial features of the ancient pre-Islamic Egyptians and in church still use their language; all the conquering Greeks, Romans, Arabs, and Turks have left them almost untouched. In view of such perseverance, there is hope that late Egyptian music might to a certain extent be preserved in the chant of Coptic churches.

[59] A. Z. Idelsohn, "Der Kirchengesang der Jakobiten," in *Archiv für Musikwissenschaft* IV (1922), pp. 364–89. Egon Wellesz, and other sources: cf. Gustave Reese, *Music in the Middle Ages, op. cit.,* p. 432.
[60] Cf. the bibliography in Gustave Reese, *op. cit.,* p. 434.

Plate 3. Members of the court orchestra of Elam, playing harps, double oboes, and a drum. Relief in the British Museum, c. 650 B.C. After Sachs.

Chanting is done by a few blind singers who sit on the ground, perform in a thin, high, and nasalizing voice and accompany themselves with the tinkle of small cymbals, much as the ancient Egyptians shook their metallic sistra. Their melodies are definitely heptatonic and, in the main, syllabic, with comparatively rare ligatures and graces. The listener is often under the impression of tetrachordal modes.

Ex. 37. COPTS   *after Newlandsmith*

But whoever attends Coptic services—as the author many times did in Cairo and in Luqsor—must be struck by the discouraging vagueness of all notes inside a fourth or a fifth and, as a consequence, will prefer to refrain from modal analysis. The question how to interpret this vagueness is difficult: is it an inherent quality of the Coptic—and hence Egyptian—style or is it a consequence of degeneration? In face of the nature of singing in general and of Oriental singing particularly, inheritance is likelier than decadence.

Ethiopian church music should in a similar way be taken into consideration. Abyssinia boasts of Jewish descent, believes that her first emperor was the son of King Solomon and the Queen of Sheba and claims that her church has preserved the melodies of Solomon's temple. History in its turn states that the first bishop of Ethiopia was a Phoenician, that is, a neighbor of the Palestinian Jews, and that about 500 A.D. Syrian monks came to that land as missionaries.

Ex. 38. ABYSSINIANS   *after Herscher-Clément*

The cantillation of Abyssinian churches has scarcely been investigated so far; but at least in its performance there is a trait reminding us of the Jewish temple: the ends of the lines are marked by shaking the sistrum, be it the ancient Jewish sistrum or, more probably, the ancient Egyptian sistrum, which in its native country has been forgotten.

Ethiopians, indeed, do not deny that there are close ties between their church music and the melodies of the Copts.[61]

❋   ❋   ❋

POLYPHONY, too, is a fascinating trait of Abyssinia, and the more fascinating as—except for the Arabian influence in the *masanqo* or improvised fiddle songs of wandering minstrels—her musical life appears to have been untouched since olden times.

Mondon-Vidailhet, a French resident of Abyssinia, an excellent observer, and the best among the very few writers on Ethiopian music, relates that "liturgical music is not exclusively homophonous. . . . In several ceremonies, I noticed that before one of the groups had ended another group had started so that their ensemble was a very harmonious music in a complicated kind of counterpoint." [62]

He tells of begging lepers who perform *lalibaloč* before sunrise at the doors of their luckier countrymen, a woman first, then a man, then both or even three; and in doing so, they sing, to translate Mondon-Vidailhet's words, in "a simple harmony, generally based on the third." [63]

A third form of musical teamwork in Ethiopia belongs to the folksongs called *zafan*: a soloist sings the verses, the chorus joins in with a refrain, and while all together sing the coda, the voices drop out one by one until only a single voice is left,[64] almost as in Haydn's Farewell Symphony where one musician after another stopped playing and left.

But a more important parallel is mentioned in the Talmudian tractate *Arachin* 2:3, which, speaking of the double pipe, adds that the final cadence came from one cane only, "to make it more agreeable." I have already discussed the question for which of several reasons the two canes blown together were less agreeable.[65] Maybe they were played in unison and caused unpleasant pulsations when not tuned with the greatest care; or else they might have played separate parts, possibly and even probably in the manner of a drone.

Droning is indeed the basic form of counterpoint wherever double pipes

[61] Cf. the bibliography in Gustave Reese, *ibid.*, p. 434. Recent contribution: J. Herscher-Clément, "Chants d'Abyssinie," in *Zeitschrift für Vergleichende Musikwissenschaft* II (1934), pp. 51–7.
[62] Mondon-Vidailhet, "La Musique éthiopienne," in Lavignac, *Encyclopédie de la Musique* I 5 v, p. 3192.
[63] *Ibid.*, p. 3181.
[64] *Ibid.*, p. 3180.
[65] Curt Sachs, *The History of Musical Instruments, op. cit.*, p. 120.

are played. The Arabian *arḡūl* and the double oboes of India, the Sardinian triple clarinet *launeddas,* and practically all bagpipes in the world provide one pipe for the melody and the other for a sustained pedal tone below the melody.

Drones, archaic in themselves, were doubtless known at least five thousand years ago. On one relief of the Egyptian Old Kingdom a double clarinet is depicted, and Sumer has left double oboes of the same time; on some pictures of the Egyptian New Kingdom (after 1500 B.C.) the piper fingers the right cane with both hands while the left cane is merely supported by the thumb, which clearly indicates that the left cane sounds a drone. On other pictures, the left hand holds the cane above the highest fingerhole; again, this cane cannot have contributed more than one single note. The holes that the player did not wish to work were stopped with wax; one pipe, excavated in Thebes and dating from the end of the Middle or the early New Kingdom, still has the stopping wax in three of its four fingerholes.

❊　❊　❊

THE HARPERS' POLYPHONY, lastly, has been discussed in my *History of Musical Instruments:* [66] a well-known relief in the British Museum represents the Elamic court orchestra welcoming the Assyrian conqueror in 650 B.C. and, among its players, seven harpists similar in all details except that they are plucking different strings. Such difference must not be considered accidental in an art work of realistic, indeed almost photographic, accuracy; nor can that single variation among otherwise uniform players be explained by an artist's formal consideration. (Pl. 3, p. 80)

Each harper plucks two strings. As the numbers of the strings plucked follow in intervals of five—the fifth, tenth, fifteenth and the eighth, thirteenth, eighteenth—the genus must be pentatonic, either with major thirds and semitones or with minor thirds and whole tones. The next question, whether the tetrachords are arranged in heptads or in octaves, is immaterial, since in the range of a score of strings, conjunct and disjunct tetrachords alternate anyway. Supposing that the fifth string sounds *A,* the tenth and the fifteenth sound *a* and *a'*; and the eighth, thirteenth, and eighteenth, *e, e',* and *e''*. The result is an empty fifth orchestrated in the modern way, the two notes being distributed among the seven players in different combinations, as double octave, octave, unison and fifth:

[66] *Ibid.,* p. 82.

First   harpist: *A–e"*
Second harpist: *e–e'*
Third   harpist: *e'–e"*
Fourth harpist: *e'–e'*
Fifth   harpist: *a'–e"*
Sixth   harpist: *a'–e"*
Seventh harpist: *(a)–e'*

The unexpected results of studying this relief encouraged me to extend examination to other ancient pictures of harpists, both in Assyria and Egypt, in which the strings and plucking fingers were represented with similar distinctness. I found portrayed: in Assyria, in the seventh century B.C., the fifth; in Egypt, from the early third millennium B.C. on, fifths and fourths, octaves and unisons.[67]

It is probable that this means an incidental stress of essential notes rather than a continuous accompaniment in parallels. Anyway, it proves the use of pentatonically tuned instruments, although this, in turn, does not necessarily imply pentatonic melodies.

[67] Curt Sachs, "Zweiklänge im Altertum," in *Festschrift für Johannes Wolf*, Berlin, 1929, pp. 168–70.

[4]

CONCLUSION

TO SUM UP: Despite an almost complete lack of direct information, conclusions by analogy and other indirect inference allow us to draw the vague outlines of how music was in the ancient Western Orient.

Large ensembles, like the court orchestras of Egypt, Babylon, and Elam and the choruses and orchestras connected with the Temple in Jerusalem suggest a high standard of musical education, skill, and knowledge.

The system they followed can to a certain degree be inferred from the instruments used: the open strings of harps and lyres imply the up-and-down principle and almost certainly a pentatonic tuning that other evidences confirm; the later long-necked lutes, spreading from a center in Mesopotamia or Iran, hint at the divisive principle.

Singing, at least in the last one thousand years B.c., was heptatonic without any trace of pentatonism. Its style as a whole was logogenic, basically syllabic, and only moderately spiced with ligatures and melismas. Melody followed ready-made patterns or was composed of carefully classified motifs, not of single notes. As a consequence, notation developed in the direction of group scripts, accents, and neumes, not of pitch scripts.

'Meter' in the Greek sense was unknown, and 'time' with regular beats existed only in dances and dance-inspired music. Religious melody was rhythmically free; it followed the irregular meters of the words by lengthening the accented syllables, even when they were phonetically short.

Besides simple solo and choir singing, music was by preference organized in the various forms of antiphony. Exactly what role polyphony played is hard to say; drones and consonant chords occurred at least on instruments.

It is important to realize that the ancient Western Orient had a music quite different from what historians of the nineteenth century conceded it. Open the first volume of A. W. Ambros' *Geschichte der Musik* in its edition of 1887 and you will find that "Assyrian music seems never to have risen above the level of a mere sensual stimulus"; that the music of Babylon "was in any case voluptuous and noisy and far from simple beauty and noble form"; and that the main task of Phoenician music was "to drown the cries of the victims who burned in the glowing arms of Moloch." What a difference from the calm simplicity and noble grandeur of Greek music!

Let us pigeonhole these rash and foolish misconceptions. Though we do not know how that ancient music sounded, we have sufficient evidence of its power, dignity, and mastership. Not the least is that the Greeks themselves claimed to be its pupils.

Section Three

EAST ASIA

1

GENERAL FEATURES

THIS SECTION deals with the music of China, Korea, and Japan; of Indo-China, from Annam to Siam; and of the Malay islands, particularly Bali and Java.

Chinese music can be traced back to the Shang Dynasty between the fourteenth and twelfth centuries B.C. Japanese music began only in the fifth century A.D., when Korean court music was adopted. In the sixth century, Japan became familiar with both Buddhism and the ceremonial music of China, though once more through Korea, while direct influence, without foreign intermediation, set in a hundred years later. China also passed on to Japan the ceremonial dances of India with their music, which were Japanized as the solemn and colorful *Bugaku*. A strong wave from Manchuria, in the eighth century, ended foreign influences on the classical music of Japan.

Japanese music is more archaic than Chinese music, although its history has been so much shorter. At first sight this seems paradoxical. But it is consistent with the general rule that things continue developing in their native country, while natural evolution comes to a standstill in foreign environments. In many respects, therefore, the music of the ancient East may be better studied in Japan than in China.

❀   ❀   ❀

THE ANCIENT MUSIC of which we know in the Far East is only a part, indeed a small part, of the music actually performed and enjoyed in those early times. We are almost in the position of those of our fellow musicologists who deal with the Middle Ages; just as these men are thrown on books exclusively written by monks for monks on monks' music, while no heed was given to secular songs or dances, China's "popular music was contrary to established literary principles, and there was no recognized precedent for it; so it was simply ignored." [1]

The few passages in which 'vulgar' music is mentioned are contemptuous.

[1] Gulik, *The Lore of the Chinese Lute, op. cit.,* p. 39.

In Confucius' words, a vulgar-minded man's performance "is loud and fast, and again fading and dim, a picture of violent death-agony. His heart is not harmonically balanced; mildness and graceful movements are foreign to him." And vulgar was the "noisy" music of the tyrants of Hia and Yin that Lü Pu-we, the poet of 'Spring and Fall' describes: "They deemed the loud sounds of big drums, bells, stones, pipes, and flutes beautiful and thought that mass effects were worth while. They aimed at new and strange timbres, at never heard of tones, at plays never seen before. They tried to outdo one another and overstepped the limits." [2]

True music or, in Confucius' words, "the noble-minded man's music is mild and delicate, keeps a uniform mood, enlivens and moves. Such a man does not harbor pain or mourn in his heart; violent and daring movements are foreign to him." [3] Music should be serene: *yüo* 'music' and *lo* 'serenity' had the same graphic symbol.

The contrast of good and bad music did not so much separate religious from secular music, but rather the esoteric music of a few sages, to whom music meant the last step in wandering the universe, from the cheap entertainment of the noninitiated. Thus Lü Pu-we "was able to speak of music only with a man who has grasped the meaning of the world." [4]

No staccato, no accelerando, no strong crescendo or decrescendo had a place in such music—nothing that aroused unrest, passion, lust. Music was the wisdom of the heart. No doubt 'good music' could be exasperating, and we do not blame Prince Wên of Wei (426-387 B.C.) for exclaiming: "When in full ceremonial dress I must listen to the Ancient Music, I think I shall fall asleep, but when I listen to the songs of Chêng and Wei, I never get tired." [5]

But whether good melodies were pleasant or boring, never has attitude toward music been more idealistic; and having so lofty a conception, the Far East has given the art a unique place in its spiritual life.

❀ ❀ ❀

MUSIC, to the Chinese, is born in man's heart. Whatever moves the soul pours forth in tones; and again, whatever sounds affect man's soul.[6] Confucius himself, the nation's spiritual paragon, was so deeply impressed by

---

[2] Lü Pu-we, *op. cit.,* V 3.
[3] Wilhelm, *op. cit.*
[4] Lü Pu-we, *op. cit.,* V 2.
[5] R. H. van Gulik, *op. cit.,* p. 37.
[6] Lü Pu-we, *op. cit.,* p. 73.

some old hymn that "for three months he did not know the taste of meat," and when he played the *ch'ing,* a man who passed his house exclaimed, "This heart is full that so beats the sounding stone." [7]

An old legend relates that the music master Wen of Cheng followed great Master Hsiang on his travels. Three years he touched the strings, but no melody came. Then Master Hsiang said: "By all means, go home." Master Wen laid the zither down, sighed, and said: "It is not that I cannot bring a melody about. What I have in my mind does not concern strings; what I aim at is not tones. Not until I have reached it in my heart can I express it on the instrument; therefore I do not dare move my hand and touch the strings. But give me a short while and then examine me." After a while he again appeared before Master Hsiang, who asked: "How about your playing?" Master Wen answered: "I have attained it; please test my playing." It was spring; and when he plucked the *Shang* string and had the eighth semitone accompany, a cool wind sprang up, and the shrubs and trees bore fruit. When it was autumn and he plucked the *Chiao* string and had the second semitone respond, a gentle, tepid breeze sprang up and the shrubs and trees deployed their splendor. When it was summer and he plucked the *Yü* string and accompanied it with the eleventh semitone, hoar frost and snow came down and the rivers and lakes suddenly froze. When the winter had come and he plucked the *Chih* string and had the fifth semitone respond, the sun began to scorch and the ice thawed at once. Finally, he sounded the *Kung* string and united it with the other four strings; then lovely winds murmured, clouds of good luck came up, sweet dew fell, the springs welled up powerfully.

Music's magical might to overcome the laws of nature has been praised in the legends of all nations. The Chinese myth is deeper: not sound as such has power—it is the heart that works the miracle, the great heart that in music finds its voice and form.

❀ ❀ ❀

THE GREAT HEART in another people's music rarely beats in unison with our own. Everyone has experienced how difficult it is to grasp the emotional qualities in the musical style of our own forefathers three hundred years back, and how much a conscientious performer is in doubt whether his interpretation rights or wrongs what the old composer had in mind.

---

[7] *The Original Chinese Texts of the Confucian Analecta,* transl. by J. Steele, London, 1861, p. 185.

But the gap between ourselves and 'exotic' music is hardly bridgeable; whoever has attended performances in the Orient knows that the natives seem unmoved when the visitor's imagination or sympathy is struck, and that, vice versa, he is cool or even annoyed when they burst into enraptured *Ya Salâm's*. Though we are denied participation in all its delights, we at least realize that music is greater and richer than our own limited musical capacity would admit. And this is a good thing to know.

As far as ancient China is concerned, emotion seems to have emanated much more from single sounds than from melodic turns. Confucius' stone slab provided one note; 'heartfelt' beating must have enlivened this one note by its power to benefit from the almost impalpable intricacies of striking and deadening, and even of interference.

In a similar spirit, Japanese flute players are still expected to enliven the individual tone, not only by a constant vibrato but also by skillfully sharpening it beyond its natural pitch.

The long zither in its two forms *Shê* and *Ch'in*,[8] often erroneously called "lute," is the outstanding representative of this esoteric music of ancient China. No singing girl, no actor were permitted to play this instrument. But a scholar was expected to keep it somewhere in his studio, even if he did not know how to play it; indeed, even if it had no strings. In lonely meditation or before a few selected friends, the player, having burnt incense and ceremoniously washed his hands, would lay the long, narrow instrument before him and begin his dreamy, delicate playing.

Few notes he would leave clear and hard; mostly, the string, after plucking, is given additional tension, so that the tone goes up for a moment or for good; or else, the stopping finger leaves the tone just plucked and rubs along the string with a wiping noise rather than a melodious glissando. Such continual wailing and sobbing, though certainly against our taste, is indispensable when East Asiatic music appeals to the heart.

And here, too, beauty

lies not so much in the succession of notes as in each separate note in itself. . . . Each note is an entity in itself, calculated to evoke in the mind of the hearer a special reaction. The timbre being thus of the utmost importance, there are very great possibilities of modifying the coloring of one and the same tone. In order to understand and appreciate this music, the ear must learn to distinguish subtle nuances: the same note, produced on a different string, has a different color; the same string, when pulled by the fore finger or the middle finger of the right hand, has a different timbre. The technique by which these variations in timbre are effected is extremely complicated: of the vibrato alone there exist

[8] Curt Sachs, *The History of Musical Instruments, op. cit.*, pp. 185-8.

no less than twenty-six varieties. The impression made by one note is followed by another, still another. There is thus a compelling, inevitable suggestion of a mood, an atmosphere, which impresses upon the hearer the sentiment that inspired the composer.[9]

The single note actually counted for more than melody: chimes, numerous in all kinds of orchestras, were mere sets of single stones, metal slabs, or bells, united in one frame, it is true, but not in any actual scale arrangement. Panpipes followed the same principle. Each verse of the Hymn to Confucius ended in a single blow on a sonorous stone which was to "receive the tone" and transmit it to the following word. Cosmological connotations were given to individual notes, not, as in the West, to melodic patterns. And notation consisted in separate pitch symbols.

At first sight, one would think that a musical world in which the exact cut of a tone is avoided rather than sought, and in which the single tone seems to matter more than its melodic relation to other tones, was little interested in accurate pitch and scale. The opposite is true. Both the moment of the single tone and its freedom could be established only on law and strictness, not on anarchy.

❊   ❊   ❊

LAW AND STRICTNESS, indeed, were imposed on music in China more than anywhere else, for "it was rooted in the Great One, the universal idea that nobody can visualize or even conceive." [10] The world itself, manifestation of the Great One, integrated time, space, energy, and sound. The world embodied eternal time in its unalterable cycle of seasons, months, and hours. It embodied eternal space, toward East and West, and North and South. It combined into a whole all substances, wood and metal, skin and stone. It was power, visible in wind and thunder, fire and water. And the world was tone in its two conceptions, as pitch and as timbre.

Time and space, matter and music were congruent and, in their congruency, merely different aspects of the same One. Their differentials, consequently, were congruent as well: a certain season corresponded to a certain cardinal point, or substance, or musical instrument, or note.[11] And the four seasons were separated from one another, not only by definite amounts of time but also by musical intervals: following the up-and-down principle, there was a fifth from autumn to spring, a fourth back to winter,

[9] R. H. van Gulik, *op. cit.,* pp. 1 f.
[10] Lü Pu-we, *op. cit.,* V 2.
[11] First described in the *Chou li.*

and a fifth to summer, producing the strange equation (already mentioned in the second section) as similar to the late Babylonian conception.

(F) Autumn
(C) Spring
(G) Winter
(China: D) Summer (Babylonia: C)

Chinese wisdom has indulged in endless co-ordinations of this kind; each instrument belonged to one of the cardinal points, substances, and powers: the bell stood for west and autumn, dampness and metal; the drum, for north and winter, water and skin. And the notes were associated with the twelve months of the year and their allegoric animals—tiger, hare, dragon, snake, horse, sheep, ape, cock, dog, pig, rat, and ox.

❋ ❋ ❋

COSMOLOGICAL CONNOTATIONS of musical conceptions are, as the seasonal equation of Babylonia shows, by no means confined to China. There are quite similar equations in India, in the Islamic countries, in ancient Greece, and even in the Christian Middle Ages: seasons, months, days, hours, planets, parts of the human body, moods, illnesses, elements, and what not are compared and associated, and finally the cosmos itself sounds in an eternal harmony of spheres.

Certain passages from the Bible have been quoted as inspired by the idea of cosmic harmony. But at best they show a certain preparedness for accepting such an idea through the general conception that "all the earth" ought to sing unto the Lord and "declare his glory among the nations, his marvellous works among the peoples." It would be a logical step from Psalm 96: 12, in which "all the trees of the wood rejoice before the Lord," to Philo, who in his *Life of Moses* exclaims: "O Lord, have the stars, united to form one chorus, the power of singing a song worthy of thee?" [12] The link between them is that question in Job 38: "Where wast thou when the morning stars sang together?"

The Book of Job is said to be late; Job himself lived in the time of the Babylonian Exile (sixth century B.C.). On the other hand, Philo ascribes the idea of cosmic harmony to the Chaldeans. Thus it is highly probable that the harmony of the spheres, developed from earlier cosmological co-

[12] Philo, *De Vita Moysis* II ¶ 239.

ordinations, was given its final shape in Babylonia and from there handed over to the Jews, the Greeks, and probably also the Egyptians.

One thing should not be overlooked: the harmony of the spheres differs basically from the original theory of co-ordination. This latter had established that a certain planet was to another planet as a certain pitch was to another pitch; the harmony of the spheres meant something quite different: the planets, or rather their spheres, resounded in actual, though imperceptible, tones.

In neither form is the idea of a functional interdependence of things musical and nonmusical self-evident; it cannot have originated spontaneously in every country between the Pacific and the Mediterranean.

Where, then, did it come to life, and when?

That we do not know. The best of all methods, to go back to the earliest evidences, fails with Asiatic sources which we sometimes are not able to date within a thousand years. Moreover, the texts of Egypt, Sumer, Babylonia, Assyria, and Persia are silent on the subject (which does not prove that cosmological connotations were unknown).

The only statement we are allowed to make is this: the earliest evidences of these cosmological co-ordinations are Chinese and Greek, and as far as Greece is concerned, the idea is doubtless due to importation from the East. But there is as yet no answer to the question whether it was indigenous to China or brought in from some other part of Asia.

❊ ❊
❊

CO-ORDINATION requires a *tertium comparationis*. Such a cosmological series as fire-red-Mars-south-summer is logical and self-explanatory in that all its members are hot. Sound, on the contrary, has no direct relation to other categories of perception, except by the most abstract of all likenesses: number and measure.

Sound in itself, however, is impalpable and unmeasurable, except by vibration numbers, which were unknown in ancient China. The only way open was to shift from sound to sound-producing devices, from tones to instruments. Pitch varied with the size of the vibrating medium, and the relation between two tones could be expressed by the proportion of two lengths of flutes or strings.

But the relativity of proportions would not do for the use of music in the co-ordinations of cosmology. The Chinese—more than any other people—

needed absolute pitch or, in other words, a standard length. Indeed, Lü Pu-we plainly states: "Music stems from measure." [13] And so intimate became the connection of music and length that the Imperial Office of Music was annexed to the Office of Weights and Measures.

This idea, again, was not confined to China. As un-Chinese and late a thinker as the Jewish poet, Jehuda Halevy (c. 1080–1140), said: "Measures, weights, the proportions of various movements, the harmony of music, everything is in number." [14]

The unit of length imposed on the standard pitch was the metrical foot that in China ruled whatever extended in length, width, and height. Music truly became a function of space; and once more the universe appeared to be one. So close became the relation of pitch tone and foot that in the tenth century A.D. some learned Chinese, called upon to renormalize the spreading confusion, earnestly questioned whether pitch depended on feet and inches or the metric foot on the pitch tone.

❋   ❋   ❋

CORRECTNESS IN MUSIC was not mainly, if at all, a musical concern. It was essential to the cosmos. Time and space, substance and power were beyond man's control. But sound he created himself; in music, he took the heavy responsibility for either strengthening or imperiling the equilibrium of the world. And his responsibility included the world's truest images, the dynasty and the country; the welfare of the empire depended on the correctness of pitches and scales.

As a consequence, the readjustment of music was one of a new emperor's first acts; for, would the preceding dynasty have been eliminated unless its music was out of harmony with the universe?

The Chinese have credited the very oldest dynasties with this order of thought. The mythical Emperor Shun, said to have come to the throne in 2285 B.C., impressed on his chief musician, so *Shu King,* the earliest Chinese chronicle, relates: " 'Kwei, I command you to regulate music. . . . The notes should accord with the measure. The reed regulates the voice and the eight instruments, and you must harmonize them all, but without disturbing the due order. Gods and men will then approve. . . .' Yearly, in the second month, he journeyed eastward, going about the territories

13 Lü Pu-we, *op. cit.,* V 2.
14 Yehuda Halevy, *Cusari,* ed. Cassel, II § 65, IV § 25, quoted from Eric Werner and Isaiah Sonne, "The Philosophy and Theory of Music in Judaeo-Arabic Literature," in *Hebrew Union College Annual* XVI (1941), p. 265.

. . . and adjusted the four seasons, the months and the first days and tested the notes of music." [15]

When the emperor wished to ascertain whether his government was right or not, he listened to the six pitches, the five tones of the scale, and the eight kinds of musical instruments, and he took the odes of the court and ballads of the village to see if they corresponded with the five tones.[16]

These ideas resulted under Emperor Wou (141–87 B.C.) in the foundation of *Yüe fu,* the Imperial Office of Music, with special sections to supervise ceremonial, foreign, aristocratic, and folk music and a complete archive of national melodies. Its chief concern, however, was the establishment and preservation of correct pitch.

[15] *The Shoo King,* transl. by W. H. Medhurst, Shanghai, 1846, pp. 10, 33 f. *The Shu King,* transl. by Walter Gorn Old, London, 1904, p. 20.
[16] Medhurst edition, pp. 69 f.

2

THE LÜ'S

"EMPEROR HUANG TI, so legend says, one day ordered Ling Lun to make pitch pipes. Ling Lun went from the west of the Ta Hia and came to the north of the Yüan Yü mountain. Here he took bamboos from the valley Hia Hi, selected those the internodes of which were thick and even, and cut them between two nodes. Their length was three inches, nine lines. He blew them and made their tone the starting note *huang chung* of the scale. He blew them and said: 'That's right.' Then he made twelve pipes. Since he heard the male and the female bird Phoenix sing at the foot of the Yüan Yü mountain, he accordingly distinguished the twelve notes. He made six out of the singing of the male Phoenix, and also six out of the singing of the female Phoenix, which all could be derived from the main note *huang chung*." [17]

Ta Hia, which the English sinologist, Giles, had believed to be a district of Bactria, was recently identified by Otto Franke as the country of the Tochars. The Tochars, who had lived on the southeastern border of the Gobi desert at least since the thirteenth century B.C., were peace-loving people and acted as agents between the Eastern and Western civilizations.[18] Pitch pipes, however, were unknown in the West, as far as we can see. It is more probable that the Occident presented China with the method of deriving notes from one another.

Later versions of the same legend offer a few more details. Père Amiot, the earliest serious writer on Chinese music, had mentioned one of them in his manuscript, but his posthumous editor, Abbé Roussel, omitted it as "irrelevant" and only called it to notice in a short footnote.[19] And just this detail is particularly illuminating. Ling Lun, it reads, found a bamboo pipe that reproduced exactly the pitch of his own voice when he spoke without passion, and this he made the *huang chung*. Here at last, Chinese tradition admits a musical fact among so many extramusical data: the

[17] Lü Pu-we, *op. cit.*, p. 478.
[18] Otto Franke, "Das alte Ta-hia der Chinesen," in *Ostasiatische Zeitschrift* VIII (1920), pp. 117–36.
[19] Père Amiot. *Mémoire sur la Musique des Chinois*. Paris, 1779, p. 86 r.

huang chung, primarily, was roughly taken from the medium pitch of a man's voice and only subsequently normalized in feet, inches, and lines.

❋   ❋   ❋

THE STANDARD TONE *huang chung,* "the yellow bell," "begot" all other tones.

Most authors, however, have misrepresented this process. Overblowing, they have said, did not result in the octave, but in the twelfth (as the pipe supposedly was stopped and did not produce even-numbered partials). The new note, mentally transposed into the lower octave, became the fifth of the standard tone. A second pipe was tuned to this fifth. When over-blown, it again yielded a twelfth which, transposed down by two octaves, formed a whole tone above the standard tone. And so on, twelfth by twelfth.

This entangled cycle of fifths with its overblown notes and its subsequent transpositions by one or several octaves up to six is neither convincing nor evidenced: none of the sources mentions blowing or hearing. They relate, on the contrary, that the pipes were cut with the aid of a ruler by alternately subtracting and adding one third of their length—3:2 and 3:4. Space under the Chou the Chinese foot was divided into nine inches, and the inch into nine lines, the standard tone had a pipe length of eighty-one lines. The following pipe was smaller by one third or twenty-seven lines. The third pipe was longer than the second by one third or eighteen lines.

Graphically:

$$\begin{array}{ccccc} & 54 & & 48 & \\ \diagup & \diagdown & \diagup & \diagdown & \diagup \\ 81 & & 72 & & 64 \end{array} \text{ and so on.}$$

The way up (musically speaking) was called an *inferior generation* (that is, coming from below), and the way down, a *superior generation.*

Theoretically, this procedure resulted in a chain of ascending fifths and descending fourths:

$$\begin{array}{ccccccccccc} & C & & D & & E & & F\sharp & & G\sharp & & A\sharp \\ \diagup & & \diagdown & \diagup & & \diagdown & \diagup & & \diagdown & \diagup & & \diagdown \\ F & & G & & A & & B & & C\sharp & & D\sharp \end{array}$$

Operations were stopped after six inferior and six superior generations, so that, again theoretically, a complete chromatic series was brought about. The six odd-numbered pitch notes (our lower line) were called *lü's* or "norms" and considered masculine, while the six even-numbered notes, later likewise called *lü's,* had names which meant "companions, intermediate, lateral" and were feminine. This shows that at the beginning the notes produced by inferior generation had no musical significance proper, or at best a subordinate significance: the series consisted of six *lü's* at equal whole-tone distances.

* * *

CONCEIVING a set of qualities as alternately masculine and feminine and their coexistence as a sequence of generations is certainly no everyday idea. And yet it strongly calls to mind the kabbalistic cosmogeny of the ancient Jews which combined the eternal masculine with the eternal feminine and cemented them into the eternally human. God created the world by ten utterances or *sphirot*. The first *sphira*—principle of all principles, the crown of all that which there was of the most high—was neither positive nor negative, but though sexless it was androgenous. This first *sphira* begot all nine following *sphirot* in successive generations. The second *sphira*, called understanding (*bīnā*), was negative and feminine; the third *sphira*, called wisdom (*hākmā*), was her child, positive and masculine. And so on.

Once more we face the striking cosmopolitism of mystic ideas. J. F. C. Fuller says of the Kabbala: "Aryan and Chaldean esoteric doctrines percolated into it. In Egypt, the mysteries of the Sun god, the Moon goddess, of Osiris and Isis, impinged upon it. Assyria and Babylon gave it much, and not a little may be traced to the Vedas, the Upanishads, the Bhagavad-Gita and the Vedantas, and much of the practical Qabalah to the Tantras more especially. In it will be found Hinduism, Taoism, Buddhism, Zoroastrianism. . . ." [20]

And in view of such spiritual cosmopolitism one might ask whether the ancient Middle East, particularly Sumer, Babylonia, and Egypt, had not some kind of *lü* system in their music. After all, with the open strings of their harps and lyres, these nations must have based their musical systems on the same up-and-down principle that the Chinese had. And then, the legends of China relate that the emperor's minister brought the *lü's* from the West.

* * *

TWICE in explaining the *lü's* we used the word *theoretically;* twice, by this word, we warned the reader against supposing that the Chinese ever had a perfect method of tuning. The foot measure itself was anything but constant; it varied between a minimum of twenty centimeters in the Chou

[20] J. F. C. Fuller, *The Secret Wisdom of the Qabalah*, London (1937).

period and a maximum of thirty-four centimeters under the Ming. The ratio of these extremes, 3:5, forcibly resulted in a musical variation within a minor sixth: if the pitch tone was *C* under the Chou, it was the *E* below under the Ming! One can easily imagine what the musical consequences were when temples and palaces preserved venerable stone and bell chimes from epochs in which the foot and pitch had been different.

So much for absolute pitch.

The relation between the *lü's* was no less faulty. The proportions 4:3 for the fourth and 3:2 for the fifth, correct in theory, failed in practice, since pitch depended, not on one but on three factors: the length of the tube, to be sure, but also its diameter and the position of the player's lips. The twelfth of the ground tone, produced by overblowing a pitch pipe [21] and generally believed to have controlled the issue, worsened rather than corrected the result. For, according to Dr. Manfred Bukofzer's experiments,[22] the overblown twelfth of stopped pipes is too high if the pipe is longer than eight inches, and too low if the pipe is shorter than eight inches. The incorrectness may amount to as much as a quarter tone.

The influence of the blowing lips was not realized in China, and the importance of the diameter was considered only in a few periods of Chinese history; in the second century A.D., for instance, the official gaugers gave all pipes the same diameter, but in the third century they gradually lessened it line by line, starting from nine lines for the *huang chung*. The very number nine, derived from the nine times nine lines of the *huang chung's* length, indicates that the diameter was determined by numeral symbolism rather than by any mathematical ratio. But even with correct measurements, the pitches would not have been entirely reliable, since the force of the breath and the exact angle at which it crossed the upper orifice of the pipe were likely to interfere with theoretical calculation.

Finally, the cycle of fifths was doomed from the very beginning, because it would graze but never hit the octave, indispensable in building scales. The reason is mathematically obvious: going on in fifths means raising the ratio $\frac{3}{2}$ to a higher power; the octave has the ratio $\frac{2}{1}$; but no power of three can ever coincide with a power of two.

In 40 B.C., the musician, King Fang, tried to correct the fault by extending the cycle of *lü's* from twelve to sixty; and about 430 A.D. somebody outdid him by continuing the cycle up to 360 fifths. The reader shall be spared the grotesque ratio that results from the 360th power of $\frac{3}{2}$—such hairsplitting

[21] Cf. Curt Sachs, *The History of Musical Instruments, op. cit.,* p. 418.
[22] Manfred Bukofzer, "Präzisionsmessungen an primitiven Musikinstrumenten," in *Zeitschrift für Physik* IC (1936), pp. 643–65, esp. p. 660.

was disproportionate to so inexact a procedure and it was also ineffective.

We are not going to describe all the futile attempts made since. Suffice it to say that the *huang chung* was uncertain from the very beginning and the struggle never came to rest. The history of Chinese pitch is a history of some twenty centuries of confusion, deception, and failure; the recipes changed, and so did the results.

❋　❋　❋

THE SET OF LÜ's has been called a "scale." Especially in its mature form, with the auxiliary *lü's* dovetailed in, it seemed to be, and consequently was described as, a chromatic scale.

This was a mistake. The twelve notes never formed a scale in the narrower sense of the word, and least of all anything resembling our modern chromatic scale with its equal semitones of one hundred Cents. In a cycle of fifths, each semitone is separated from its neighbor by seven times the interval of a fifth, or $7 \times 702 = 4,914$ Cents, which of course must be lowered by four octaves or $4 \times 1,200 = 4,800$ Cents. The result is 114 Cents for the semitone. But since the whole tone amounts to 204 Cents, the complementing semitone cannot have more than ninety Cents. Far from being well tempered, the set of *lü's*—at least as it should be were it correct—is an alternation of major and minor semitones which the Western ear can hardly tolerate.

Moreover, the old discrimination between superior and inferior generation persisted both in arrangement and name: the Chinese, who understand the universe as the harmonious balance of *yang* and *yin,* the masculine and the feminine principle, called the six odd-numbered *lü's* "male," and the six even-numbered "female." The legend related above tells this in its own way: it ascribes six of the *lü's* to a male bird, and six to a female bird. So definite was the contrast that musical instruments, tuned to the *lü's,* never mingled the two sets: in stone and bell chimes the male *lü's* were provided by an upper row, and the female by a lower row of slabs or bells; and panpipes, which at first were nothing but complete sets of pitch pipes, consisted either of male or of female pipes only, or, if combined, had the two sets kept apart in two wings.[23] In the Occidental conception, such instruments would play continuous melodic lines through all kinds of intervals. The Chinese, on the contrary, aimed at single notes only, the

---

[23] Cf. Curt Sachs, *The History of Musical Instruments, op. cit.,* pp. 168, 169, 176, 177.

selection of which depended on the season and the particular rite of the day rather than on musical considerations.

❀   ❀   ❀

THE CONFUSION of the series of *lü's* with a scale—a "dim" scale indeed, as the Koreans qualifyingly call it—had been made long before, and in a way interesting enough to be related. That legend of the minister's errand to the West is completed by a tradition that the male bird sang his notes in an ascending, and the female bird hers in a descending, succession.

The symbolism of male and female scales is obvious: the male sex was in many civilizations represented by an upward pointing symbol, and the female sex by a descending one, just as in our books on biology or botany. But there was a far more important discrimination of ascending and descending scales: ascending scales, as a rule, were instrumental, whereas descending scales were vocal. It is not difficult to find the reason. A primitive singer does not begin in the low register of his voice to climb up higher and higher; he normally starts from the high register and descends to the lower limit of his range. Players behave differently. A piper's scale is brought forth by opening the fingerholes hole by hole; it is ascending. In the same way, lutanists, fiddlers, and players of fretted zithers depart from the open string and pass to the higher notes of the stopped string. Indeed, the second part of the seventh of the books called *Yo tse* relates that in the ancient worship of heaven and earth the instruments played in an ascending series of *lü's*, and the voices sang in a descending series of *lü's*.[24]

This contrariness, still in use under the T'ang (618–907 A.D.), had been simplified by the end of the sixteenth century: Prince Tsai Yü assumed that all vocal keys were a fourth higher than the corresponding instrumental keys; voices and instruments used two different keys a fourth apart, and when playing together they performed throughout in parallel fourths; the voices would sing in *F,* while the instruments played in *C* below. This was exactly the contrapuntal form of the *organum* of the early Middle Ages, in which the *cantus* was sung above, while the *organum* (originally meaning "instrument") accompanied in parallels a fourth lower. In a similar way, the Siamese play parallel fourths on their gong chimes.[25]

[24] Mrs. Timothy Richard, *Paper on Chinese Music,* Shanghai (1899), p. 5.
[25] Cf. Carl Stumpf, "Tonsystem und Musik der Siamesen," in *Beiträge zur Akustik und Musikwissenschaft, Heft* 3, 1901; the same in *Sammelbände für Vergleichende Musikwissenschaft* I (1922), pp. 172 f.

❀   ❀   ❀

IN JAPAN, the twelve *lü's* are known as *ritsu*—a term that must not be confused with the name of one of the foremost melodic modes of the country. Pitch pipes, as in China, exist but are not important in musical practice. Generally, the *ritsu* are fixed on the ground of the up-and-down principle; players of the unfretted long zither *koto* stretch the first string to an appropriate pitch; then they tune the sixth string to the upper fourth and the eighth string to the upper fifth, go back by a fourth to the third string and up by a fifth to the tenth string, and so on.

The pitch itself "is within limits arbitrary: for a loud singer it is tuned up, for a singer with a small voice it is tuned down. But the normal pitch of the note is approximately middle *C*." [26] The latest Japanese source indicates, as pitch tone, the lowest *d'* of the vertical flute *shakuhachi* at 292 vibrations.[27] It is to be noted that the Middle East too uses *d'* as pitch tone and also derives it from the lowest note of its vertical flute.

[26] Francis Piggott, *The Music and Musical Instruments of Japan,* 2nd edition, Yokohama-London, 1909, p. 85.
[27] Hisao Tanabe, *Japanese Music,* Tokyo, 1936.

3

THE SCALES

THE NORMAL SCALE of the Far East is pentatonic without semitones. It consists of three whole tones and two minor thirds, the thirds being alternately separated by one or by two whole tones, just as in the series of black keys on our pianos.

The scale is usually presented in the form *kung* (do), *shang* (re), *chiao* (mi), *chih* (sol), *yü* (la), (*kung*) (do).

These five notes were tied into the network of cosmological connotations much in the same way as the twelve *lü's*. There was close interrelation between the

Notes	*kung*	*shang*	*chiao*	*chih*	*yü*
Cardinal points	North	East	Center	West	South
Planets	Mercury	Jupiter	Saturn	Venus	Mars
Elements	wood	water	earth	metal	fire
Colors	black	violet	yellow	white	red

This scale is generally said to have originated from picking out five of the *lü's*. Such misrepresentation should not be repeated indefinitely. In the first place, *lü's* formed intervals out of tune and therefore unusable for scales. Secondly, the scale itself must have existed before the artificial system of *lü's* was constructed. Thirdly, the *lü's* in their earliest arrangement consisted of two entirely independent sets of six whole tones each, without the characteristic minor thirds, fourths, or fifths in either set of the scale. Picking out the five notes necessary to the scale would have meant jumping to and fro and picking at least two, if not three, of the five notes from the merely auxiliary female set which at the beginning hardly counted at all. This does not make sense.

In any case, deriving scales from systems is putting the cart before the horse: all over the world, scales have been abstracted from living melodies and integrated in systems.

The 'picking' out holds true only for the tonic *kung*, which indeed, as far as ritual music was concerned, had to be one of the *lü's*. The *huang chung* was selected as the tonic when sacrifices were presented to heaven;

but the melodies were transposed to the fifth for sacrifices to the earth; to the second, for the sun; to the sixth, for the moon. Moreover, all melodies were shifted monthly by one *lü,* so that the same melody, played in January in, say, *E,* would be transposed to *F* in February.

No sources ever speak of conforming the other four notes to four *lü's.* Quite independently, they follow one of the two methods of developing scales from a starting tone, either the cyclic principle or the divisive principle. Indeed, the long zither *ch'in* follows both principles at once: it has open strings tuned by ear in a cycle of just fifths and fourths, but only for the accompaniment. The melody string, on the other hand, is fretted in an unusual way: instead of actual raised frets which start from the upper end, thirteen little mother-of-pearl studs, inlaid in the soundboard to mark the stopping places, are symmetrically arranged from the center toward the two ends, and that at one half of the total length, in one and two thirds, in one and three quarters, in one and four fifths, in one and five sixths, and in one and seven eighths. The seven strings consisted of a varying number of silk threads—48, 54, 64, 72, 81, 96, 108—reproducing, in the numbers of their threads, the musical ratios of eight to nine or 204 Cents (the whole tone) and twenty-seven to thirty-two or 294 Cents (the minor third). Thus the open strings obeyed the up-and-down system, while the melody string followed the divisive system. Consequently, the melody and its accompaniment had different major thirds, different minor thirds, and different seconds.

This discrepancy was certainly not due to insensitive ears. Even a norm instrument like the *chuen,* made in the last century B.C. for tuning bell chimes (and probably also its huge prototype, the *kyun* of the Chou Dynasty), united the same two principles: a wooden soundboard, nine feet long, supported thirteen strings, twelve of which were open and the thirteenth, in the middle, was stretched along a calibrated scale. This scale, however, differed from the symmetrical arrangement of the studs on the *ch'in;* a picture that Prince Tsai Yü published seventeen hundred years later—after either an old picture or an actual specimen—shows twelve marks in a single series at proportionately decreasing distances.

❈   ❈
❈

MODAL ARRANGEMENTS of the Chinese pentatonic scale are best characterized in Japanese theory. There, the pentatonic octave of three seconds and two minor thirds appears under two clearly defined forms: *ryo* and *ritsu.*

Ryo, called the Chinese and male mode, starts with two consecutive seconds, say *CDE GA C,* and might be symbolized numerically (by its characteristic opening notes) as 123; it has *C* as the finalis, and *G* as the confinalis. A good and easily accessible example is the Chinese song "The Haunts of Pleasure" or "The Fifteen Bunches of Flowers" on page 42 of J. A. van Aalst's *Chinese Music.*

Ex. 39. CHINESE SONG   *after van Aalst*

Ritsu, called "female" and preferred in Japan, is very different. It forms an octave of two disjunct fourths, each of which is divided by a filling note closer, sometimes to the upper, sometimes to the lower end. Accordingly, the *ritsu* scale appears in two forms, *DE GAB D* and *D FGA CD.* The numeric symbols for these would be 124 and 134, and for *ritsu* in general, 1·4 (with either 2 or 3 as a filler). Our examples are a Japanese song and the beginning of the Chinese Hymn to Confucius, probably the oldest preserved piece of Far Eastern music:

Ex. 40. JAPANESE SONG   *after Noel Peri*

Ex. 41. HYMN TO CONFUCIUS

This makes a total of three modes, which may be represented in this way:

124:	*G A C D E G*
134:	*A C D E G A*
123:	*C D E G A C*

To judge from sources of the Chou Dynasty, there were seven loci for modal inversions of the pentatonic scale probably before the scale itself was given seven notes. But this modal wealth was scarcely more than a theoretical construction; musical theory, all over the ancient civilizations, exhausts the number of possible variations and combinations without ever caring for the realities of musical life.

❀   ❀   ❀

THE ARRANGEMENT *CDE GA* (123) has generally been considered the original, standard form from which the other modal arrangements were derived by the usual toptail inversion.

This is a mistake; the 123 scale differs basically from any 1·4 scale. The latter, forming in tetrachords, conjunct or disjunct, and resulting in heptads or octaves, goes back to primitive patterns in which under the normative power of the fourth an original third nucleus grows a second affix or, inversely, a second nucleus grows a third affix in order to attain to a fourth.

A 123 scale, on the contrary, is practically always hexachordal; there are no sevenths or octaves. Nor does it form in tetrachords; indeed, the very fourth is wanting. Instead, the fifth acts as the normative power: two thirds, superimposed, settle down in a pentachord; the lower third is filled in, and the sixth is scarcely more than a neighboring note returning to the fifth.

This entirely different nature of the 123 scale is evident from melodies of primitive peoples in which the elements show better than in the elaborate songs of China. One of the best examples is the following melody from Greenland:

Ex. 42. EAST GREENLAND

Farther back, two four-tone patterns precede the 123 scale: one, with the lower third filled in, but without a sixth (123·5), appears in this Song of Fate performed by the Voguls in West Siberia:

Ex. 43. VOGULS, SIBERIA   *after Väisänen*

The other, with the sixth, but without fillers (1·3·56), may be represented by a vocal melody from the Solomon Archipelago:

Ex. 44. SOLOMON ISLANDS   *after Hornbostel*

Consequently, this structure must have been very old; but it hardly begot the entirely different 1·4 structure.

* * *

JAPAN OPPOSES a national scale of its own to the so-called Chinese scale. It is pentatonic as well, but not 'anhemitonic': each of its tetrachords has an undivided *major* third above and a semitone below.

This impressive scale appears in three 'tunings,' which actually correspond to the three aspects of Greek modes, Hypodorian, Dorian, and Hyperdorian:

Hirajoshi: A B C E F A

(conjunct tetrachords with the supplemental octave below; *hypo*)

Kumoi(joshi): E F A B C E

(disjunct tetrachords)

Iwato: B C E F A B

(conjunct tetrachords with the supplemental octave above; *hyper*)

The first in importance is Hirajoshi; the second, Kumoi. Hirajoshi is the mode of the following nursery song:

Ex. 45. JAPANESE NURSERY SONG   *after Noel Peri*

Presto

A solo on the long zither *koto*, played in a death scene in the tragedy *Kesa*,[28] illustrates Kumoi:

Ex. 46. KOTO SOLO FROM THE JAPANESE TRAGEDY 'KESA'
after Abraham and Hornbostel

[28] After Otto Abraham and E. M. von Hornbostel, "Tonsystem und Musik der Japaner," in *Sammelbände der Internationalen Musikgesellschaft* IV (1903), p. 351 and *Sammelbände für Vergleichende Musikwissenschaft* I (1922), p. 223.

Modulation is frequent. The first of the two following examples shows the passage from Kumoi (disjunct tetrachords) to Hirajoshi (conjunct tetrachords); the second modulates inversely from Hirajoshi to Kumoi:

Ex. 47. JAPANESE SONG *after Noel Peri*

Ex. 48. JAPANESE SONG *after Noel Peri*

All books agree in the ill-considered assertion that the Japanese flattened two notes of the Chinese scale in order to spice an all too lifeless pattern—man has always been inclined to interpret as offshoots things that he happened to learn at a later date.

The idea of spicing is suspiciously Western; it smells of modern virtuosoship and snobbery. From a psychological standpoint one has, on the contrary, to concede that a greater contrast of intervals, bearing witness to stronger emotional tension, is scarcely ever a later development. This is confirmed by a highly significant fact: Japanese folk music never accepted the Chinese scale, but, in spite of court and temple rituals, has again and again come back to the major thirds and semitones.

The situation is somewhat similar in Korea; they have a pentatonic scale of the 123 type and 'flatten' the third: *DEF AB,* and this scale, too, occurs exclusively in folk music.[29]

The major-third scale, therefore, is doubtless a *substrate*—an old, inherited design that in all times has glittered through foreign varnishes.

❀   ❀   ❀

KINDRED SCALES have existed outside Japan and Korea.

India has them by the score in all possible combinations and arrangements—with two major thirds, or one major and one minor, or even one major and two minor thirds. It is hard to tell how many of them are due to

Ex. 49. INDIAN RĀGA MALAHĀRĪ *after C. R. Day*

[29] C. S. Keh, *Die Koreanische Musik*, Strassburg, 1935, p. 15.

a later desire for completeness, rather than to musical necessity; in any event, four of the scales enumerated in Bharata's *Nātyaśāstra,* India's earliest source of music, already have either two or at least one major third: *Arṣabhī, Ṣāḍjodīśyavatī, Dhaivatī, Niṣādī.* Possibly the second and third of these scales are meant to have the *F* sharpened (which according to Bharata's own statement was in several cases necessary).

Mongolia, too, uses major-third scales,[30] though apparently no longer always in pure form: our example, printed from Carl Stumpf's short monograph on Mongolian music,[31] contains a *D* that obviously belongs in a later stratum:

Ex. 50. BURIAT MONGOLS   *after Stumpf*

Even Greece knew the strong flavor of major-third pentatonics; a later chapter will discuss the vital role of its Hellenic form, the so-called enharmonion.

And the ancient Egyptians also tuned their temple harps to the major-third scale.

The presence of these scales in Mongolia, with evidences in East Asia, India, Egypt and Greece, hints at a possible origin in Central Asia. This assumption is corroborated by major-third scales among Moroccan Berbers, who seem to stem from Central Asia and to have preserved many traits of Central Asiatic civilization—the house with several stories, for instance.[32]

❊   ❊   ❊

THE MALAY ARCHIPELAGO clings to the major third more than any other country outside Japan. In West Java, the most archaic part of the island, singers perform in scales with two major thirds, such as (descending):

$$\underbrace{398 + 94}_{492} + 210 + \underbrace{402 + 96}_{498} \text{ Cents}^{33}$$

---

[30] Ilmari Krohn, "Mongolische Melodien," in *Zeitschrift für Musikwissenschaft* III (1920), p. 71.

[31] Carl Stumpf, "Mongolische Gesänge," in *Vierteljahrsschrift für Musikwissenschaft* III (1887), p. 303, and in *Sammelbände für Vergleichende Musikwissenschaft* I (1922), p. 110.

[32] E. M. von Hornbostel und R. Lachmann, "Asiatische Parallelen zur Berbermusik," in *Zeitschrift für Vergleichende Musikwissenschaft* I (1933), pp. 4–11.

[33] Jaap Kunst, *De Toonkunst van Java,* 's Gravenhage, 1934, vol. I, p. 318.

That is to say, two disjunct tetrachords, each of which consists of a perfect major third above and a semitone below—the exact likeness of a Japanese Kumoi scale.

In similar arrangements, a great many single instruments and entire orchestras of West Java have scales with one or even two major thirds. Specialists may evaluate the exact measurements in the West Java chapter of Jaap Kunst's book.[34]

The classical major-third genus of the archipelago, used all over Java and the neighboring island of Bali, is *pelog*. This scale can hardly be rendered

Ex. 51. JAVANESE PELOG   *transcribed by Curt Sachs from Decca 20124 A*

original ¼ tone lower

by a standard pattern of Cent numbers. Two conjunct tetrachords form a heptad; each tetrachord consists of a major third above and a semitone or so below. Variation, however, is very great. The thirds and the seconds, even on the same instrument, are rarely of the same sizes; one second would measure 91 Cents, and the following second 176 Cents; and an approximately major third of 376 Cents would coexist with a fourthlike third of 488 Cents. The tetrachords are larger, and often much larger, than a just fourth.

To understand this lack of regularity, I should like to refer the reader to the end of the division on Shades in the Greek section of this book, page 215.

Malayan scales are indeed very free, to put it mildly. Both pitches and distances have an amazing latitude even within the same instrument, and it is a mere chance to find a just fourth. Such failure in a music-loving country would be inexplicable unless we knew that the cycle of fifths was just as little known as the harmonic division of strings. The orchestras of the archipelago consist in fact of idiophonic instruments which did not admit any palpable relation of length and pitch; the other classes are only represented by one or two drums and a casual flute or (Arabo-Persian) fiddle. Whenever one asks for Balinese or Javanese tuning methods, the answer is that some old gong founder owns a few highly respected metal bars inherited from a remote ancestor and uses them with more or less accuracy as pitch standards. In other words, scales have not been con-

[34] *Ibid.*, pp. 197, 199, 288, 290, 309, 311, 312, 318.

structed, but copied and recopied throughout the centuries with ever growing incorrectness; the archipelago has a musical tradition, but no musical
science.

❀   ❀   ❀

Two ARCHAIC TYPES of Javanese orchestras, called *munggang* and *ƙodoƙ
ngoreƙ,* have a restricted range of only one tetrachord of the *pelog* kind:
(descending) *E C B.* They are particularly shrouded in mystery and ven-
erated, and therefore have been considered to be very old—older than
pelog itself.

I must confess that I am not convinced. The first orchestra in *munggang*
tuning is said to date from the fourth century A.D. Is this really 'old'? Can
we earnestly believe that at so late a time, more than a thousand years after
the era of *pelog*-like scales in Greece, the Javanese, although they were advanced enough to form orchestras, still had not progressed beyond three-
tone melodies—notwithstanding whether they lived under East Asiatic or
Indian influence or were left to themselves? I believe the reasoning that a
heptad of two tetrachords must have been preceded by a single tetrachord
is a bit too cheap. Nor do I see any confirmation in other instances.

Pelog is often misrepresented as a heptatonic scale; the thirds, unin-
formed authors say, are brought about by skipping two of the seven notes.
It is the other way around: in order to allow for modal rearrangements
within the same range, instruments are given seven notes, two of which
can alternate with their neighbors. Thus there are seven loci for five degrees
of the scale, and there is no more 'skipping' than when we leave out the
black keys in playing *C* major.

The question of mode is not quite easy. Once there were three modes:
nem or *bem, limå* or *pelog,* and *barang.* Written in *A,* for the sake of simplicity, they would read:

Nem: (*A*) *B C*   *E F*   *A*
Limå: *A   B*   *D E F*   *A*
Barang: *B   C*   *E F G*

But Dr. Jaap Kunst and, with him, Dr. Manfred Bukofzer, who was
kind enough to send me his unpublished notes, insist on the rather insignificant role of mode and particularly on the neglect of *limå.* Still, *limå* seems
to have at least an historical importance. One cannot overlook the fact that
nem, with its conjunct tetrachords plus an additional tone below, cor-

responds to Japanese Hirajoshi. And *limå* would be a perfect Kumoijoshi, with its disjunct tetrachords, if it had its *B* flattened. From Dr. Bukofzer's material, I gather indeed that this *B* is nearly always flatter by about a quarter tone than it should be. This looks suspiciously like a compromise between the two modes. Such compromise would probably have a parallel in the Western Orient where the neutral third of Zalzal of Bagdad (d. 791) and of Persian lutanists has been attributed to facilitating the transition from conjunct to disjunct tetrachords.[35] The final loss of *limå* might be due to a certain feeling against disjunct tetrachords.

❊   ❊   ❊

SALENDRO OR SLENDRO, the other great genus of the Malays, considered masculine in opposition to the 'female' *pelog,* is generally described as an octave divided into five steps of equal size, each step coming to six fifths of a tone, or 240 Cents. This is on the whole true, though exact equality is never attained: steps vary between 185 and 275 Cents. These extremes, however, are exceptions; the first optimum is around 231 Cents, and a second optimum is around 251 Cents.

Ex. 52. JAVANESE SLENDRO   *transcribed by Curt Sachs
from Decca 20124 B*

The picture changes when from recent instruments we turn to very old pieces, excavated from the soil of Java and still reliable because their metal bars have kept a constant pitch. While no modern metallophone includes any step wider than 275 Cents, old specimens generally have one of a larger size, between 300 and 310 Cents [36] and a smaller large step besides of around 280 Cents.

Here are unmistakable traces of an ancient octave divided into three seconds and two minor thirds—a division that at least every Westerner believes he hears anyway.

But the traces of ancient thirds also testify to a temperament tending to efface the difference between thirds and seconds. Of the two thirds in each

[35] Antoine Dechevrens, *Etudes de Science musicale, 2ᵉ Etude, Appendice IV,* Paris, 1898, p. 8.
[36] J. Kunst en C. J. A. Kunst-v. Wely, *De Toonkunst van Bali,* Weltevreden, 1925, II, pp. 476, 477.

octave only one reaches or exceeds the standard distance of three hundred Cents; the other is smaller in the first two examples, while in the third example it has actually been assimilated into the augmented seconds.

The exact bearings of the *slendro* scale might also be taken in virtue of the fact that all features common to the Javanese and the Balinese civilizations appear in a more archaic stage of development in Bali. Consequently, a comparison between Javanese and Balinese *slendro* tunings must be expected to throw light on the evolution of that system. At first sight, they do not differ very much; the distances from tone to tone seem to be just as arbitrary in Bali as they are in Java. Nevertheless, the trouble of evaluating the four average distances on a greater number of carefully measured instruments, both in Bali and in Java, yields a definite result. The Bali average, from tone to tone, is:

        219 250 228 260   Cents
(Sums: 469 697 957   Cents)

The Java average is:

        236 240 248 227   Cents
(Sums: 476 724 961   Cents)

There is less temperament in Bali; the distance of 697 Cents practically coincides with the perfect fifth.

Slendro has been believed, even in Java, to be older than *pelog*. This is highly improbable; indeed, there is a definite indication of the contrary: one among the Javanese notes is called *limå,* "the fifth," and one *nem,* "the sixth." But they are so only in *pelog;* in *slendro* they are the fourth and the fifth note. The terminology must have been created for *pelog* and later transferred to *slendro*.

※　　※　　※

THE QUESTION OF MODE is not easily answered. Java had three *slendro* modes, but they have no importance today, and even their distinguishing features are nearly forgotten. They are played on the same instruments and in the same range and scale and only differ in their main notes, which in the orchestra are emphasized by single strokes of the large gong. But not even these chief notes are beyond doubt. Dr. Jaap Kunst found the second note of the (ascending) octave used as the key note of the mode *nem* in 64.2 per cent of all *nem* melodies; the fourth note for *sangå* in 84.7 per cent; the fifth note for *manjurå* in 59 per cent—against 41 per cent of other chief notes.

This means disintegration. But it also shows an original start from different notes of the scale—as in the Indian *grāmas* and the European hexachords—which must have resulted in difficulties when the necessity of playing all modes on the same one-octave instruments forced the Javanese musicians to project the three scales into the same range: thirds would be necessary where the instrument provided seconds, and vice versa.

And this might be the key to solving the awkward *slendro* problem. Just as our *equal temperament* was due to the need of transposition, the *slendro temperament* could easily be understood as a compromise of seconds and thirds. This, in turn, could account for the decline of the modes which after all depended on the difference, not on the assimilation, of the two kinds of intervals.

It seems that the modes or, better, the melodies ascribed to the modes, matter today only from the standpoint of choosing the adequate time for performance: pieces in *nem* are to be played between seven and midnight; *sangå* is the right mode for the early morning between midnight and three and for the afternoon between noon and seven; *manjurå* belongs to the hours between 3:00 A.M. and noon.

This time table is unmistakably Indian.

The name *salendro* points also to India. It probably stemmed from the Sumatran Salendrå Dynasty, which ruled Java almost to the end of the first thousand years A.D. and had come from the Coromandel Coast in South India. Thus it might be wiser to connect *slendro* with *rāgas* like *madhyamāvatī, mohana,* or *haṃsadhvanī* than with the Chinese scale.

❀   ❀   ❀

SIAM, CAMBODIA, BURMA close the ring of East Asiatic scales. They have the strong tendency toward equal temperament that the *slendro* arrangement shows, without in the least effacing the contrast between tones and thirds. This is achieved by dividing the octave into seven (theoretically) equal parts, each of which would, if perfect, measure 171.4 Cents.

The actual justness of these distances is of course questionable, since the ear without physical and mathematical help is not capable of correctly dividing an interval. However much Carl Stumpf [37]—who himself had an

---

[37] Carl Stumpf, "Tonsystem und Musik der Siamesen," *loc. cit.,* and in *Sammelbände für Vergleichende Musikwissenschaft* I (1922), pp. 129–77.

excellent ear—wondered at the relative accuracy with which Siamese musicians tuned their instruments, the distances that Alexander J. Ellis measured [38] varied from 90 to 219 Cents.

The Siamese use these seven equidistant notes as loci for pentatonic scales by skipping two of them at a time, thus creating the clear contrast between short tones of 171.4 Cents and neutral thirds of 343 Cents. The skipping places determine the modal structures:

$$I \quad II \quad III \quad — \quad V \quad VI \quad — \quad I$$
$$I \quad II \quad — \quad IV \quad V \quad VI \quad — \quad I$$
$$I \quad — \quad III \quad IV \quad V \quad — \quad VII \quad I$$

(The eighth note is not an end, as our octave, but the starter of another heptad.)

Singers do not pay much heed to this temperament. The following operatic aria in almost Western intervals alternates with orchestral ritornelli in Siamese tuning:

Ex. 53. SIAMESE OPERATIC SOLO   *transcribed by Curt Sachs from*
Decca 20127 B

original ½ tone higher

PALACE AND TEMPLE MUSIC, in China as well as in Korea and Japan, have rejected the infixed semitone since, far from soothing the passions, it filled the soul with sensual lust.[39] Still, the allegedly skipped loci have been given a certain place in secular music, though at first only in the way of alternation. The mode that the Japanese call *ritsu* occurred, as we have seen, in two distinct forms, 12·456·8 and 1·345·78, say *DE GAB D* and *D FGA CD*. Thus the two purely pentatonic forms of *ritsu* required a full seven-tone set. Still, melodies followed one of the two pentatonic patterns without ever combining them.

This restriction was subsequently suspended: composers were allowed to mingle the two forms in the same melody, provided that the critical notes were kept alternative without ever touching and forming semitones:

[38] A. J. Ellis, in the latter publication, pp. 36–42.
[39] Keh, *op. cit.*, p. 39.

Ex. 54. JAPANESE SONG   *after Noel Peri*

Finally, even this last ban was lifted, at least in folk music.

The *ryo* scale 123, on the other hand, was heptatonized in a more directly way by the insertion of a *sharpened* fourth and a major seventh: $F\,G\,A^b\,C\,D^\sharp\,F$.

Similarly, the Japanese cleave their major thirds into two seconds: $A^\sharp\,F\,E^d\,C\,B\,A$.

Neither scale became strictly heptatonic. The additional notes kept a transitional, auxiliary character and had not even the privilege of individual names: the Chinese called them by the name of the note directly above with the epithet *pièn,* which means 'on the way to,' 'becoming.'

❊   ❊   ❊

A STORY, recorded in contemporary sources, shows how far the Chinese were from an actual heptatonic scale: Between 560 and 578 A.D., a man from Kutcha in East Turkistan astonished his Chinese listeners by playing 'justly' a complete major scale on his lute *p'i p'a.* Its notes were called *sochiba, sadalik, badalik, kichi, shachi, shahukalam, shalap, panjam, dzilid-zap, hulidzap.* Some of these terms are obscure, some are obvious. Professor Nicholas N. Martinovitch, whose opinion I sought, was kind enough to suggest the following equivalents: *scattering, sonorous, exchanging, small, sprinkling, royal word, hanging, the fifth, strong tremolo, very strong.* "Of course," he writes, "I cannot be sure in my suggestions, for the corruptions of these words are too great."

At about the same time, another source claims that the twenty-eight 'foreign modes'—whatever they might have been—could not be fixed by means of the Chinese pitch pipes, but only by the strings of the *p'i p'a.*[40] In other words, the newly imported Western music followed the divisive not the up-and-down principle. Still, the cross flute *ti* also adopted a Western major scale. Altogether, heptatonic melodies have been more frequent in the north than in the south of China.

[40] Gulik, *op. cit.,* p. 39.

Indeed, even Japan has known a major scale, *Champa*. In 763, music from Champa, that is Cambodia, is first mentioned as played at a banquet of the Imperial Court. But the Cambodian style in Japan was assimilated four hundred years later into the Chinese style, and it is not possible to tell whether the original Champa music had or had not the major scale that the modern Japanese designate by this name.[41]

The evolution of East Asiatic scales now begins to stand out. It starts from strictly pentatonic scales with thirds of any size. In a second stage, heptatonics appear in the form of seven loci for strictly pentatonic scales. In a third, the two 'skipped' loci are admitted to the scale, though only as passing notes. Finally, they are fully incorporated.

Temperament had a parallel evolution. *Pelog* represents a pretemperamental stage. In China and Japan, on the contrary, scales have been rather well tempered to whole and semitones and to minor and major thirds. In *slendro,* the original minor thirds and whole tones have more and more been assimilated, resulting in five nearly equal six-fifths of tones in the octave. In Siam, Cambodia, and Burma, on the other hand, seven loci have been assimilated to form almost equal seven-eighths of tones, five of which are actually used in melodies.

[41] Cf. Noel Peri, *op. cit.,* and Paul Demiéville, "La Musique čame au Japon," in *Publications de l'Ecole Française d'Extrême-Orient, Etudes Asiatiques,* I (1925), pp. 200, 225.

4

MELODY AND RHYTHM

SCALE AND MODE, though not exclusively instrumental, have been established on instruments; in vocal music they best show in those styles that depend on the collaboration of instruments. It must be emphasized that the Far East, however, knows singing styles entirely independent from instruments and consequently from the rigidity of scales and modes. We need not discuss Buddhist cantillation. But a section on East Asiatic music would be incomplete without mentioning that peculiar recitative that found its perfection in the Japanese *nō*.

The *nō* in its present form only reached its peak about 1500 A.D. It is an archaic lyrical drama, derived from ecstatic rituals of the past, but laid in a worldly atmosphere and performed by a few masked actors in a strict unity of word, melody, and dance. Its singing, far from the freedom so dear to modern Occidentals, runs to no more than nine stereotype, perpetually recurring, patterns: the first appearance of the main dramatis persona, the account of the second person's journey with which he introduces himself, and so on. This is done in a uniform cantillation on one note, which, however, is interrupted by melodic formulas intoned in the uncertain, gliding manner, with subsequent sharpening that we know from Japanese zithers and flutes. These formulas are indivisible units, each of which has its individual name such as 'revolving,' 'color,' 'tension' (like the tropes in Jewish cantillation). When chanting is resumed, it will jump to a level a fourth lower, and even to another fourth—*a-e-B,* or drop to the next whole tone and then jump down by one or by two fourths—*a-g-d-A.*

Rhythm is just as irrational as intonation, and even when a melodic formula suggests a stricter meter, the singer tries to destroy this impression by a kind of rubato. Only on the lower level are both rhythm and intonation more apt to be steady.

The orchestra, sitting on the stage, is formed by one stick-beaten and two hand-beaten drums and a transverse flute. As a rule, the drummers strike an even rhythm though the voice is free. Now and then, the flute joins in and soars above the voice; but its melody is neither co-ordinated nor even correlated to the song: the two parts are not supposed to be heard together, but to coexist, in a magical, not in an aesthetic, sense.

With our present terminology it is not possible to give an adequate idea of the strange vocalization of the East. Koreans expect at least their geishas to sing in a low register.[42] In general, "only children and coachmen sing from the stomach"; [43] Far Eastern singing is nasal, compressed, explosive, by preference high in pitch, often ventriloquially veering to the lowest register, and continually interspersed with glissandi. Unusual as it appears to our ears at the beginning, it rapidly affects even the unprepared Westerner as the perfect counterpart of the mask that the singer wears: it conceals his identity, indeed his human nature, and from the world of everyday lifts him to the sphere of heroes, gods, and demons. Once we have experienced this mythic atmosphere, we begin to realize the limitations of the Western 'natural' style which is unable to contrast Wotan, the father of the gods, and Hans Sachs, the shoemaker of Nürnberg.

The Chinese opera in its classical form was ruled by its texts. It could not be otherwise. Monosyllabic languages have a few hundred syllables to express ten thousand things and notions; so each syllable has many different meanings. Understanding depends on special intonation, on the rising, level, or falling inflection of the voice.

Melody is under the necessity of following these inflections; words set to music against their natural speech melody would be less intelligible than an interrogative sentence that drops at the end would be in some European opera.[44]

Thus the vocal music of classical China was strictly logogenic. A musical vocabulary provided a stock of appropriate single notes for the level tone and of groups of notes for each of the three 'tones,' which again were subdivided into 'male' and 'female' forms, the latter being slightly different and a tone lower.

❁ ❁
❁

MONOSYLLABIC LANGUAGES are not favorable to quantitative meter; long and short are much less vital than in composite words. True, poetry (and doubtless music) followed definite meters during the T'ang Dynasty, in which the Chinese were particularly fond of elegant form. To give an

[42] Keh, *op. cit.*, p. 20.
[43] O. Abraham and E. von Hornbostel, "Tonsystem und Musik der Japaner," *loc. cit.*, p. 212.
[44] Cf. John Hazedel Levis, *Foundations of Chinese Musical Art*, Peiping, 1936.

example: a poem of the eighth century A.D., "The Drinker in the Spring,"
is given the following affected meter: [45]

```
  ⌣   ⌣   ⌣   ⌣   ⌣
  —   —   —   —   —
  ⌣   ⌣   —   ⌣   ⌣
  —   —   ⌣   —   —
```

But then, the period of the T'ang was widely open to influences from India
and the Middle East, and this poetic style may be due to foreign paragons.

As a rule, Chinese has imposed the qualitative, strong-weak principle
on poetry and music, with the syllable as the time unit or beat. Since Chinese verses are extremely short—four, five, or six monosyllables as a rule—
each verse is musically rendered by one measure of as many beats, not, as
elsewhere, by a whole phrase.

Such musicopoetical forms are either asymmetrical and rhapsodic (*ch'i*)
or else symmetrical (*shi*). The purest realization of the symmetrical form is
the Hymn to Confucius, main piece of the Confucian liturgy, which probably represents the earliest preserved stage of Chinese music. Temple singers
perform it in incredibly long-drawn notes of equal value, each of which
carries one monosyllable of the text. Four such notes form a verse and eight
verses a strophe. Once more, the single note proves to be the generative
cell of Chinese music (Ex. 41).

❋   ❋   ❋

QUALITATIVE RHYTHM ('time'), though often running against the accents of
spoken words, is, outside the Far East, common in Tibet and among the
Turkish peoples including Tatars, Kirghizes, and Bashkirs. Four-beat
measures prevail in the same vast area.

There are exceptions, though. Both Korea and China have preserved
folksongs in three beats, and the Chinese themselves had odd and even
mixed measures in the first millennium. But these again have been attributed to foreign influences.[46]

Rhythm is certainly less important than in other countries. The great
number of percussion instruments in all parts of the Far East should not
mislead our judgment. Most of them do not serve rhythm at all; rattles,
scrapers, bells, and stones had other tasks. The drums themselves were
struck with sticks and therefore served time beating better than elaborate
rhythmic patterns.

[45] Heinz Trefzger, "Das Musikleben der Tang-Zeit," in *Sinica* XIII (1938), p. 58.
[46] Heinz Trefzger, *ibid.*, p. 59.

It would be a mistake, however, to compare such time beating with the crude four beats of our big band drums. In the oldest preserved style, the classical Sino-Japanese *bugaku* dances, the strong accent is on the last beat, which is emphasized by a stamp of the dancers and by a powerful stroke on the drum prepared by a soft stroke on the half-beat before: one, *two*, three, *and FOUR*.

Bugaku is supposed to be of Indian origin, and Chinese and Japanese music on the whole were under Indian influence in the second half of the first millennium A.D. And yet the most typical trait of Indian music, its sophisticated rhythmical patterns or *tālas*, had no chance in the East. In 860 A.D., someone wrote a treatise on drumming in China, with over one hundred 'symphonies,' which doubtless were Indian *tālas*; but nothing came of this, and not one of the Far Eastern styles has preserved the slightest trace of such patterns. The three rhythms used in Tibetan orchestras, and kept up in percussion even when the other parts are silent,[47] are obviously not Far Eastern, but deteriorated Indian patterns.

The elaborate polyrhythm of Balinese cymbal players that Mr. Colin McPhee has recently described is not Far Eastern either. "The cymbal group may include as many as seven players each with a different-sized pair of cymbals, performing a different rhythmic pattern. The same rhythmic motives can be heard at times during the rice-stamping, when the steady pounding of the poles in the wooden trough is accompanied by various syncopated rhythms beaten against the sides or ends of the trough."[48]

[47] T. Howard Somervel, "The Music of Tibet," in *The Musical Times* LXIV (1923), p. 108.
[48] Colin McPhee, "The Technique of Balinese Music," in *Bulletin of the American Musicological Society* no. 6 (1942), p. 4.

5

NOTATION

NO LOWER CIVILIZATION finds the way to musical or other scripts; the mental horizon is narrow, and knowledge is limited in range; oral tradition has become almighty, and memory, unburdened and unchallenged by other means of preservation, is trained to a hardly believable degree.

Many particular circumstances had to contribute before the earliest forms of writing relieved tradition and memory. Only one of them was valid for music: the fear that in times of distress tradition might weaken and, by an inexact rendition of the sacred songs, endanger the efficacy of worship.

A remarkable example is the musical notation invented in the island of Bali by learned Hindu-Javanese who in the sixteenth century A.D. had escaped from the Mohammedan conquest of their native Java and wished to preserve their traditional music from oblivion in a new country without tradition.

It consisted in a kind of shorthand: the five notes *dang, ding, dung, dèng, dong* were simply rendered by the little symbols for the vowels *a, i, u, è, o,* without indicating rhythm.[49]

While alphabets seem to have had a relatively uniform evolution, from realistic pictures to abstract symbols and from concepts to sounds, musical notation followed different principles from the very beginning, and most peoples used several systems at once. There were *tonal notations,* indicating the individual notes by symbols taken from the ordinary alphabet; *tablatures* or fingering notations to lead the player's hand whatever the notes produced might be; *neumes,* which graphically depicted the melodic steps as directions rather than as groups of two or three distinct pitches; *group notations,* in which conventional groups of notes were designated by call syllables or nicknames.

The Far East has had musical scripts at least since the beginning of our era; particularly interested in individual pitches, it has above all favored *tonal notation.* This is in the strictest sense true with the players of stone and bell chimes who, unconcerned with melody proper, strike one slab or bell at a time, each of which produces one of the *lü's.* Logically, the pitches

[49] J. Kunst en C. J. A. Kunst-v.Wely, *De Toonkunst van Bali, op. cit.,* pp. 47–68.

are known by the first syllables of the *lü* names: *huang* (*chung*), *ying* (*chung*), *wu* (*i*), and so on. Like all Chinese notations and the ordinary script itself, the symbols are arranged in descending columns which progress from the right to the left.

Singers, on the contrary, more concerned with melody than with absolute pitch, use the five syllabic symbols which denote the pentatonic scale: *kung, shang, chiao, chih, yü,* written below or on the right of the corresponding syllable of the text. Absolute pitch is not neglected, though; a head note indicates to which *lü* the fundamental note *kung* shall be tuned (exactly as we do in the case of our clarinets "in *A*" or horns "in *F*"). (Pl. 4, p. 142)

The same kind of notation is customary with the players of the lute *p'i p'a* and of all pipes. Most of these instruments had a comparatively recent Western origin, and at the beginning their players probably were Mongols. As a consequence, they replaced the complicated Chinese by the simpler Mongolian characters. When voices and lutes perform the same melody, both the Mongolian and the Chinese symbols are written under each syllable of the text.

❋   ❋
❋

EAST ASIA also had rudimentary *neumes* for those melodies in which the curve mattered more than the individual pitches. A dash, ascending from left to right, indicated 'upward'; a horizontal dash, 'level movement'; a dash, descending from left to right, 'downward.' A × between two of these dashes allowed for either of them. Or a little white circle meant level movement, and a black one, an oblique movement, which in turn had to be specified by additional syllables as either falling or rising. Sometimes the composer halved this circle; white above and black below meant a more or less level movement but freedom to make it oblique; black above and white below denoted the contrary.

The unavoidable manual counterpart of neumes is not missing. The Chinese use the hand to memorize the four types of tonal movement in phonetics; they touch the third phalange of the forefinger to indicate *p'ing,* the level tone; the tip of the same finger, for *shang,* the rising tone; the tip of the ring finger, for *ch'ü,* the falling tone; and the third phalange of the same finger, for *ju,* the (musically meaningless) dialectal shortening of any of the foregoing three movements.[50] The similitude of Guido of Arezzo's famous hand is obvious.

[50] John Hazedel Levis, *Foundations of Chinese Musical Art, op. cit.,* p. 17.

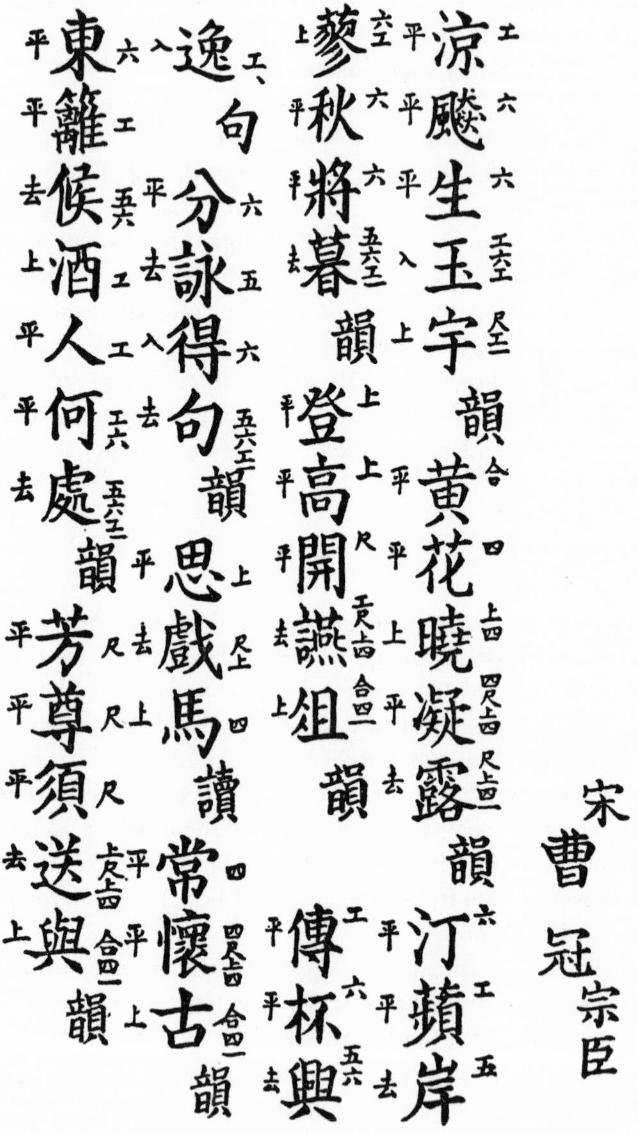

宋 曹冠 宗臣

涼颸生玉宇韻黃花曉凝露韻汀蘋岸

蓼秋將暮韻登高開讌俎韻傳杯興

逸句分詠得句韻思戲馬讀常懷古韻

東籬候酒人何處韻芳尊須送與韻

Signs for rhythm were shared with the other forms of notation. But in general it sufficed to mark the end of a phrase, the phrase itself being determined by the number of syllables in the verse, each of which coincided—at least in principle—with a musical beat. Occasionally one syllable might take more or less than a beat; such abnormal cases were either ruled by tradition or left to the singer's personal taste.

❁   ❁   ❁

TABLATURES were used by players of long zithers and flutes to indicate what their fingers should do in order to produce the required notes, rather than the notes themselves which were unchangeably fixed in making or tuning the instruments. Figures beside the syllables of the text denoted the strings to be plucked. A figure right in the middle of the column prescribed the thumb; shifted to the left, it indicated the forefinger; to the right, the middle finger. Not even what we might call graces depended on the player's taste, as in older European music. So vital in East Asiatic music is the delicate vacillation that dissolves the rigidity of pentatonic scales that all possible artifices have carefully been classified, named, and, by the syllabic symbols of their names, embodied in notation: *ka* (to quote the terms of Japanese koto players); that is, sharpening a note by pressing down the string beyond the bridge; *niju oshi,* sharpening by a whole tone; *é,* the subsequent sharpening of a note already plucked and heard; *ké,* sharpening it for just a moment and releasing the string into its initial vibration; *yū,* the same, but making the relapse very short before the following note is played; *kaki,* plucking two adjoining strings in rapid succession with the same finger; *uchi,* striking the strings beyond the bridges during long pauses; *nagashi,* a slide with the forefinger over the strings; and many others.

This tablature includes two symbols that do not belong in the domain of

---

PLATE 4. Chinese Notation. After John Hazedel Levis.—The script runs downward; the vertical columns read from right to left. The four columns with large symbols are the text, each symbol representing one (monosyllabic) word. The small signs on either side of a column indicate the melody. The right-side symbols denote the exact pitches of every beat and word: the first one, at the upper right corner, a'; the second and third ones, c''. The following group of three, flanking the fourth word of the text, designates a ligature $a'-c''-a'$ on one beat. The fifth group means the ligature $g'-a'$ on one beat plus a rest—the horizontal dash—that marks the end of the phrase. The left-side symbols are neumes, the first three indicating level movement, the fourth rising and falling, the fifth rising movement.

graces: *kaké* is a frequent phrase of five notes, two of which are plucked
with the forefinger, two on a lower string with the middle finger, and the
fifth with the thumb on a higher string; *hazumu* is a short falling phrase,
consisting of a dotted note on the tenth string, followed by two notes on
the ninth and eighth strings. These signs belong in the category of *group
notation*.

Recent investigation has made clear that this tablature is a Chinese transcription of Sanskrit symbols used in India.[51] Indeed, the graces of long
zithers, unparalleled in East Asiatic music, are nothing else than the *gamakas* of India, imported with the sway of Buddhism during the Han
Dynasty and given to the technique of Chinese zithers, which became the
favorite instruments of meditative Buddhist priests and monks.

※   ※   ※

NONE OF THESE SCRIPTS indicates time values. Rhythm was often left to
instinct and tradition;[52] or else the composer added a special notation for
the beats. But this notation is rather inconsistent and still relies on the ear
more than on the eye.

The Chinese write small circles beside the corresponding notes to indicate the fourth beats of the bars, and often mark the first, second, and third
beats by simple dots. Quarter notes, consequently, always had a dot, while
many eighth notes were not marked at all. Thus a rudimentary mensural
notation branched off from the beat notation: the dot, properly meaning a
beat, came to designate a quarter note, while half notes were given two and
whole notes three dots.

Japanese notation is more consistent: all downbeats are given circles,
alternately with single and with double periphery (to facilitate reading),
while the even upbeats are indicated by smaller circles. When eighths or sixteenths occur in koto scores, the figures denoting the string to be played
are placed between the circles, either halfway or, for those following a
dotted note, nearer to the subsequent circle.

Some koto players have used mensural symbols: a full circle for the
whole note, an upright semicircle for the half note (like a *D*), a quarter
circle (like the upper part of a *D*) for the quarter note.[53]

Tempo is left unwritten. It varies, however; though not within the same
piece; different tempi are supposed to contrast, not to blend.

[51] Cf. Heinz Trefzger, "Das Musikleben der Tang-Zeit," *loc. cit.,* p. 52.

[52] Wang Guang Ki (Kuang-chi Wang), "Ueber die chinesischen Notenschriften," in *Sinica*
III (1928), pp. 110–23.

[53] Mueller, "Einige Notizen über die japanische Musik," *loc. cit.,* p. 19.

[6]

POLYPHONY

EAST ASIATIC CHORUSES always sing in unison—just as ancient Greek choirs did. The curious fact that in Buddhist worship every singer chants the same words in the same rhythm in whatever tonality he prefers [54] is no exception; while the strange, never ceasing drones used in the choral singing of Tibet belong in the Indian, not in the Chinese sphere of Tibetan civilization.

A singer's accompanist, on the contrary, is expected to follow behind by an irrationally small particle of time, as an aide avoids riding abreast of his general. This is particularly the practice of Japanese flutists; but even so, nearly all East Asiatic accompaniment depends on shifted phrases, on canonlike anticipation and retardation. The singer displays a rich, ornamental realization of some melodic pattern, and the player, having this same pattern in mind, gives the singer all the freedom required and carefully tries to follow. His notes come in the correct—though not pedantically precise—order, but are delayed when the voice unexpectedly restrains its ornaments and are ahead when the singer dwells upon a phrase. In a more recent stage, this unavoidable discordance has become a highly appreciated means of expression, in which the continuous friction of seconds and sevenths is probably not perceived as a dissonance in any Occidental sense.

In the sacred music of China, such accompaniments have to a great extent been simplified. One rule of classical music reads: while the singer holds a whole note, the long zither plays thirty-two thirty-second notes and the mouth organ adds one inhaling and one exhaling half note. The stringed instruments always accompany in broken chords formed by the unison, fourth and octave or unison, fifth and octave, in strict parallels with the singer.

Japanese koto players have more freedom; they now support the voice, now fill the gaps in rhythm left by the singer's sustained notes, thus producing chords of octaves, perfect or diminished fifths, fourths, thirds, and even seconds.

The Occidental word *harmony,* however, scarcely applies here. These

[54] C. A. Wegelin, "Chineesche Muziek," in *China* IV (1929), p. 143.

concords of two or three notes are not 'functional'; they do not add a third dimension to musical space, nor do they create an emotional atmosphere. In practically all cases, they add to the singer's notes other notes that the singer has just abandoned or that he is going to strike up; they are melodic present, past, and future superimposed, and nothing, after all, but piled up heterophony.

The same is true with the chords of the mouth organ—the instrument called *shêng* in Chinese and *shô* in Japanese. I have described it as a piece of wood cut in the shape of a gourd.

The neck serves as a mouthpiece and air conduct, while the body forms a windchest to feed the pipes. Thirteen or more slender canes of different length (the highest measuring sixteen to twenty inches) project upwards out of the windchest in a circular arrangement; inside the windchest each pipe has a side hole which is covered by a thin metal tongue.

The player blows both a melody and, on other pipes, an accompaniment in chords.

In the court music of Japan old harmonies are preserved which were brought to the country a thousand years ago from China; some comprise three notes, some five, some six. Only two of the eleven usual chords correspond to occidental minor triads; the others consist of the notes of pentatonic scales sounding simultaneously (for instance: *DE FGA*) or in other combinations, as *B C D E F A*. These complicated harmonies are in modern China replaced by simple parallels of fourths and fifths. In both cases, the melody is below its accompaniment, as in ancient Greece and the earlier part of the European Middle Ages.[55]

The problem of East Asiatic polyphony is not solved but clarified by the contrast of *right* and *left music*.

The motley influences that had acted on Japanese music up to 800 A.D.—Manchurian, Korean, Chinese, Indian—could obviously not be blended into one organic style. So the Japanese disintegrated them in the ninth century into two separate styles. Manchurian and Korean influences were united in the so-called right music, with the cross flute *koma fuye* and the big hourglass drum *san no tsuzumi* as the distinguishing instruments. Chinese and Indian influences, on the contrary, formed the so-called left music, with the cross flute *ô teki*, the mouth organ *shô*, and the small cylinder drum *kakko* as the distinguishing instruments. Beside these instruments, both styles shared the oboe *hichiriki*, the lute *biwa*, the zither *sôno koto*, as well as the larger drum *taiko* and the small gong *shôko*.

The essential distinction, however, was in the relations of the two leading

[55] Curt Sachs, *The History of Musical Instruments, op. cit.*, p. 183.

instruments, the flute and the oboe: while in the left, Chinese music they
played in unison with the chords of the mouth organ; in the right, Manchurian music they played in counterpoint.[56]

The court orchestra of the Mikado, which boasts that it has preserved
the unaltered tradition of the first millennium A.D., performs in a very
elaborate form of polyphony. Its timbre is light and clear, since none of its
five melodic instruments reaches below the middle of the one-lined octave.
One mouth organ and one vertical flute play the melody high up in the two-
lined octave, and a cross flute doubles them an octave above. All three of
these wind instruments play heterophonically, now joining, now sepa-
rating, forming thirds or even grinding seconds, and their vacillating curve
becomes even more unsteady as the flutes are constantly driven up by irrational microtones. Below this strident clamor, the lute follows the same

Ex. 55. JAPANESE COURT MUSIC   *after Mueller*

---

[56] Hisao Tanabe, *Japanese Music, op. cit.*, p. 15.

trend, in fourths or other chords, and the zither koto joins in with a short, dry ostinato motif. Of the two drums, the *kakko* contributes rolls and both single and repeated blows, while the *taiko* adds some single strokes; the gong marks the beginning of each bar with a single blow. The author failed in the attempt to write down the score from a phonograph recording. Our example follows the score published by Dr. Mueller, who had the opportunity to test each individual player.[57]

[57] Mueller, "Einige Notizen über die japanische Musik," *loc. cit.,* 31–3.

ORCHESTRAS

ORCHESTRAS WERE SOUNDING BRIDGES between the macro-
and the microcosmos, between the world of gods and ancestors and the
world of the living, since they embodied all classes of instruments, each
of which stood for an element, a cardinal point, a season, a planet, a substance: the stone chime for northwest and stone; the bell chime for west
and fall and metal; the long zither for south and summer and silk; the
flute for east and spring and bamboo; the trough and the tiger for southeast
and wood; the drum for north and winter and skin; the mouth organ for
northeast and gourd; the globular clay flute for southeast and earth.

Kwei, Emperor Shun's chief musician, "said, when they tapped and beat
the sounding stone, and struck and swept the *ch'in* and *shê,* in order to
accord with the chant, then [the spirits of] the ancestors and progenitors
came down and visited. The guests of them filled the principal seat. And
the host of nobles virtuously yielded [place to one another]. At the bottom
of the hall were the pipes and the tambours, which were brought into unison or suddenly checked by the beaten trough and the scraped tiger, while
the mouth organ and the bell indicated the interludes." [58]

The size of an orchestra mirrored the rank and power of its owner. In
the shadow of gigantic imperial orchestras, the Chou Dynasty (1122–255
B.C.) allowed the high dignitaries only twenty-seven (mostly blind) men,
sitting on three sides of a square, while the ordinary noblemen had no more
than fifteen players in one straight line.

The Han Dynasty had, in the years 58 to 75 A.D., three orchestras: one for
religious ceremonies, the second for the archery of the palace, and the third
for banquets and the harem. The total number of their members was 829.
The court also retained a large military band.

Orchestras included singers and dancers. The dancers' group, with weapons for war themes, and with feathers and flutes for peaceful subjects,
closely followed poetry and music by forming the writing symbols of the
text.

❊ ❊ ❊

[58] *The Shoo King,* transl. by W. H. Medhurst, *op. cit.,* p. 46.

THE T'ANG DYNASTY (618–907 A.D.), deeply interested in fostering the arts, seems to have brought the court orchestras to their highest evolution. Six of them were 'standing,' and eight, 'sitting.' All together, they numbered from five to seven hundred members.

Several graphic ground plans illustrate the arrangement of some of these orchestras. In one of them the conductor has 20 oboes before him; then 200 mouth organs in a second tier; 40 flutes and 128 lutes in a third tier; 120 harps in a fourth tier; 2 stone chimes are to his left, and to his right, 2 bell chimes; and an undisclosed number of drums behind the 4 chimes.

Another diagram shows that choruses occupied the left and the right of the orchestra from the front to rear. On a third diagram, the dance orchestra of forty-four players is arranged in a circle with an inscribed square; twenty *ya* drums form the circle, while twenty-four performers with stamping tubes, clapper tubes, and drums are drawn up alternately in the square.

The court musicians were provided by an Imperial Academy of Music, the Garden of Pears. Its female section, the Garden of Everlasting Spring, trained several hundred young ladies under the personal supervision of the emperor, and it was also open to girls of outstanding beauty, though lesser musical gift, who were admitted with the title of auxiliary musicians.

A part of the female court orchestra, performing before Emperor Ming Huang (713–756) and his mistress, is depicted on a recently discovered delightful painting of the eighth century A.D. The conducting lady agitates a clapper, and in the rear a girl strikes a big drum; the other instruments— harps, long zithers, and lutes, transverse flutes, oboes, and mouth organs, metallophones and hourglass drums—are played in pairs.[59] (Pl. 5, p. 160)

Besides all these indoor orchestras, the imperial court entertained a huge outdoor band. It consisted of a vanguard with 890 players of gongs, cymbals, drums, and wind instruments, plus forty-eight singers; and a rear guard of 408 musicians in similar arrangement; that is, in all no less than 1,346 men.[60]

The Korean court in King Setjo's time (1457–1468) entertained 572 players and choir singers and 195 apprentices, and as late as 1897 the emperor had 772 musicians.[61] (Pl. 6a, p. 161)

❀ ❀ ❀

---

[59] Cf. Heinz Trefzger, "Das Musikleben der Tang-Zeit," *loc. cit.*, p. 68.
[60] Maurice Courant, "Essai historique sur la musique historique des Chinois," in Lavignac, *Encyclopédie de la Musique.*
[61] C. S. Keh, *Die Koreanische Musik, op. cit.*, p. 17.

THE CHINESE COURT indulged also in the diversity, not only in the sizes, of its orchestras. The aristocracy, like all higher civilized groups, had a strong taste for exotic timbres and experienced the unique stimulus that imagination receives from foreign music. The emperors appreciated presents of singing and playing girls from allied kings, just as the Egyptian pharaohs had done before. Confucius once took his departure from court as a protest, when "the people of Ts'e sent Loo a present of female musicians, which Ke Huan received, and for three days no court was held" [62]—a protest that reminds one of the pronouncement of the great Jewish philosopher and physician, Maimonides (1135-1204), that secular music ought not to be tolerated, and by all means not when performed by a singing female.[63]

Such delight in foreign music was seasoned with imperialistic pride in times of expansion. Whenever a country had been conquered, native musicians were sent to the Chinese court to form a national orchestra—not merely on occasion or as a solitary tribute, but as a permanent institution alongside those already in existence, much as a conquered country's escutcheon would be incorporated in the victor's coat of arms.

Of the so-called Seven Orchestras entertained in 581 A.D., one had come from Kaoli, a Tungus country; another from India; a third from Buchara; a fourth from Kutcha in East Turkistan, with twenty performers of mostly Western instruments, which had been established as early as 384 A.D. and was so much in favor that the emperor tried to bar it. Individual musicians from Cambodia, Japan, Silla, Samarkand, Paikchei, Kachgar, and Turkey mingled in them. The 'scholars,' puristic defenders of the 'ancient' music, protested; but in vain.

The number of court orchestras was increased to nine in the seventh century; but some Cambodian musicians, engaged in 605, were sent back because their instruments were too primitive. In 801 or 802, the emperor hired thirty-five Burmese musicians, and between the year 1000 and the end of the monarchy, two more Mongolian bands and a Ghurka, an Annamese, a Tibetan, and an Islamic orchestra were added.

Japan was no less receptive than China. In 809, the Imperial Academy of Music included twenty-eight masters of foreign styles—Cambodian, Chinese, Sillan, and others.[64]

* * *

[62] *The Original Chinese Texts of the Confucian Analecta, op. cit.,* p. 237.

[63] Cf. Eric Werner and Isaiah Sonne, "The Philosophy and Theory of Music in Judaeo-Arabic Literature," in *Hebrew Union College Annual* XVI (1941), p. 281.

[64] Cf. Paul Demiéville, "La Musique čame au Japon," in *Publications de l'Ecole Française d'Extrême-Orient, Etudes Asiatiques* I (1925), pp. 199–226.

ORCHESTRAS, now almost extinct in China, Korea, and Japan (except the Mikado's court orchestra), have survived in the southeast of Asia, particularly in Java and Bali, and are there the centers of musical practice. Their common name, in the Malayan Islands, is *gámelan,* from *gamel,* 'to handle.'

A gamelan is utterly different from a modern orchestra. Western orchestras are bodies of musicians, playing for almost all kinds of occasions, buying the latest models of instruments, using them when they have been expressly prescribed, and changing even within the same work. Malayan orchestras, on the contrary, are bodies of instruments, mostly inherited from times past and imposed on both players and composers. Composite as they are, they form unalterable units with so personal a character that they bear individual names with the title *kjahi,* 'sir.' Most courts possess quite a number of them; the Sultan of Soesoehoenan owns at least twenty-nine full gamelans, each of which is assigned to special tasks.

Large gamelans consist of three sizes of metallophones with slabs resting on the sound box and three sizes of metallophones with suspended slabs, the various sizes being tuned an octave apart; three corresponding sizes of gong chimes; two sizes of xylophones; up to a score of small and large gongs; two hand-beaten drums; a flute, and a fiddle. In the glittering peal of this strange orchestra, as I wrote in my *History of Musical Instruments,* one can distinguish the plain and solemn melody of the basses, its paraphrase and loquacious figuration in the smaller chimes, and the punctuation of the gongs, of which the smaller ones mark the end of shorter sections while the powerful basses of the large gongs conclude the main parts. The two drums guide the changing tempo.

❀　❀
❀

CAMBODIA, SIAM, AND BURMA, the Indo-Chinese countries between the archipelago and China, complete the province of orchestral music, as opposed to the vast area where chamber music prevails in the Middle and Near East.

The Siamese accompany their theatrical performances with orchestras generally composed of two flutes, two gong chimes, two metallophones, two xylophones, a single gong, and three large drums. The strict gemination of the melodic instruments against three drums is reminiscent of the Chinese orchestra of women during the T'ang Dynasty just mentioned. The dominant metallic timbre, on the other hand, relates the Siamese orchestra to the Malay gamelan. The comparatively large share of drums, however, indicates the neighborhood of India.

Still further from Javanese ideals is the women's orchestra of Cambodia, in which the three Malayan sets of idiophones, the xylophone, the metallophone, and the gong chime, are matched by stringed instruments: a large zither, a Chinese lute, and an Arabo-Persian fiddle.[65]

Burma uses orchestras chiefly to accompany her shadow plays, the *pwe*. These orchestras are small; they consist of two pairs of clappers, two pairs of cymbals, a gong chime arranged in a circular framework around the squatting player, a similar drum chime, a big drum suspended from a gallows, and two oboes blown with such energy and endurance that often an assistant is in readiness to support the collapsing player. (Pl. 6*b*, p. 161)

These penetrant oboes, which lead the melody instead of the tinkling gongs of Java and Bali, are definitely Indian. But still more Indian is the unparalleled drum chime of, normally, twenty-four carefully tuned drums, suspended inside the walls of a circular pen, which the player, squatting in the center, strikes with his bare hands in swift, toccatalike melodies with stupendous technique and delicacy.[66]

And now we turn to India proper.

[65] Illustration in Curt Sachs, *Die Musikinstrumente Indiens und Indonesiens*, 2nd ed., Berlin, 1923, p. 9.
[66] Illustrations in Curt Sachs, *Die Musikinstrumente Birmas und Assams*, München, 1917, Plate 2; *Die Musikinstrumente Indiens und Indonesiens, ibid.*, pp. 4, 5.

Section Four

INDIA

THE ROOTS of music are more exposed in India than anywhere else. The Vedda in Ceylon possess the earliest stage of singing that we know, and the subsequent strata of primitive music are represented by the numberless tribes that in valleys and jungles took shelter from the raids of northern invaders. So far as this primitive music is concerned, the records are complete or at least could easily be completed if special attention were paid to the music of the 'tribes.'

But the following stratum is entirely wanting: we are not permitted to watch the slow transition from folksong to art song, from hundreds of tribal styles to one all-embracing music of India.

The facts and ideas that appear in the earliest Sanskrit sources prove that this process had long ago come to an end. They show music as the center of all religious rites, court ceremonials, and private entertainments. They show a nation so deeply fond of music that in its belief the gods themselves were ardent musicians and Śiva in his enthusiasm had exclaimed, "I like better the music of instruments and voices than I like a thousand baths and prayers." [1] They picture a country where musical practice had settled down in many strata, from the slave-girl up to "sweet-voiced" eunuchs and to famous masters, and where singing, playing, dancing were not wanting in a well-bred lady's education.

No music from those times is left. Still, when we read in Bharata's classical book of the twenty-two microtones in ancient Indian octaves, of innumerable scales and modes, and of seventeen melody patterns with their pentatonic and hexatonic varieties and chromatic alterations, we realize that music at, or even before, the beginning of the first century A.D. was by no means archaic. Indeed, there is no reason to believe that India's ancient music differed essentially from her modern music, which is closer to our Western taste and comprehension than any other Oriental music. The strange division of the octave into twenty-two microtones still persists, although their sizes have changed; melody follows mode and *rāga* exactly in the same way as it did two thousand years ago; and the difference, within this homogeneous style, between ancient and recent music may after all not be much greater than the present difference between the more archaic Carnatic style in the South and the Hindustani style of the North.

Away from art music, India has had its Vedic cantillation.

[1] Bharata, ch. 36:27 (Grosset, in *Encyclopédie de la Musique, op. cit.,* p. 260).

THE VEDIC CHANT

THE VEDA is the whole of the (pre-Buddhist) religious wisdom of India, collected in four books: Rig-Veda, the Veda of verses; Sāma-Veda, the Veda of melodies; and two others, Yajur-Veda and Atharva-Veda. The Rig-Veda is the earliest section. Although its origin and date are not fully established, modern specialists believe that its older parts already existed between two thousand and one thousand B.C. when the Aryans arrived from the northwest and began to invade and conquer India.

The Vedic ritual culminated in the solemn Soma drink offering which was assisted by four priests, each with one of the Vedas: the high priest, who conducted the ceremony with the Atharva-Veda; the Adhvaryu, who murmured incantations from the Yajur-Veda; the Udgātar, who sang from the Sāma-Veda; and the Hotar, who performed from the Rig-Veda in a style that might be equally well described as reciting and chanting.

Early recitation probably used only two notes. The grammarian Pānini, who lived in the fourth century B.C., wrote unmistakably: "A vowel pronounced at a high pitch is called *udātta;* pronounced at a low pitch, it is called *anudātta;* their combination is called *svarita."* This is a phonetic statement; but it concerns recitation and cantillation as well, since the Rig-Veda is provided with the graphic symbols of the same three terms. Ancient Sanskrit had indeed the three pitch (not stress) accents that the Greeks and Romans knew as *oxýs* or *acutus, barýs* or *gravis,* and *perispómenos* or *circumflexus.*

The *svarita,* however, was just as uncertain in its meaning as the circumflex; contrary to Pānini's statement, and at least after his time, the *svarita,* instead of being the combination of *udātta* and *anudātta,* became an appoggiatura falling from a higher tone or semitone to the *udātta,* so that the later form of Vedic chant was a three-tone melody with the stress on *udātta.* Occasionally, the high note was given a syllable without being tied to the middle note by a ligature; but even so it was invariably followed by the middle, never by the low, tone.

❋　❋　❋

THE SĀMA STYLE ignores rhythm; long and short notes follow the natural meter of the words, and the last note before a breath is strangely accented. Modern Sāma singers of the south distinguish sixteen time values from one to sixteen units in steady progression; the shortest, *anudruta,* is said to equal "four instants, or thirty-two moments, or 16,384 atoms."

Melodically, there are two entirely different Sāma types. The archaic type is limited to the three notes of the Rig-Veda, with emphasis on the middle note.

EX. 56. INDIAN CANTILLATION, ARCHAIC STYLE

after Felber

The more recent type, indicated as early as about 400 B.C., is by some scholars said to represent an adaptation to pre-existent melodies, often by inserting meaningless syllables. It has the range of a sixth, although there

EX. 57. INDIAN CANTILLATION, LATER STYLE   *after Felber*

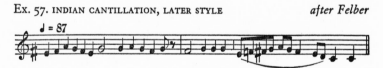

were theoretically seven notes. But the first and highest was seldom if ever used; for, in the words of the book *Sāmavidhānabrāhmaṇa,* "the gods live on the highest note of the Sāma, the men on the first of the following." Consequently, the Hindus spoke of one plus six, not of seven notes and gave number one either to the note that was actually second or to both the first and the second note: they called *kruṣhṭa* the note of the gods, and to the rest, in descending order, gave the names *prathama,* 'first,' *dvitīya,* 'second,' *tṛtīya,* 'third,' *ċaturtha,* 'fourth,' *mandra,* 'fifth,' *atisvārya,* 'sixth,' or similar terms. If they used figures to write these notes, they arranged them in the sequence 1 1 2 3 4 5 6 or 11 1 2 3 4 5 6, without 7, though they occasionally availed themselves of the latter to designate a special kind of ligature.

A. C. Burnell, editor of the fourth book of the Sāma-Veda,[2] describes

---

[2] A. C. Burnell, *The Ārsheyabrāhmaṇa,* Bangalore, 1876.

this *yama* scale as (descending) *F E D C B A G*. But in spite of much discussion it has not yet been ascertained whether absolute pitch and a steady scale were required in the ancient rites. Phonographically recorded Sāma songs differ both from Burnell's indications and from one another. But they are too rare to give sufficient evidence.[8]

The two Sāma styles differ widely.

The three-tone melodies of the archaic style are the freer. They vary short motifs without running in regular beats or observing stricter rules of symmetry; nor do they always conform to the syllables of the text. Most distances are bridged over by a kind of glissando.

The six-note melodies of the more recent type are often based on several motifs and uniform meters and regular structures. They also follow the syllables of the text more closely and avoid continuous gliding.

The difference hints at an interesting chronology of chanting. In the passage from recitation to singing, a speechlike glissando from pitch to pitch came before the pitches were well detached from one another. In a similar way, meter and structure became less 'natural' and were reduced and normalized.

The only problem is the increasingly syllabic character of melody. But it should be evident that the partition of syllables was an analytical abstraction posterior to the conception of undivided sentences.

❋   ❋   ❋

No WILLFUL ALTERATION of either the text or its presentation has ever been permitted lest the magic power of the Veda might weaken, and the style in which it is chanted today may on the whole be authentic in spite of its degeneration and all the local and eral variants that nothing human can escape in the lapse of four thousand years.

The Vedic style would not have been preserved in its relative integrity without certain expedients to support oral tradition.

One of these was raising, leveling, and bowing the head as comovements with the higher, the middle, and the lower tone. When the original range of two or three notes was enlarged, Sāma singers gave up the metaphorical reflex motion, resorted to counting the notes of the Veda scale, and accordingly called them by ordinal numbers: the first, the second, and so on. Since in the ancient world counting has consistently been facilitated by

[8] Erwin Felber and Bernhard Geiger, "Die indische Musik der vedischen und der klassischen Zeit," in *Sitzungsberichte der Kais. Akademie der Wissenschaften in Wien, Phil.-Hist. Kl.* CLXX (1912), no. 7.

PLATE 5. Chinese women's orchestra performing before Emperor Ming Huang (713–756 A.D.). From a silk scroll in Dr. Otto's collection, Canton. After Heinz Trefzger.—The conducting lady agitates a clapper, and in the rear a girl strikes a big drum; the other instruments—harps, long zithers, lutes; transverse flutes, oboes, mouth organs; metallophones and hourglass drums—are played in pairs.

PLATE 6A. Korean orchestra. After Sachs.—Note the stone and bell chimes in their upright stands.

PLATE 6B. Burmese orchestra. After Sachs.—In front: gong chime, drum chime, barrel drum; in the rear: oboes, cymbals, clapper.

touching the fingers, the Hindus devised several methods of finger counting, and among them the one later used in medieval Europe under the
nickname of "Guido's hand": with the right index they touched a certain
place on the left hand where the note to be sung was located. There were
five such places: the small finger, for the lowest note; the lower end of the
forefinger, for the following note; then the ring finger; and finally the index again for both the fourth and fifth notes.

These indications cannot be accepted without question. In the first place,
the notes indicated belong to the scale of ordinary music, not to Vedic cantillation. In the second: why is the middle finger omitted while both the
small finger and the index are used twice?

❀　❀　❀

As a notation in a narrower sense, North India uses figures, as we saw,
and the South, syllables taken from the ordinary alphabet, *ka, ki, ko, ku, kai,*
kau, and many other consonant-vowel combinations. Only a few of these
indicate single notes: *ta* means the fourth note of the descending scale; *na*
demands a ligature of the first and the second note and dwelling on one of
them; *cho* indicates the second, third, and fourth notes in succession; *ke*
stands for a group of no less than seven notes. Two hundred and ninety-
seven such indicatory syllables are known.

Once more a syllabic script, taken from the current alphabet, is coupled
with religious texts; once more it stands for sacred, inviolable melodies;
once more it designates stereotyped groups of notes. The only difference is
their place in the manuscripts: here, they are set right within the text, after
the first syllable of a line and also, but seldom, in the middle. Both positions
are illustrated in the beginning of the first *sāman,* TA, CHO, and NA
being musical symbols:

> *o TA gna i*
> *a CHO ya hi NA vi ito i*

To this form, discovered and discussed by A. C. Burnell,[4] Richard Simon
was able to add another,[5] in which each *parvan* of the text was followed by
the melody; for example:

> *barhā-iṣā auhovā* ṬA KHĀ ŚI RI

---

[4] A. C. Burnell, *The Ārsheyabrāhmaṇa, op. cit.,* Introduction.
[5] Richard Simon, "Notationen der vedischen Liederbucher," in *Wiener Zeitschr. für die*
Kunde des Morgenlandes XXVII (1913), p. 346.

Burnell calls the South Indian letter notation "the oldest," that is, older than the figures used for the same purpose in North India. To his philological reasons one might add the general fact that South India has preserved the older forms of tradition more faithfully than the North which again and again was exposed to conquest and immigration on a large scale.

The possible relation of this script to Ethiopian and Babylonian notations was discussed in a paper that the author read in 1939 at one of the meetings of the International Congress held by the American Musicological Society in New York.[6]

[6] Curt Sachs, "The Mystery of the Babylonian Notation," in *The Musical Quarterly* XXVII (1941), pp. 62–9.

[2]

PICTORIAL AND LITERARY EVIDENCES

PICTORIAL EVIDENCES of the earliest Indian music are rare. The most ancient phase of Indian culture, the so-called Indus civilization of the third millennium B.C., seems to have left only one musical trace: a frequent ideogram of its puzzling script apparently represents a vertical arched harp of the type common in early antiquity between the Nile and the Ganges.

After a gap of two thousand years, information becomes safer and ampler when, under the influence of Greek art, Indian sculptors in North and Central India begin to carve reliefs on the walls of temples and burial mounds, many of which depict musical scenes. These important sources have recently been made accessible in an outstanding French publication.[7] (Pl. 7, p. 176)

Pictorial evidences, however, tell little of the musical style in ancient India. Still, they prove two facts. One is the important role of hand-beaten drums, which has been characteristic of India to this day and indicates a strong dependency on motor impulse and rhythm. Secondly, the only stringed instrument is the arched harp; therefore the classical *viṇā*, so often mentioned in poetry and musical theory, must in antiquity have been a harp before the name passed to the present tube zither and eighteen other instruments [8] at the end of the first thousand years A.D. The soundboard of leather, mentioned in several ancient sources, confirms this statement.

The typical group of girls accompanying dancers with harps and drums was exclusive until in the first century A.D. the Indo-Scythic courts of the northwest entertained male musicians with lutes, lyres, and double oboes. The two latter species disappeared soon enough, since the Greek influence in music was small or none; but the lute was accepted. Cymbals appeared between the fourth and sixth centuries, and the *viṇā* in the older of its two modern forms only in the seventh century.

❈ ❈ ❈

[7] Claudie Marcel Dubois, *Les Instruments de Musique de l'Inde ancienne*, Paris, 1941.
[8] Cf. Nārada, *Sangīta-maḳaranda*, ed. Telang, Baroda, 1920.

LITERARY EVIDENCES are fortunately more abundant than in most countries. Poetical works like the great national epos *Rāmāyaṇa* [9] describe India's musical life in the times of Plato without refraining from technicalities; ancient dictionaries give some help, too; above all, there are special treatises on music in prose and in verse, not always easily comprehensible nor free from later additions, but well detailed and on the whole very useful.

Unfortunately, their ages are rather uncertain, and misdatings have been frequent. "The Ocean of Music," *Sangīta Ratnākara,* by Śārngadeva, "the greatest of Indian musical authorities and one who still inspires reverence in the minds of India's musicians," was, not long ago, dated at about 200 A.D. and "considered to be the oldest reliable musical work extant." [10] Today, we know that Śārngadeva lived no less than a thousand years later, in the thirteenth century.

Actually the oldest, and certainly the most important, treatise on ancient music are the seven chapters 28–34 in Bharata's unique book on the theatrical arts of India, the *Nātya-śāstra,* of which only the twenty-eighth has been translated.[11] This excellent source would be even more valuable if we knew its approximate date. Most critics agree in establishing it as the earlier centuries A.D.; a recent bibliography, however, shifts it tentatively to the fourth or even fifth century B.C.[12] Whatever its date may be, Bharata's book testifies to a well-established system of music in ancient India, with an elaborate theory of intervals, consonances, modes, melodic and rhythmic patterns.

[9] P. C. Dharma, "Musical Culture in the Rāmāyaṇa," in *Indian Culture* IV (1937), pp. 447–53.

[10] C. R. Day, *The Music and Musical Instruments of Southern India and the Deccan,* London, 1891, p. 13.

[11] Sanskrit text, French translation, and commentaries: Jean Grosset, "Contribution à l'étude de la Musique hindoue," in *Bibliothèque de la Faculté des Lettres de Lyon* (1888) v. 6. English translation (incomplete): E. Clements, *Introduction to the Study of Indian Music,* London, 1913, pp. 49–51. Sanskrit text, German translation, and commentaries (incomplete): Bernhard Breloer, *Die Grundelemente der altindischen Musik,* Diss. Bonn, 1922.

[12] M. S. Ramaswami Aiyar, "Bibliography of Indian Music," in *Journal of the Royal Asiatic Society of Great Britain and Ireland,* 1941, p. 237.

3

SCALES

INDIA'S SCALES are numberless. Still there has been a kind of standard scale, referred to in the very earliest sources, the *Rikprātiśakhya* and the *Rāmāyaṇa* epos (both about 400 B.C.): *shaḍja, ṛśabha, gāndhāra, madhyama* ('middle'), *panchama* ('fifth'), *dhaivata,* and *niśāda,* generally abbreviated to *sa ri ga ma pa dha ni.*

The seven names indicate in the first place steps, not notes. This unusual conception probably has the same reason that Mr. Coomaraswamy gives for the frequent portamento of singers and players: in India the interval counts more than the note.[13]

As an inevitable expedient, the names of the steps were also given to the notes that limited them. But a step has two limiting notes, and the question is which one to prefer. In modern India it is the lower note: *sa* means the note *C* with the whole tone above (*C–D*). In antiquity, it was the other way around: *sa* meant the note *D* with the whole tone below. The contradiction is probably due to the conflict between descending vocal and ascending instrumental scales.

Instead of an elaborate notation, Indian musicians write the musical syllables themselves, just as the Chinese do, which is particularly easy since the alphabets derived from the Sanskrit script *nāgarī* provide ready-made symbols for syllables, not single consonants. Notation consequently differs according to the musician's native script; the symbols he uses may pertain to the Hindustani, Bengali, Telugu, Malayalam, or whatever script the district favors. The ancient Tamils, on the contrary, used their seven long vowels instead of syllables,[14] which was in exact parallel with Egyptian and Greek invocations.[15]

Signs for time values, formerly used in connection with the note symbols, have been given up as too complicated. Today, the original symbols

---

[13] Ananda Coomaraswamy, "Indian Music," in *The Musical Quarterly* III (1917), p. 167.

[14] N. Chengalavarayan, "Music and Musical Instruments of the Ancient Tamils," in *Quarterly Journal of the Mythic Society,* n.s. XXVI (1935), p. 80.

[15] Franz Dornseiff, *Das Alphabet in Mystik und Magie,* Berlin, 1925. C. E. Ruelle, "Le Chant gnostico-magique des sept voyelles grecques," in *Congrès International d'Histoire de la Musique,* Paris, 1914.

may be modified in order to distinguish longer and shorter notes, although without exact time values.

Musical punctuation is indicated by special signs for repetition and for the end of a period.

*　　*　　*

THE ANCIENT ORGANIZATION of this scale was startling. All distances were subdivided—the semitones into two elements and the whole tones into either three or four, in all twenty-two elements or *śrutis*:

$$
\begin{array}{ccccccccc}
D & E & F & G & A & B & C & D \\
\underbrace{3\ \ \ 2\ \ \ 4} & & & 4 & \underbrace{3\ \ \ 2\ \ \ 4} \\
\underbrace{9\qquad\quad 4\qquad\quad 9} \\
22
\end{array}
$$

There has been much pondering over the puzzling problem of why and how the Hindus came to a division into twenty-two parts. Twenty-four quarter tones would have been comprehensible; but twenty-two? To ask such a question means to be prejudiced by the modern idea of equal temperament.[16]

Actually, the *śrutis* were not units but, on the contrary, of three different sizes necessitated by the very nature of Indian scales.

The two essential features of these scales are their shape and their transposition.

India's standard scales depended on the divisive principle; they had major whole tones of 204, minor whole tones of 182, and semitones of 112 Cents.

These ingredients appeared in several arrangements according to the mode required, and the modal scales could be transposed to any pitch. The incessant readaptation of the octave required facilities for changing semitones or major whole tones into minor whole tones, of adding and cutting off adequate portions.

All permutations in these 'give-and-take' operations were feasible with only three elements: (*a*) twenty-two Cents or a 'comma,' the difference between the major and the minor whole tone (204–182 Cents); (*b*) seventy Cents, the difference between the minor whole tone and the semitone;

[16] Cf. E. M. von Hornbostel und R. Lachmann, "Das indische Tonsystem bei Bharata und sein Ursprung," in *Zeitschrift für Vergleichende Musikwissenschaft* I (1933), pp. 73–91.

(*c*) ninety Cents, the difference between the semitone and the comma. Consequently, there were for

the major whole tone: $90 + 22 + 70 + 22 = 204$ C.,
the minor whole tone: $90 + 22 + 70 = 182$ C.,
the semitone: $90 + 22 = 112$ C.

The give-and-take operation also indicates the exact sequence of the twenty-two *śrutis:*

D		E		F			G			A		B		C			D
112	70	22	90	22	70	22	90	22	90	70	22	90	22	70	22	90	22	70	112

The first and last steps of 112 Cents, minimum steps with which any modal scale begins and ends, are not split in this operation.

❊   ❊   ❊

Two FUNDAMENTAL SCALES or *grāmas* appear in Bharata's treatise: *sa-grāma* and *ma-grāma*. And at once difficulties begin.

Bharata at first (in *śloka* 25) defines *sa-grāma* as the scale of 324 4 324 *śrutis,* but later (in the following *ślokas* 26–29) describes it as 432 4 432: he has shifted the series by one digit to the left without explaining the contradiction.

After all, he probably did not contradict himself; if any passage in Bharata's much rehandled book looks like a later addition, it is this unexpected, unnecessary, and contradictory restatement. The theory of scales and modes leaves no doubt that *sa-grāma* started from the note *sa* and was a D-mode.

Ma-grāma, the other fundamental scale, differed, according to Bharata's first definition, in nothing but the shift of one 'standard' (*pramāṇa*) *śruti* (of 22 Cents) from *G–A* to *A–B:*

	D	E	F	G	A	B	C	D
Sa-grāma		3	2	4	4	3	2	4
						!			
Ma-grāma		3	2	4	3	4	2	4

How could so tiny a difference cause and justify the existence of two fundamental, indeed opposite, scales? A great many authors have been unable to solve this puzzling problem, and some of them have denied outright, and despite the detailed indications in ancient treatises, that *ma-*

grāma ever existed. This denial was indeed a poor move, and unnecessary, too.

The actual nature of *ma-grāma* follows from the second passage in Bharata's treatise: the scale started from *ma* and was organized in 434 2 432 *śrutis*, which series must, in accordance with the correct *sa-grāma*, be shifted by one digit to 342 4 324 *śrutis*.

Sa-grāma	D	E	F	G	A	B	C	D
	3	2	4	4	3	2	4	

Ma-grāma				G	A	B	C	D	E	F	G
	(3	2	4)	3	4	2	4	3	2	4	

Within the range of the *sa-sa* octave, *ma-grāma* would indeed differ by that one *śruti* only. The actual difference was apparently the major third and the minor seventh. But this is not the whole truth:

Sa-grāma is the plagal, and ma-grāma the authentic form of Indian scales.

Ma-grāma is said to have disappeared from practice in the sixteenth century.[17] That the plagal form was actually more important seems to be confirmed by Śārngadeva (thirteenth century), who relates that in the third part of the *ālāpa*—the improvised introduction of a *rāga*—the singer begins with the tonic and uses only three notes above and then descends to notes of the octave below before developing the upper tetrachord.

One should not dismiss the question of *grāmas* without considering that Bharata's second statement (which I believe to be a later addition) mirrors the more recent stage of Indian music: *sa-grāma* has become a C-mode and *ma-grāma* an F-mode.

This latter scale is described in the very earliest source in Tamil language, the *Tivākaram* (third century A.D.).[18] The scale, it reads, contains 4 432 432 *śrutis*. This is an F-mode, too, and—a remarkable fact—in the exact arrangement of the *sa-grāma śrutis* from *ma* on.

This suggests that Bharata's text was possibly rehandled as early as antiquity, and it may confirm the idea that Bharata himself wrote his treatise much earlier.

❀   ❀   ❀

[17] N. S. Ramachandran, "The Evolution of the Theory of Music in the Vijayanagara Empire," in *Dr. S. Krishnaswami Aiyangar Commemoration Volume* (1936), p. 392.

[18] Herbert A. Popley, *The Music of India*, Calcutta, 1921, p. 31.

A THIRD SCALE, *gāndhāra-grāma* or *ga-grāma,* has been an unsolved mystery. It is not mentioned in Bharata's book and had in the thirteenth century A.D. already "withdrawn to Indra's heaven" when the great theoretician Śārngadeva wrote his *Sangīta Ratnākara.*

I say, "not mentioned," without adding "yet." It is inadmissible to conclude from Bharata's silence that the *ga-grāma* was devised after his time. Two more facts warn against such a rash conclusion. First, ancient Tamil works even refer to four modes instead of Bharata's two.[19] Second, there is the story of Supriya.

One of the Buddhist legends relates how a famous musician, Supriya, was able to play, on one string, in the French translator's words, *"sept notes avec vingt-et-un tons et demi-tons."* [20] I do not know exactly what Mr. Feer fancies tones and semitones to be. The Sanskrit text does not suggest any such things; it speaks of seven *svaras* and twenty-one *mūrchaṇas.*

This word, as the next paragraph will show, unmistakably means modal toptail inversions of the *grāmas,* each *grāma* having seven of them. Consequently, there must have been a third *grāma* in the time of the Hundred Legends. Unfortunately, we do not know the date of these legends; but they were translated into Chinese as early as the third century A.D., and the original may have been written one or two hundred years before.[21]

I refrain from dragging the reader through the maze of contradictory descriptions in the later Sanskrit literature and of modern attempts to interpret them. Those interested in the evasive *ga* scale are referred to the latest controversy between Mr. Fox Strangways and Mr. Ramaswami Aiyar.[22]

This uncertainty suggests another question. We know that two basic principles have shaped scales all over the world: the cyclic principle with its equal whole tones of 204 and semitones of 90 Cents, and the divisive principle with major whole tones of 204, minor whole tones of 182, and large semitones of 112 Cents.

Bharata's system derives from the divisive principle, and this, in turn, stems from stopped strings. But the earlier part of Indian antiquity had no stringed instrument except the open-stringed harp; no lute, no zither provided a fingerboard. India must have had the up-and-down principle, and it cannot but be hiding somewhere.

---

[19] Popley, *ibid.,* p. 34.

[20] "Avadāna-Çataka," transl. by Léon Feer, in *Annales du Musée Guimet* XVIII (1891), p. 76 (17th tale).

[21] J. S. Speyer, "Avadānaçataka," in *Biblioteca Buddhica,* St. Pétersbourg, 1902, III, I v.

[22] A. H. Fox Strangways, "The Gāndhāra Grāma," in *Journal of the Royal Asiatic Society for Great Britain and Ireland,* 1935, pp. 689–96; M. S. Ramaswami Aiyar, "The Question of Gramas," *loc. cit.,* 1936, pp. 629–40.

But, after all, does not the system of *śrutis* serve equally well the purposes of either principle? Does it not even allow for a smooth transition? Transfer, in a 'divisive tetrachord,' one standard *śruti* (22 Cents) from *F–E* to *E–D*, and you have the two major whole tones and the minor semitone required in the up-and-down system:

$$D \qquad E \qquad F \qquad G$$
$$182 \qquad 90 \qquad 204$$
$$\longleftarrow 22$$

We certainly do not know whether the cyclic principle had anything to do with the *ga-grāma*. But at least we must suppose that this principle still existed when the *śruti* system was being formed.

❋　❋　❋

THE MŪRCHAṆAS were scales of more specific nature than the *grāmas*. There were fourteen, seven belonging to *sa-grāma,* and seven to *ma-grāma*.

For a moment one might think they were transpositions of the two basic scales. But several reasons are against such an interpretation. Transposition along the octave would imply five sharps and one flat, while Bharata mentions only the two first sharps. Moreover, Bharata expressly describes how a *mūrchaṇa* can be transposed into its upper fifth or lower fourth by sharpening *F*, which would be meaningless with seven transpositions. Lastly, Bharata states that there were *also* some *mūrchaṇas* with sharps (or flats). Consequently, the normal *mūrchaṇa* must have had naturals.

The mūrchaṇas were modal toptail inversions.

It is probable that the number fourteen was rather due to systematic completeness than to the necessities of musical practice. The discussion on *jātis* will show that only seven were in actual use.

Tānas were hexatonic and pentatonic versions of these fourteen scales, with one or two notes omitted. Bharata enumerates no less than forty-nine hexatonic and thirty-five pentatonic versions, in all eighty-four *tānas,* that is, twelve forms, each in seven tonalities.

Players of stringed instruments had two ways of performing incomplete scales; one consisted in passing lightly over the intermediate note between a lower and a higher note, or vice versa; the other, in leaving the intermediate note untouched. However, "when the intermediate note is being touched and held, there is *mūrchaṇa*." In other words, the notes in question could be either skipped, or touched slightly, or even played in the usual way; there was no strict distinction between complete and incomplete scales.

Speaking of incompleteness and omission is in a way embarrassing. Mostly, the conception of "omitting" notes stems from the naïve belief of historically untrained minds that patterns usual in the person's own time and country are 'natural' and therewith timeless, so that archaic stages are easily mistaken for abnormal varieties.

Here, however, things are different. Classification, especially in the Orient, starts from actual facts, but is thorough in its accomplishment regardless of practice. The nearly one hundred *mūrchaṇas* and *tānas* were almost certainly products of theoretical construction rather than of musical necessity. Only a few of them appear in the melodic patterns that shall be discussed next.

4

RĀGAS

THE STRICTNESS of mathematical laws and hairsplitting classifications, however, has to a remarkable degree been counterbalanced by artistic freedom—in India as elsewhere. Deviations from the rule were not only considered admissible, but necessary to make a melody more expressive and human. Theory has often tried and always failed to get hold of them.

Nothing could be more Oriental than the continuous adjustment of variation and stabilization, of spontaneity and tradition, of freedom and law. Primitive singers seldom are able to repeat the same melody in exactly the same form; their originality and their mood at the moment of singing, the factor of detrition and other circumstances—all these influences bar stereotype reproduction; every performance means actual re-creation.

The high civilizations of the Orient have to a great extent preserved the flexibility of melodic patterns, and singers are in certain respects not only allowed but actually expected to offer individual interpretations.

Such freedom, unknown in the modern West, was checked by fetters equally unknown. Melodies were conceived and performed in the limits of a certain *rāga* and varied only in so far as its laws remained intact.

Rāga means 'color' or 'passion' and denotes a pattern of melody with a well-defined mood and a modal scale in which every note has its individual place as the starter, the predominant, the center, the final.

The 'predominant' *aṃśa*, originally identical with the starter, is neither what we call a tonic nor a dominant. It is not even conditioned by the structure of the scale and sometimes differs in various melodies of the same *rāga*. Modern *Bilāval*, for example, the counterpart of our major mode, has the tetrachordal skeleton *C–F–G–C*, but the predominant *E*. Its role becomes perfectly clear from our Examples 58 to 62: in *Bihāg*, it is *E;* in *Bhairava, A;* in *Bhairavī, C;* in *Mālkos, C*.

Certain melodic characteristics often join the obligatory traits of a *rāga*. Modern *Bilaharī*, for instance, requires the copious use of the turn *A C B A*.

The easiest way to make Westerners understand what melodic patterns are is to compare them with the architectural orders of the Greeks. Hellenic architects obeyed the rules of the Doric, or the Ionic, or the Corinthian style. Each implied certain proportions of the columns, the ground motives of the capitals, the equilibrium of cornices, friezes, gables, and numberless other qualities. The artist's latitude was small and his inventiveness restricted to detail work and general harmony.

Oriental music has been ruled by the same idea of submitting individual creative power to the binding force of ready-made patterns.

❊ ❊ ❊

THE BINDING POWER of the *rāgas* is mirrored in a legend from the *Adbhuta Rāmāyaṇa*:

> Once upon a time the great Rishi Nārada thought within himself that he had mastered the whole art and science of music. To curb his pride the all-knowing Vishnu took him to visit the abode of the gods. They entered a spacious building, in which were numerous men and women weeping over their broken limbs. Vishnu stopped and enquired from them the reason for their lamentation. They answered that they were the *rāgas* and the *rāgiṇīs*, created by Mahādeva; but that as a rishi of the name of Nārada, ignorant of the true knowledge of music and unskilled in performance, had sung them recklessly, their features were distorted and their limbs broken; and that, unless Mahādeva or some other skilful person would sing them properly, there was no hope of their ever being restored to their former state of body. Nārada, ashamed, kneeled down before Vishnu and asked to be forgiven.[23]

The interesting point is that this legend represents an almost literal replica of a satire, in one of Pherekrates' comedies, against the then modern music in Greece after the Peloponnesian wars and its protagonist Timotheos of Miletos. A woman, dejected, ragged, and limping, answers sympathetic questions: "I am Music, and once I was well off. But now Timotheos and others have manhandled me, oh, friend.—What Timotheos?—The Redhead from Miletos.—Timotheos, too, maltreated you?—He is the worst of all; his notes crawl about like ants, against melody, in the highest pitch, and he has chopped me like cabbage and stuffed me with a stinking mixture. And when I was alone, he overcame me, stripped me, and fettered me with twelve strings. . . ."

In India, this idea of personalizing musical sounds and patterns and making them react to violation in a human way has been developed in a great many versions. One of the most attractive is the story of the king of apes, Hānuman, who was very proud of his musical attainments, and foolishly boasted about them. Rāma, the hero of the Rāmāyaṇa epos, de-

[23] Herbert A. Popley, *The Music of India, op. cit.,* p. 8.

vised a plan to humble him. In the jungles there dwelt a noble rishi who caused the Seven Notes to become embodied in seven lovely nymphs. Rāma took Hānuman into the vicinity of the abode of the rishi, and Hānuman, wanting to show off his qualifications, proudly took up the *vīṇā* and began to play. Just then the seven lovely nymphs or notes passed by them; they were going to fetch water. Hearing the music, one stopped, swayed and fell dead. Hānuman had sung that note incorrectly. The sister notes were comfortless and moaned and lamented her death piteously: the rishi, seeing all this, smiled, took up the *vīṇā* and struck the notes loudly. As soon as the dead note was played correctly it revived and gaily rejoined its sister notes and there was much rejoicing. Hānuman, thoroughly ashamed of himself, hung his head and performed penance for his silly vanities.[24]

❋   ❋   ❋

EXACTNESS AND SKILL were not only a question of art; careless performances endangered the extramusical potentialities of the *rāgas*. For each of them had its cosmic connotations, indeed had forceful secret energies that worked on man and nature.

A singing girl, by exerting the powers of her voice in a certain *rāga,* once drew down from the clouds timely and refreshing showers on the parched rice crops of Bengal and thereby averted the horrors of famine.

Whoever, on the other hand, attempted to sing the rāga *Dīpaka* was to be destroyed by fire. The Mohammedan Emperor Akbar [sixteenth century A.D.] ordered Naik Gopaul, a celebrated musician, to sing that *rāga:* he endeavored to excuse himself, but in vain; the Emperor insisted on obedience: [Naik Gopaul] therefore requested permission to go home and bid farewell to his family and friends. It was winter when he returned, after an absence of six months. Before he began to sing he placed himself in the waters of the Jumna till they reached his neck. As soon as he had performed a strain or two, the river gradually became hot; at length it began to boil; and the agonies of the unhappy musician were nearly insupportable. Suspending for a moment the melody thus cruelly extorted, he sued for mercy from the Monarch, but sued in vain. Akbar wished to prove more strongly the powers of this *rāga:* Naik Gopaul renewed the fatal song: flames burst with violence from his body, which, though immersed in the waters of the Jumna, was consumed to ashes! [25]

The *rāgas* also worked on, and belonged to, certain hours of the day and seasons of the year. A musician in Emperor Akbar's time sang one of the

---

[24] Atiya Begum Fyzee-Rahamin, *The Music of India,* London, 1925, p. 87.
[25] Sir W. Ouseley, "Anecdotes of Indian Music," in *The Oriental Collections* I and in Sourindro Mohun Tagore, *Hindu Music from Various Authors,* 2nd ed., Calcutta, 1882, I, 166.

night *rāgas* at midday: the powers of his music were such that it instantly became night, and the darkness extended in a circle round the palace as far as the sound of his voice could be heard.[26] I need not remind the reader of the similar legend from China related in the Far Eastern section.

The connection with a certain hour of the day is still respected. "No musician, unless specially ordered, will sing any *rāga* out of the proper time of day apportioned for it. . . . It would be considered improper to make any change. Even in educated circles among Hindus it would be thought a display of ignorance to call for a particular *rāga,* unless for some special reason, at an improper season." [27]

Connotations with the signs of the zodiac, the planets, the days of the week, the seven heavens, seasons, elements, colors, voices of birds, human complexions, sexes, temperaments, man's ages, and what not, exceed even Chinese proportions. A complete list is printed in Atiya Begum Fyzee-Rahamin's book. The attributions, however, have not been consistent in all parts of the country.

The theory of psychological effects can be traced back to early times. The Rāmāyaṇa (c. 400 B.C.) expects *rāgas* to arouse one of the nine sentiments: love, tenderness, humor, heroism, terror, anger, disgust, surprise, tranquillity.[28] Bharata's twenty-eighth chapter ends with the promise "to indicate the sentiments that the *rāgas* affect," but the twenty-ninth chapter has not yet been edited.

Unfortunately there is no answer to the question how all these physical and psychological energies work, or on what account they are attributed to certain notes or *rāgas;* for neither the *rāgas* themselves nor their connotations are the same in the north and the south of the country, and in both parts they differ from those indicated in the ancient treatises on music. Tradition is hopelessly lost. Every local school has a terminology of its own, and when a northern musician associates the rāga *Srī* with love and evening twilight, a man from the south will rebuke him and relate it to grandeur and the hours between noon and 3:00 P.M.

This confusion frustrates any deeper insight into the relation of the musical and the extramusical qualities of the *rāgas.*

*　*　*

[26] *Ibid.,* pp. 165 f.
[27] C. R. Day, *The Music and Musical Instruments of Southern India and the Deccan, op. cit.,* p. 45.
[28] P. C. Dharma, "Musical Culture in the Rāmāyaṇa," *loc. cit.,* pp. 447–53.

EVIDENCE OF RĀGAS appears in the earliest sources of Indian music, though under different names. The Rāmāyaṇa (c. 400 B.C.) as well as Bharata and even the much later Nārada call them *jātis,* and both Bharata and Nārada mention eighteen of them. Bharata, however, already knows the word *rāga* as the distinctive color given to the *jātis* by sharps and flats.

The very existence of accidentals (which cannot be gathered from the ancient terminology) makes the old descriptions vague and calls for inter-pretation.

Bharata explains in detail that only seven of his eighteen *jātis* are pure and simple; eleven are combinations of two or more simple *jātis.* Four out of the seven belong to the *sa-grāma,* and three to the *ma-grāma.*

What was their characteristic difference?

An attempt to reconstruct the ancient *rāgas* logically starts from the modern *rāgas* which almost certainly must have preserved some of their forerunners. Among the ten groups in use today, one is quite irregular, three belong to the so-called Gypsy scale, and the other six, to the three pairs of tetrachordal scales we call by their Greek names Dorian and Hypo-dorian, Phrygian and Hypophrygian, Lydian and Hypolydian.

It is hard to believe that these modes, in universal use in antiquity, should have been wanting in India until more recent times, the more so since the Hindus themselves claim the tetrachordal character of their scales. That they hide among the *jātis* is the more probable as the numbers are sugges-tive: seven simple *jātis,* like the classical modes of Greece (the above-named plus Mixolydian), and three of these authentic or *hypo,* again as in Greece. Moreover they follow stepwise like the Greek scales, notwithstanding Bharata's different arrangement. Our survey is confined to the seven pure modes; it neglects the hexatonic versions, but includes the pentatonic forms. Brackets make the conjunct and disjunct tetrachords evident.

The Hindus, however, although they speak of tetrachords all the time, seem to have lost the knowledge of conjunction. Instead, they interpret conjunctional scales as being composed of two unequal tetrachords—just as the Arabs do.

Natural *jātis,* says Bharata, are the so-called simple *jātis* with all the steps 'complete,' that is, with the *śruti* numbers prescribed for both *grāmas.* But there were also artificial *jātis* with one, two, or more notes altered.

This definition seems to leave unlimited possibilities. But actually most arrangements of whole and semitones ever used in Indian scales are real-ized in the seven simple and eleven complex scales as they stand.

THE SEVEN PURE JĀTIS

Pancamī

A B C D E F G A

A B   D E   G A

Modern *Asāvarī*
Hypodorian

Madhyamā

G A B C D E F G

G A B   D E   G

Modern *Khamāj*
Hypophrygian

Gāndhārī

F G A B C D E F

F G A   C D   F

Modern *Yaman*
Hypolydian

Ārsabhī

E F G A B C D E

E F G ? B   D E

Modern *Bhairavī*
Dorian

Šadjī

D E F G A B C D

D ? F G A B   D

Modern *Kāphī*
Phrygian

Nišādī

C D E F G A B C

C   E F G   B C

Modern *Bilāval*
Lydian

Dhaivatī

B C D E F G A B

B C   E F G   B

Modern ————
Mixolydian

Some alterations, for this reason, might have departed from diatonics and given birth to those augmented seconds that characterize the chromatic gender of the Greeks and the so-called Gypsy scales of later Hindu music, like the rāga *Bhairava*:

EX. 58. RĀGA BHAIRAVA   *after Abraham and Hornbostel*

THE NUMBER OF RĀGAS, already indicated as sixty in a Sanskrit-Tibetan dictionary of the seventh century A.D.,[29] increased, at least in theory, to several hundreds, indeed, thousands; the ancient Tamils calculated the total as 11,991.[30]

Any enumeration would be both impossible and useless. A survey of the groups actually in use will prove more helpful. And there is no want of native classifications; quite to the contrary, there are too many.

The most interesting, typically Oriental division is used in the north: five great *rāgas* have sprung from Śiva Mahādeva's five heads, and a sixth one, from Parvatī, his wife; each of the six great *rāgas* has five wives or *rāginis* and eight *putras* or sons with eight daughters-in-law or *bharyas*. In all there were 132 *rāgas*.

A recent method of classification, based on musical traits and probably the best ever devised, was indicated by N. V. Bhātkande in Bombay.[31] This is its outline.

All *rāgas* are organized in ten groups according to the scale on which they are built:

1) *Bilāval* group: the octave consists of two disjunct tetrachords; both have the semitone above, as in the Lydian octave of the Greeks. Our two examples present one of the heptatonic patterns, *Bihāg,* and, from Udai Shankar's repertoire, the pentatonic pattern of this group, *Durgā:*

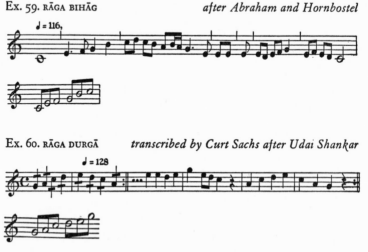

Ex. 59. RĀGA BIHĀG   *after Abraham and Hornbostel*

Ex. 60. RĀGA DURGĀ   *transcribed by Curt Sachs after Udai Shankar*

29 Ananda Coomaraswamy, "Indian Music," *loc. cit.,* p. 166.
30 N. Chengalavarayan, *op. cit.,* p. 81.
31 Popley, *op. cit.,* p. 55.

2) *Yaman* group: the same scale with a sharpened fourth; Hypolydian.

3) *Khamāj* group: the upper fourth has the semitone in the middle, and the lower fourth, above; Hypophrygian.

4) *Bhairava* group: both tetrachords have augmented seconds (the so-called Gypsy scale Ex. 58).

5) *Pūrvī* group: the same, except for an augmented fourth; no Greek analogy.

6) *Mārvā* group: the lower fourth similar, the upper fourth regular with the semitone above.

7) *Kāphī* group: both tetrachords have the semitone in the middle; Greek Phrygian.

8) *Āsāvarī* group: the upper fourth has the semitone below and the lower tetrachord in the middle; Greek Hypodorian.

9) *Bhairavī group* ('ascetic'): both tetrachords have the semitone below; Greek Dorian. My two examples illustrate *Bhairavī* proper and its pentatonic version *Mālkos:*

Ex. 61. RĀGA BHAIRAVĪ   *after Lachmann*

Ex. 62. RĀGA MĀLKOS   *transcribed by Curt Sachs after Udai Shankar*

10) *Toḍī* group: the upper fourth has an augmented second, while the lower fourth is augmented and has the semitone below.

The members of a group differ mostly in the number of notes. In the first group, for example, rāga *Bilāval* has the complete major scale; *Bihāg* jumps from *C* to *E* and from *G* to *B;* *Durgā* passes from *D* to *F* and from *A* to *C* and thus is a pentatonic scale of the 124 type.

From a Western standpoint, we should prefer a different arrangement of the ten groups: a first unit, comprising the six diatonic groups (1) to (3) and (7) to (9), and a second unit, comprising the scales with augmented seconds (4) to (6) and (10). But Bhātkande was right from an Indian standpoint, as we shall see in what follows.

❋   ❋   ❋

BHĀTKANDE'S CLASSIFICATION takes into consideration the hours of the day at which the *rāgas* are supposed to be sung.

Most Hindus divide the day into six periods: (*a*) 4:00 to 7:00 A.M. and P.M., when day and night separate, (*b*) 7:00 to 10:00 A.M. and P.M., after the separation, and (*c*) 10:00 to 4:00 A.M. and P.M., before the separation.

Musical attribution is ruled in the following way: the two groups of hours in (*a*) require those *rāgas* that have the augmented second D♭–E; (*b*) those that have D, E, and A natural; (*c*) those that have both E♭ and B♭.

The two periods of hours that form a pair are musically differentiated by the position of the predominant: a predominant in the lower tetrachord denotes the hours between noon and midnight; a predominant in the upper tetrachord those between midnight and noon.[32]

There is no consistency, however, either in the division of the day or in the association of certain *rāgas* with certain hours. Another system is based on eight periods of three hours each and proceeds with the *rāgas* in the following way: [33]

1) From 6:00 to 9:00 A.M. one plays slow, dreamy, pure rāgas, established on the Gypsy scale, like *Bhairava*.

2) From 9:00 A.M. to noon: *Āsāvarī* and *Bhairavī* rāgas, with three and four flats.

3) From noon to 3:00 P.M.: *Kāphī* rāgas with two flats.

4) From 3:00 to 6:00 P.M.: *Pūrvī* and *Mārvā* rāgas, with augmented second and fourth.

5) From 6:00 to 9:00 P.M.: *Yaman* rāgas, major with an augmented fourth.

6) From 9:00 P.M. to midnight: major rāgas of the *Bilāval* group.

7) From midnight to 3:00 A.M.: pentatonic rāgas with three flats, like *Malkōs*.

8) From 3:00 to 6:00 A.M.: pentatonic rāgas, like *Hindolam*, in which all the notes of *Malkōs*, except the first and its octave, are sharpened.

[32] Popley, *op. cit.*, pp. 63 f.
[33] Fyzee-Rahamin, *op. cit.*, p. 76.

The general idea is clear: *rāgas* have most flats in the quietest hours, extending from midnight to the hot time of the day, and reach a majorlike character in the cooler time between six and midnight.

❋ ❋ ❋

THE RĀGA, strictly speaking, also requires a drone or pedal note to emphasize the 'predominant.' In vocal music, an accompanying lutanist plucks it softly on the four thin wire strings of the *tamburi,* a large, long-necked lute without stopping frets, of Indo-Persian character, the place of which, alas, is often taken by a European harmonium.

To provide drones in instrumental music, recorders, oboes, bagpipes, and the clarinets of snake charmers are geminated to form pairs, in the hands of either one or two players. One pipe plays the melody, while the drone pipe has all fingerholes but one stopped with wax [34] or no fingerholes at all, exactly in the manner of Western Asia and Egypt. Fox Strangways heard two oboe players at Tanjore: "They took it in turns to play chanter and drone. When the second was asked to surcease from droning, the first said he felt 'like a ship without a rudder.'" [35]

❋ ❋ ❋

GAMAKA OR ORNAMENTATION has been "life and soul" of Indian music. "Music without *gamakā*" Somanātha (c. 1600) claims, "is like a moonless night, a river without water, a creeper without flowers." Mr. Coomaraswamy, more definite, though less poetical, says: "The Indian song without grace would seem to Indian ears as bald as the European art song without the accompaniment which it presupposes." [36] But I like particularly the way Mr. Stoll briefly puts it: "Without *gamakas* a melody cannot smile." [37]

The English translation "ornament," however, wrongs the *gamakā*. Indian graces are not glued on some melody like trills and mordents in recent Western music. They are the very pulse and breath of melody and give the individual note its weight, shade, and meaning.

In a way, Indian performance reminds one of skillful penmanship as opposed to printing. It avoids the rigid array of separate letters, but joins

[34] Curt Sachs, *Die Musikinstrumente Indiens und Indonesiens, op. cit.,* pp. 155, 158, 159, 165–7.
[35] A. H. Fox Strangways, *The Music of Hindostan, op. cit.,* p. 46.
[36] Ananda Coomaraswamy, *op. cit.,* p. 167.
[37] Dennis Stoll, "The 'Graces' of Indian Music," *loc. cit.,* p. 169.

them in one long dash of the pen that the writer's mood and motor impulse vivify in spirited turns and flourishes.

And one more point should be understood: while East Asiatic music stresses the single, indeed the isolated, note, Indian music emphasizes the step or even the interval—not as a jump from note to note, not as the fusion of two notes in one chord, but as the actual unit of melody. Therefore the individual note leads to the next note portamento, or else, if there is no melodic progression, it is rapidly deflected. Such a deflection may comprise a larger interval, but often only the *śruti* nearest at hand, and frequently such turns would require, in Dennis Stoll's words, "an aural microscope for our uncultured Western ear in order to grasp them in detail." [38]

The ornaments for the *vīṇā*, the *sarōd*, and other plucked instruments have been neatly classified and even written down in special symbols: glissando up and down with the stress put on the beginning, not on the end; a wail by deflecting the string right after plucking; a weak echo produced by relifting the finger; flattening a note by pressure of the nail and plucking with extraordinary strength; and many other refinements.[39] We hinted at India when we were discussing the similar style connected with instruments of the Far East. Whoever listens to phonograph recordings of this kind of ornamentation will often be at a loss to decide whether he hears a Chinese performing on a *ch'in* or a Hindu playing the lute *sarōd*.

Singers likewise indulge in numberless kinds of trills, portamentos, appoggiaturas, backfalls, and mordents, and sometimes dissolve single beats in more than a dozen pearling notes. To speak the truth, singers of the ordinary type often overdo ornamentation. They

appear to have an idea that the highest form of their art consists in introducing as much grace as possible, whether it adds to the beauty of their songs or not; in fact, they try to disguise the real melody as much as possible by embellishments of their own, and so in nine cases out of ten it is quite impossible to follow either the air or the words of a song, since the singer is only anxious to exhibit what he fondly imagines to be his skill.[40]

The strangest aspect of ancient *gamakā* appears in Nārada's surprising classification of *rāgas* into three groups: the first includes those sung with a quivering voice throughout; the second, those with partial quivering; the third, those without any quivering.

[38] *Ibid.*, p. 168.

[39] Cf. Richard Simon, "Die Notationen des Somanatha," in *Kgl. Bayerische Akademie der Wissenschaften, Sitzungsberichte der philolog. Klasse*, 1903, Heft III, pp. 452–60.

[40] C. R. Day, *The Music and Musical Instruments of Southern India and the Deccan, op. cit.*, p. 60.

We would dismiss this unique tripartition as awkward and beyond our comprehension. But then, it should strike a note familiar to students acquainted with the music of the Catholic Church, which among the melodicles that the neumes symbolize has two, *quilisma* and *pressus,* expected to be performed *tremula voce.* These are late European traces of a once important form of Oriental singing which was still in bloom in India in the eighth century, indeed, was observed in the Vedic chant as late as the seventeenth century and is customary to this day among certain Mongol tribes who sing throughout with a bleating tremolo voice.[41]

*   *   *

Singing, in its skill and ethics, was emphasized as nowhere else in the ancient world. India's national epos Rāmāyaṇa, composed in the third or fourth century B.C., expects a singer to know the science of music, to have a sweet voice, to sing in the natural register, and to have a range of three octaves. It recommends him to eat sweet fruits and roots in small quantities, insists on his singing exactly as taught without any ingenious attempts to improve the master's composition or supplement it by flourishes, and strictly forbids him to take money or any other remuneration.[42]

In later times, both northern and southern treatises on music dedicate long paragraphs to the study of human physiology [43] and to what a good singer was supposed to achieve and what to avoid. The positive part of these enumerations is less interesting. We take it for granted that the singer be able to hold his breath, and that his voice be sweet and entertaining, not very loud nor very weak, but deep and rich.

The negative part, however, strikes us as singularly up to date, and nobody can read these endless lists of rules without a smile of recognition: that one should not sing with closed teeth; with fear; with the mouth wide open; with eyes tightly closed; with a nasal twang; with all the words jumbled up together and rolling in the throat so as to be incomprehensible; with a contracted stomach; with a plaintive or weeping expression, or with raised eyebrows; that the singer should not shake his head, move his eyes, swell his neck, gape, or show his teeth; that he should not crane his neck like a camel, or make frantic gestures with his hand. And many others.[44]

[41] Cf., for example, Joseph van Oost, "La Musique chez les Mongols des Urdus," in *Anthropos* X/XI (1916/17) pp. 363, 385.
[42] P. C. Dharma, "Musical Culture in the Rāmāyana," *loc. cit.,* pp. 447–53.
[43] C. Tirumalayya Naidu, *Gana Vidya Sanjivini,* 1896, p. 12.
[44] Fyzee-Rahamin, *op. cit.,* p. 71; Chengalavarayan, *op. cit.,* p. 82.

[5]

RHYTHM AND FORM

INDIAN RHYTHM in its marvelous wealth and importance shows better than the system of the Western and the Eastern Orient the two basic forms of rhythmic organization: meter and time.

The Roman orator Fabius Quintilianus has given the shortest definition: *Metrum in verbis modo, rhythmus etiam in corporis motu est*—"Meter exists only in words, and rhythm—read: time—in the motion of the body." [45]

Time, originating from pace and carriage, is 'qualitative'; it organizes melody in a rhythmical series of stressed and unstressed notes, independently of their lengths and therefore counted by regular beats. The numeric symbols of times are fractions: $\frac{4}{4}$ means that the first out of every four regular beats is stressed, and that the beats have the average tempo of human steps; $\frac{4}{8}$ means the same type of stress, while the tempo is double.

Meter is 'quantitative'; it organizes melody (like verse) in a rhythmical series of long and short notes. Counting a long note as two shorts—which is typical in all meters—the numeric symbol of meters is sums: a dactyl would appear as $2 + 1 + 1$ and an iamb as $1 + 2$, which means that the group or foot or measure consists of long-short-short or of short-long.

Over and over the two forms of rhythm have overlapped—in modern Western music no less than in ancient Oriental melody.

South India's musical meter, *ákshara,* faithfully respected the numberless foot patterns in which the arrangement of long and short was classified.

To help with this classification, the Hindus have fabricated the imposing word *yamātārājabhānasalagām.* Each three consecutive syllables, counting from the first, the second, the third, etc., syllable, indicate one meter:

yamātā	◡ — —
mātārā	— — —
tārāja	— — ◡
rājabhā	— ◡ —
jabhāna	◡ — ◡

---

[45] Fabius Quintilianus, *Institutio oratoria* IX iv.

bhānasa — ⌣ ⌣
nasala ⌣ ⌣ ⌣
salagām ⌣ ⌣ —

In addition, using the two last syllables only:

lala ⌣ ⌣
lagā ⌣ —
gāla — ⌣
gāgā — —

Symbols for rests occur, but only—like the medieval *punctus divisionis* —to define groups of three units, which, for lack of accents, could not otherwise be distinguished from even-numbered combinations.

An example of poetical meter in Indian music is the following fragment of a praise of the divine ape, Hānuman, in which every short syllable is rendered by an eighth note, while syllables long either by a long vowel or by two consecutive consonants are given quarter notes: [46]

van - de   san-tam   śrī - ha-nu-man-tam

It should be emphasized that meter in itself was in India closer to life than anywhere else, since up to the nineteenth century it ruled all kinds of written language.

❊   ❊   ❊

INDIA'S MUSICAL TIME has seldom the simple form of modern Western rhythm. One form of time, *ekā,* corresponds to our $\frac{4}{8}$, and the north has some simple patterns, allegedly introduced by the Mohammedans: *dhīma* = $\frac{4}{8} + \frac{4}{8} + \frac{4}{8} + \frac{4}{8}$ or $\frac{4}{2}$, and *dādra* = $\frac{3}{8} + \frac{3}{8}$ or $\frac{6}{8}$.

But in expressing these rhythms as sums of fractions, we have already passed to the most characteristic organization of Indian melody—the rhythmic patterns or *tālas.*

The simplest explanation of *tāla* might be: a rhythmic pattern that combines the essential features of both meter and time. Its numeric symbols consequently are sums of fractions.

The above-mentioned $\frac{6}{8}$ would give an idea of *tāla,* since it combines two three-beat groups in the metric relation of a spondee. But the true *tāla* avoids equivalence of its members.

[46] After Erwin Felber and Bernhard Geiger, *op. cit.,* p. 109.

The space occupied by a pattern is called *vibāgha,* a term that we translate by 'period.' The subsequent periods, repeating the first one, follow without any interruption. A period is composed of one, two, three, or four *angas* or 'members,' each one of which may be the size of one, two, three, four, five, seven, or nine units of time or beats.

South Indian theory indicates the current patterns in the following survey:

Ekā	3	<u>4</u>	5	7	9
Rūpaka	2+3	<u>2+4</u>	2+5	2+7	2+9
Jhampa	3+1+2	4+1+2	5+1+2	<u>7+1+2</u>	9+1+2
Triputa	<u>3+2+2</u>	4+2+2	5+2+2	7+2+2	9+2+2
Mathya	3+2+3	4+2+4	5+2+5	7+2+7	9+2+9
Dhruva	3+2+3+3	4+2+4+4	5+2+5+5	7+2+7+7	9+2+9+9
Ata	3+3+2+2	4+4+2+2	<u>5+5+2+2</u>	7+7+2+2	9+9+2+2

The underlined symbol indicates which of the five *jātis* or varieties of each *tāla* is the most frequent and does not need any distinctive epithet.

The first horizontal row denotes one-member periods (or simple measures) of three, four, five, seven, nine time units or beats; in our notation:

$$\text{♩., ♩ , ♩\_♪, ♩.\_♪, ○\_♪}$$

The second row indicates two-member periods of two plus three, four, five, seven, nine units.

And so on.

Permutation is admitted; *Dhruva* reads 2+4+4+4 or 4+4+2+4 as well. Moreover, all members may be split and dissolved into units.

Skillful drummers go as far beyond the regular patterns as they want; one of them, Simhanadana, has been credited with a monstrous pattern of a hundred units in members of two, four, and eight.

❊   ❊   ❊

RHYTHMIC PATTERNS appear as early as Bharata's book (Chapter 31) and at that time must already have passed through a long period of evolution.

Bharata knows five patterns, two of which are pure and three mixed. Of the pure rhythms, one has eight time units:

and one ten time units:

Of the mixed patterns, one has six time units:

while two have twelve time units each:

and

All five patterns appear in three versions: simple (as written); double, with time values twice as long; and quadruple, with values four times as long.

It is difficult to understand the actual meaning of these patterns unless we know about Indian time beating, and the syllabic abbreviations used to describe it in notation.

Classical practice had two kinds of beats, silent and audible. Of eight beats altogether, four were silent gestures of the hands and four were audible slaps.

The silent gestures were: (a) *ā*, palm upward and the fingers bent; (b) *ni*, palm downward and the fingers stretched out; (c) *vi*, hand to the right, palm upward and the fingers stretched out; (d) *pra*, palm downward and the fingers bent.

The audible beats were: (a) *dhru*, snapping the fingers; (b) *śa*, slapping (as the thigh) with the right hand; (c) *tā*, slapping with the left hand; (d) *sam*, slapping with both hands.

Every unit of time was accompanied by an indicative movement. Every member was given one loud beat, in the simple as well as in the enlarged versions of the patterns. If a member contained more than one unit, the second and following units were given silent gestures.

In performing these movements, the hands alternated from member to member: *śa* as the audible slap indicated that also the silent gestures of the same member were made with the right hand; *tā* prescribed the same for the left hand, and *sam*, both hands.

The fingers, too, alternated. In duple time, the four parts of a period were denoted by pointing first with the small finger and successively adding the ring finger, the middle finger, and the index. This was different in other rhythms.

These details are somewhat irrelevant here. The important point is that in antiquity the audible slap did not mark the beginning, but the end of a member; for example:

Simple pattern ♩. ♪♩ ♩ ♪♩.
Silent gestures *s s*   *s*   *s*   *s s*
Audible beats   *A A*   *A   A A*   *A*

Once again, the ancient Indians did the opposite of what we would do: just as they named the steps of their octaves for their upper notes, they emphasized the last, not the first, beats of their rhythmic patterns; indeed, they gave the greatest stress—*sam*, both hands slapping—to the very last quarter note of a period. Actually, the audible beat did not stress, but warn. It cannot be compared to the accented downbeat of our conductors, but rather to the jerk in their arms that prepares the downbeat. Once more, the shifted emphasis shows that Indian rhythm is basically different from the stressed beats of our musical style.

With the knowledge of what roles were assigned to audible and silent beats, we realize that the 'mixed' triple pattern mentioned by Bharata

is not what it seems to be: three equal beats, as in our $\frac{3}{4}$ time, which indeed would not fit in the Indian picture. The beat notation reads *ni śa śa*, meaning that the first beat is a silent gesture, and the other two, audible slaps. This indicates that the two first quarter notes form one member:

It was beyond the means of classical notation to indicate values higher than three eighths or dotted quarter notes. So they had recourse to two quarter notes instead of one half note (as in plain song) and explained their actual meaning by the distribution of silent and audible beats.

One more question arises from studying the beat forms: Bharata's plain triple pattern in its simple version reads

which again implies a symmetrical and therefore suspect rhythm. Now both the double and the quadruple version indicate, by their audible beats, the asymmetrical arrangement

Is the first version a copyist's mistake?

But then, were the members of those early patterns rigidly arrayed or permutable as they are in modern *tālas?* Could a pattern like 2 + 2 + 1 + 3 just as well appear as 1 + 2 + 2 + 3 or in any other sequence?

If so, it would be easy to rearrange one of Bharata's two six-unit rhythms. But then it would not differ from the other six-unit rhythm, which thus would no longer be a ground pattern. Permutation could hardly have been permissible in Bharata's time.

On the other hand, the combination of four- and three-unit rhythms led to numberless complex patterns up to seventeen units, among which those with five, seven, nine, ten, and eleven units were particularly in favor.

The vital quality of Indian rhythm is fully developed: there is no division into equal beats, as in our music; an $\frac{8}{8}$ measure is not divided into two halves and four quarters, but is the total of, say, three members with 3 + 2 + 3 or with 5 + 2 + 1 eighths. Since there is no accent of force on the first units of members or periods, this smooth, fluctuating rhythm is to our even time as the flight of a soaring bird to the gait of a horse.

The rhythmic patterns are given so much attention that the composer seldom fails to indicate the *tāla* after the *rāga:* a certain piece would be headed *Mālsarī rāga* and *Sūlphāḳatā tāla,* or *Bilāval rāga* and *Tīntāl tāla.*

The importance of rhythm in India becomes particularly evident in the unique role of her drums. Musical scenes depicted on the earliest reliefs in times B.C. prove that two thousand years ago they were just as indispensable as today; in 1051 A.D., the Rajarajeśvara Temple at Tanjore had no less than seventy-two drummers among its one hundred and fifty-seven musicians; [47] and in the sixteenth century, Emperor Akbar's band consisted of one pair of cymbals, twenty-three wind instruments, and forty-two drums.

The drummer who accompanies a singer uses either one drum with two heads or two drums with one head each. The heads are in both cases hand-beaten and tuned to different pitches; besides, each head in itself yields two notes, since the central part, loaded with a circular paste, sounds lower than the outer ring.

Usually, the player drums the regular 'audible' beats with his right hand on a skin tuned in the tonic *sa,* and the 'empty' beats or *khalis* with his left hand on the other drum head in lower *pa,* as:

But skillful drummers do not rest satisfied with so easy a technique; instead, they develop counterrhythms without ever violating the *tālas.* A favorite form is the counterpoint within the same *tāla:* the right hand plays the pattern in regular time, including the *khalis,* while the left hand plays it in 'augmentation' twice as slowly:

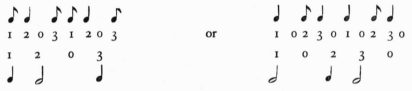

Often, however, the two hands play different *tālas,* one in ordinary time and the other in augmentation; for instance:

The two patterns may even overlap:

[47] Fox Strangways, *The Music of Hindostan, op. cit.,* pp. 79 f.

Tempo and agogics were fixed in classical times with all the methodical precision of Indian classifications. The Hindus had three main tempi in the ratio 1:2:4, and three shades in each of them. Within these nine tempi, certain forms of accelerando and rallentando were admitted.

* * *

THE MUSICAL FORMS of ancient India are unknown. But it seems admissible to date back, in a general way, the common traits of later forms and particularly those characteristics that the north shares with the south. There is scarcely a doubt that two thousand years ago the accompanied song was —to say the least—placed foremost in musical life; and since the vital essence of melody was the *rāga* with all its implications, just as it is today, the modern way of shaping musical structure in the spirit of *rāga* was probably followed in antiquity as well.

The spirit of *rāga,* the carefully maintained balance of freedom and law, has led to a dual form in art music: the antithesis of *ālāpa* and *rāga* proper.

The first part, *ālāpa,* is an improvised introduction in which the singer rehearses the essential traits of the *rāga* in question, its scale, the notes particularly stressed, the appropriate ornaments—both for his own benefit and to facilitate the listener's comprehension. This is done without words or rhythmic strictness in two first movements. Words and rhythmic pattern are introduced in a third movement, but still with more freedom than the *rāga* proper would admit.

The desire for freedom and virtuosoship has to a certain extent inverted the roles of *ālāpa* and *rāga;* performers occasionally would dwell an hour on the *ālāpa* and give the *rāga* not more than fifteen minutes. The south, more conservative than Hindustan, has not allowed the *ālāpa* to exceed the limits of a mere introduction. Its hypertrophy thus appears to be a modern development that should not be mistaken for a heritage from antiquity.

The second part or *rāga* proper is built in various forms, all of which are 'static' rather than dynamic and follow the rigid rules of verse and strophe. Within this pattern monotony is avoided either by a rondolike insertion of 'episodes' before the main subject is resumed or by variations. The pattern itself is doubtless ancient. But we are not able to tell whether in antiquity it followed the rondo or the variation type.

Whatever the form, it relied on soloists or small, intimate ensembles. "It is the chamber music of an aristocratic society, where the patron retains musicians for his own entertainment and for the pleasure of the circle of his friends." [48] Orchestras are not properly in the Hindu's line. In truth, modern theaters have built up some kind of orchestra, and a few contemporary musicians indulge—like Udai Shankar—in those delightful coloristic effects which so much appeal to the Western taste. But at the bottom, Indian music has been, and probably will be, chamber music, performed by a singer, accompanied with the delicate double drone of the tamburi; or by two fiddles and two hand-beaten drums; or by a vīṇā, a violin, and a drum.

[48] Coomaraswamy, *op. cit.*, p. 163.

PLATE 7A. Indian dancers, drummers, and harpists. Relief from the temple at Bharhut, c. 200 B.C. After Claudie Marcel Dubois.

PLATE 7B. Indian dancer and players with drums, transverse flute, lute, and harp. Relief from Pawaya, first centuries A.D. After Coomaraswamy.

PLATE 8. The Skolion of Seikilos. From a tomb stele at Tralles in Asia Minor, c. 100 B.C.—The skolion begins on the sixth line. The notes, placed above the corresponding syllables of the text, are taken from the current alphabet and belong to the so-called Vocal Notation. The dashes above some of these notes are rhythmic symbols.

[6]

CONCLUSION

INDIA'S MUSIC was never insulated. It has taken and given. In the retinue of Buddhism, it had a decisive part in forming the musical style of the East, of China, Korea, and Japan, and with Hindu settlers it penetrated what today is called Indo-China and the Malay Archipelago.

There was a westbound exportation, too. The fact, of little importance in itself, that an Indian was credited with having beaten the drum in Mohammed's military expeditions might at least be taken for a symbol of Indian influence on Islamic music. Although complete ignorance of ancient Iranian music forces us into conservatism we are allowed to say that the system of melodic and rhythmic patterns, characteristic of the Persian, Turkish, and Arabian world, had existed in India as the *rāgas* and *tālas* more than a thousand years before it appeared in the sources of the Mohammedan Orient.

In exchange, India's music has been indebted to contributions from the West.

Again, the picture must be pieced together out of tiny scraps of information. The South Indian frame drum *tambaṭṭam* was known in ancient Babylonia under the Semitic name *timbutu;* the strange South Indian stick zither *kinnari* shared its name with King David's *kinnor,* the Hebrew lyre; *vīṇā,* a foreign word, as its spelling implies, and in times B.C. indicating the arched harp, had for at least three thousand years been the name of the Egyptian harp.[49]

Direct reports give evidence of musical exchanges. The diary of a navigator at the beginning of the first century A.D., the *Periplus Maris Erythraei,* relates that India in his time imported *mousiká* from Egypt; Eudoxios of Cadiz ships "musical girls" (*mousiká paidiskária*) to India; and the geographer Strabo[50] advises his readers to present Indian rajahs with musical instruments or pretty singing girls from Palestine or Alexandria in order to win their favor. Palestine even sent pipers; the Acts of St. Thomas, written before 230 A.D., tell how a piper came down to the place where the apostle

[49] Curt Sachs, *The History of Musical Instruments, op. cit.,* p. 153.
[50] Strabo, *Geography* XV, i, 55.

landed in India, "stood over him and played at his head for a long time: now this piper-girl was by race a Hebrew." [51]

But in all times the Indus Valley was the most vital gateway. In ever new waves it conveyed to India most of the instruments in use today, and above all, at a very late time, the long-necked lutes, such as *tamburi* and *sitâr*, which from time immemorial had existed in Mesopotamia and Iran. The name *tamburi*, it is true, appears in a late Sanskrit masquerade as *tumburu-vīṇā* (just as Babylonian priests distorted Semitic terms into Sumerian in times in which this sacred language was no longer spoken), and linguistically untrained natives have not hesitated to confer on this beautiful instrument the aureole of a genuine Indian origin and a venerable age of five thousand years because of its spurious Sanskrit name. Actually, long-necked lutes do not appear in any literary or pictorial source down to the end of the Middle Ages.

Any Greek influence on Indian music, on the contrary, is more than doubtful, although Alexander the Great's campaign (333 B.C.) had inaugurated a cultural interchange with Greece. Indian and Greek scales were certainly similar in many respects; but this was hardly avoidable since they were based on tetrachords in both countries. The drum accompaniment, so vital in Indian music, had no analogy in Greece, and one ought to be very careful in comparing the rhythmical patterns of India with the metrical combinations of Greek melody. Also, while Islamic theory abounds in Greek terms and quotations from Greek authors, there is not the slightest mention of anything Greek in Hindu theory.

The most important factor against assuming direct Greek influence is the dissimilarity of instruments. India possessed none of the instruments of Greece, neither lyres nor pipes of the aulos type. Instead, Indian reliefs in Hellenistic times, essentially created under the influence of Greek sculptors, depicted arched harps and tubular drums, which in turn were not known in Greece.

The following section will show how different were the ways of Greek musicians.

[51] *Acta Apostolorum Apocrypha,* ed. Lipsius-Bonnet, II ii 108.

Section Five

GREECE AND ROME

NO MORE than a dozen Greek melodies are preserved, and several among them are mere fragments. But long before the first relic was discovered, the interest in Greek music outweighed the fascination of any other period of music history. Indeed, Greek music itself was to a great extent history. For practically all writers on Greek music, beginning with those who immediately followed the classical age, quoted and interpreted the theories of the past more than those of the present, and this kind of tradition, often misunderstood and marred, was handed down to the Middle Ages and kept and assimilated into our own days without any interruption.

It is hard to see what the unique appeal of Greek music has meant. The overwhelming role of Greek civilization in two thousand years of European education is probably the main thing. But this would not account for the intensified interest in our own time, which in a way has swerved from the exaggerated idolatry of classical antiquity.

Two reasons for this, however, might exist besides a purely humanistic concern. First, the fact that nowhere else has a complete theory of melody been created, and least of all in our own world, in which melody has been drowned in harmony and polyphony.

The second reason is the changing position of Hellenic music. Though Greece was geographically a part of Europe, its music was largely Asiatic. The Greeks themselves admitted, indeed emphasized, this fact. They credited Egypt, Assyria, Asia Minor, and Phoenicia with the invention of the instruments they used, named two of their main tonalities after the Asiatic countries Phrygia and Lydia, referred to Egypt as the source of their musicopedagogic ideas, and attributed the creation of Greek music to Olympos, the son of Marsyas the Phrygian.

With the rise of comparative musicology, it has dawned on us that music historians of earlier generations were doomed by their ignorance of Oriental music to misinterpret the sources.

Greek music, appearing in a new light, seems interesting enough to justify a retrial. In resuming the discussion we are in a unique position through the unprecedented accumulation of written, painted, and sculptured testimonies, through a quite well-preserved theoretical system, an easily decipherable notation, and even a little stock of actual melodies.

[1]

THE SOURCES

THE RELICS of Greek music number eleven, some of which are fragmentary.

O. Pindar's First Pythian Ode, allegedly fifth century B.C., was published in 1650 in Father Athanasius Kircher's *Musurgia Universalis*. But no source could be found, and the piece, obviously written in a style later than Pindar's time, is probably fraudulent.[1]

1. The first stationary song of the chorus (*stasimon*) from Euripides' tragedy *Orestes* (fifth century), written on papyrus and fragmentary.[2]

2. A fragment, possibly from a tragedy, written on a papyrus from about 250 B.C. in the Museum at Cairo.[3]

3-4. Two hymns in honor of Apollo, engraved in stone in the Athenian treasury at Delphi about the middle of the second century B.C.[4]

5. Skolion or drinking song by the 'Sicilian' Seikilos, composed in the second or first century B.C. and engraved on a column at Tralles in Asia Minor.[5]

6. Paean on the older Ajax's suicide and two other fragments on a papyrus in Berlin, written down about 160 A.D. but probably, indeed almost certainly, older.[6]

7. Hymn to Helios.

8. Hymn to Nemesis.

9. Hymn to the Muse, probably all three composed in the second century A.D. by Mesomedes (or the last perhaps by Dionysios) and published,

---

[1] Otto J. Gombosi, "The Melody of Pindar's 'Golden Lyre,'" in *The Musical Quarterly* XXVI (1940), pp. 381–9.

[2] K. Wessely, *Der Papyrus Erzherzog Rainer*, 1892.

[3] Carlo del Grande, "Nuovo frammento di musica greca in un papiro del Museo del Cairo," in *Aegyptus* V (1936), p. 369.

[4] Théodore Reinach in *Fouilles de Delphes* III ii (1912); Otto Crusius, "Die delphischen Hymnen," *Ergänzungsheft zum Philologus* LIII (1894).

[5] *Bulletin de Correspondance hellénique*, 1883; Otto Crusius in *Philologus*, 1891; Philipp Spitta, "Eine neuaufgefundene altgriechische Melodie," in *Vierteljahrsschrift für Musikwissenschaft* X (1894), pp. 103–10.

[6] W. Schubart, "Ein griechischer Papyrus mit Noten," in *Sitzungsberichte der Königlich Preussischen Akademie der Wissenschaften* XXXVI (1918), pp. 763–8. Albert Thierfelder, "Ein neuaufgefundener Papyrus," in *Zeitschrift für Musikwissenschaft* I (1919), pp. 217–25. Hermann Abert, "Der neue griechische Papyrus mit Musiknoten," in *Archiv für Musikwissenschaft* I (1919), pp. 313–28. Rudolf Wagner, "Der Berliner Notenpapyrus," in *Philologus* LXXVII (1921), pp. 256–310.

though without transcription, as early as 1581 in Vincenzo Galilei's *Dialogo della Musica antica*.[7]

10. Hymn from Oxyrhynchos in Egypt, third century A.D., on papyrus.[8]

11. A small instrumental piece by an anonymous composer, of unknown date, in an anonymous treatise on music.[9]

❋ ❋ ❋

NUMEROUS GREEK TREATISES on music, later quotations from lost treatises, and casual passages in the books of nonmusical Greek and Roman authors supplement the few lifeless notations with discussions of the laws and problems, the task and evolution of what the Greeks thought was their noblest art.

The earliest approach was made by physicists. Pythagoras' much mentioned role is vague; but Lasos of Hermione (c. 500 B.C.), Pindar's teacher, is unmistakably credited with discovering vibration as the cause of sound. Archytas of Tarentum (c. 400 B.C.) saw that there were even two forms of vibrations on which the perception of sound depended: stationary waves in the sound-producing instrument, and progressing waves in the outer air to convey them to the ear. Greek music theory culminated in Aristoxenos of Tarentum (c. 320 B.C.). He was no less a scientist than his predecessors; but he passed beyond sound production to sound sensation and became the earliest music psychologist. His "Principles," "Elements," and "Rhythmics" exist at least in a fragmentary form. Shortly after him, the so-called Pythagoreans, led by Euclid (c. 300), tried to find the exact mathematical ratios of the intervals as they presented themselves on the calibrated string of the monochord.

The theory of music reached another peak in the second century A.D. with Nikomachos, Arabian-born Neo-Pythagorean, and with the famous geographer Ptolemy, librarian of the great Library at Alexandria, who in his *Harmoniká* left the standard mathematical work on music. The importance of Aristides Quintilianus' *Perì mousikês* in three books has only recently been fully realized. Its ample information is supplemented in the slightly later *Harmonikè eisagogé* of Gaudentios.

Among the books of late antiquity, we are particularly indebted to the

[7] Friedrich Bellermann, *Die Hymnen des Dionysius und Mesomedes*, Berlin, 1840. Janus, *Scriptores Musici*, 1895, pp. 462 ff. Théodore Reinach, *La Musique grecque*, 1926, pp. 196 ff.

[8] Grenfell and Hunt, *The Oxyrhynchos Papyri* XV, London, 1922, no. 1768. Hermann Abert, in *Zeitschrift für Musikwissenschaft* IV (1922), pp. 524–9. Théodore Reinach, in *Revue musicale* III 9, pp. 8 ff.

[9] Fridericus Bellermann, *Anonymi Scriptio de Musica*, Berol., 1841, p. 98.

Alexandrian Alypios (c. 360 A.D.), whose comprehensive survey of Greek notation made possible the decipherment of Greek music; and to King Theodoric's unfortunate chancellor Boethius, who concluded musical antiquity with a presentation in five books *De Musica* which for a thousand years was considered the musical bible of the West.

Most of these treatises touched upon the history of music. Glaukos of Regium and Herakleides Pontikos laid its foundations in the fourth century B.C. The golden age of the historical branch of musicology was the second century A.D. The so-called Baedeker Pausanias inserted important sections on the music at the ancient Pythian games and on folksongs in his description of Greek curiosities; the encyclopedist, Julius Pollux, gave, in his *Onomastikon,* important abstracts from authors since lost. The outstanding men were Athenaios, in the discussions of his *Deipnosophists,* and Plutarch, in a special Dialogue *Perì mousikês,* in which actual lectures on the various epochs of Greek music were assigned to the guests at an imaginary banquet.

The details from Plutarch, Athenaios, and the other writers are scattered throughout this Greek section. One point, however, might be stressed at once: the division of Greek music history into two main periods.

The earlier period, which we would call classical but which Plutarch defined as the era of "beautiful" music, was characterized by economy, simplicity, and dignity. It came to an end when the generation of about 440 B.C. began to sacrifice simplicity to virtuosoship, and dignity to vulgar taste.

This was written more than five hundred years later. And yet we do not know whether Plutarch's judgment was fair and firsthand or just a repetition of contemporaneous opinions and a mirror of the universal unwillingness to do justice to 'modern' art.

❊   ❊   ❊

MUSIC HISTORY is deeply indebted to these men for having transmitted to posterity a mass of musical facts unique in their superabundance. Unlike Oriental authors, they have shown us the rough outlines of an evolution in the fifteen hundred years of ancient life. Owing to them, we distinguish a primeval period in which blended the songs of Grecian tribes and their Asiatic, Thracian, and Cretan neighbors; a classical period of national Greek music, inaugurated in the seventh century B.C. by the Lesbian Terpander; and a postclassical, 'modern' period from about 450 B.C. on, when subjectivism, characteristic of the time before the Peloponnesian war, led to the revolutionary art of Phrynis of Mytilene and his disciple, Timotheos of Miletos. A sample of the bitter criticisms against these pioneers has been given on page 173.

The questions that Greek writers on music suggest, however, far outnumber those that they answer. The main trouble is the impossibility of aligning the facts in chronological order: admittedly or otherwise, the ancient authors drew knowledge and opinions from sources antedating their own epochs by generations and even centuries and mingled them carelessly with contemporaneous ideas.

This fatal confusion of times, men, countries, and styles has mixed up terminology. Words like *harmonia, eidos, tonos, tropos, sýstema* were anything but clean-cut and are misleading rather than helpful. As a consequence, the historiography of Greek and Roman music has been particularly exposed to misinterpretation.

Unfortunately, the monopoly and undivided sway of classical philology had no altogether good results. Nobody would rail at so venerable a branch of scholarship. But it has been misused as a charter for 'emendation': whenever the philologist did not understand some word or sentence, he supposed the text corrupt and 'corrected' it until he, a man of the nineteenth century and patron of the philharmonic society of his town, was able to associate it with his own musical background and experience. The various 'critical' editions of Plutarch's Dialogue on Music should be a lesson: Plutarch's unobjectionable statement that owing to certain mechanical devices some musicians were able to play twelve tonalities on five strings was boldly corrected to seven strings by Burette, to nine strings by Ulrici, and to four tonalities on eleven strings by Reinach!

Not all philologists, including philologizing musicologists, were sufficiently aware that words weigh little unless one knows their meaning. What is the significance, say, of *in* and *sub,* when we learn that in a double pipe one tube was *incentiva* and the other *succentiva?* Large dictionaries provide a disconcerting number of renderings for both of these two prepositions, and picking out the proper ones is mere guesswork unless one has facts at hand.

The only facts in the field of our vision are parallels outside ancient Greece, and we may add as well: outside post-Hellenic Europe. The double pipe of the Greeks, scarcely ever played in early medieval Europe, is, with an *incentiva* and a *succentiva* tube, still a common instrument across the vast span between Morocco and the Malay Archipelago. To this day, Arabs, Nubians, Ethiopians, and Negroes use the lyres of antiquity. Should they not know more about playing them than Europe, which did away with the last remainders of the ancient lyre more than a thousand years ago? Pentatonic melodies, with major and with minor thirds, have had no place in the evolution of European music; but they still exist in Japan, China, and India in daily practice.

Is it really admissible to interpret the numberless dark passages in Greek authors with the conceptions of modern European music? Or is it not more logical and promising to ask for information where tradition is still alive?

While fanatical philologists, pluming themselves on their ignorance rather than on their achievements, have not been willing to confuse the "pure" music of their protégés with the hideous cacophonies of "savages," advanced philologists have agreed that the essential features of Greek music were misinterpreted. In the meantime, modern music historians, trained by comparative musicology to avoid the pitfalls of projecting modern ideas upon ancient and Oriental music, have taken the lead toward a revolutionary reorientation in every sense of the word.[10]

[10] Cf. D. B. Monro, *Modes of Ancient Greek Music*, Oxford, 1894. J. F. Mountford, "Greek Music and Its Relations to Modern Times," in *Journal of Hellenic Studies* XL (1920). Curt Sachs, "Die Griechische Instrumentalnotenschrift," in *Zeitschrift für Musikwissenschaft* VI (1924), pp. 289–301; and "Die Griechische Gesangsnotenschrift," in *Zeitschrift für Musikwissenschaft* VII (1925), pp. 1–5. R. P. Winnington-Ingram, *Mode in Ancient Greek Music*, Cambridge, 1936. Otto Johannes Gombosi, *Tonarten und Stimmungen der antiken Musik*, Kopenhagen, 1939.

[2]

NOTATION

THE CRITICAL ATTITUDE of the author of this book springs from his own struggles with the tangle of a notation unique in the world.

The Greeks used two different systems of notation: an obviously earlier one, generally called the instrumental notation, and a later vocal notation. We understand both of them and are perfectly able to transliterate them into modern notation. Their actual pitches, though, are of necessity unknown, and our custom of calling the center *a* is conventional if not arbitrary. It seems, indeed, to be rather high since it places the ranges of all pieces preserved between *b'* and *e♭*. On the other hand, it is practical, since it allows us to transcribe the ancient melodies with as few sharps and flats as possible.

This international agreement was unfortunately endangered when, at the beginning of this century, Hugo Riemann destroyed the consistency of the Greek system. He lowered the vocal notation (almost exclusive in our relics) because, as he said, the former interpretation favored Hypolydian and wronged Dorian, which (allegedly) was in all times the main scale of the Greeks; and the German school did not hesitate to follow. The consequences were catastrophic: while the old interpretation had allowed the transcribing of the relics of Greek music without any signature or else with one flat or sharp (Seikilos' Skolion: two sharps), the Neo-German shift charged them with from four to no less than seven sharps.

In the meantime I was able to prove that Riemann's reasoning was in all points erroneous.[11] Thus we eliminate his and his followers' impressive tonalities and restore the old simple keys.

❀　　❀
　❀

THE INSTRUMENTAL NOTATION was used for the *mesauliká,* interludes for pipes between vocal sections, and for the *kroúmata,* pieces for stringed instruments without singing.[12] It consisted of letters belonging to archaic

---

[11] Curt Sachs, "Die Griechische Instrumentalnotenschrift," *loc. cit.*
[12] Aristides Quintilianus, *op. cit.,* p. 26.

alphabets, but differed from any known letter notation: the notes B and E
were given two symbols each; all other notes of the diatonic scale had three
symbols, or rather one letter written in three positions: erect, prone, and reversed. The erect signs designated the diatonic naturals (corresponding to
our white keys), and both the flattened and the reversed signs meant sharps.

There were several puzzling questions, however. Hellenic composers
never used erect signs for both B and C or for both E and F in the same
melody. When these neighboring notes appeared together, the Greeks
wrote C with the flattened sign of B, that is, as B♯, and F with the flattened
sign of E, that is, as E♯. Why? But when they needed either a sharp before
another sharp—say G♯ before F♯—or a whole tone above a natural—say
C♯ above B—they used the reversed signs of G or C. Once more: why?

The author gave the answer many years ago: *"the lyre, chief instrument
of the Greeks, was pentatonic without semitones and preserved its archaic
tuning even when the number of its strings was increased beyond five. The
script devised for such an instrument, indicating fingering rather than
notes, was a tablature, not a pitch notation."* [13]

With a pentatonic *accordatura,* the lyre had either a *b* or a *c′* string, but
never both together; and the same is true of the *e* and *f.* When a lyre had
a string tuned to *b,* any *c′* was artificially produced by pressing the *b* string
with one of the fingers. This was indicated by the flattened symbol. When
a melody contained both *g♯* and *f♯,* the forefinger was engaged in stopping
one of the two strings, and the other had to be sharpened with the middle
finger. This was indicated by the third, reversed, symbol. In melodies with
both *b* and *c♯,* the latter was duly stopped on the *b* string with the middle
finger—exactly as it would be stopped on a European lute as a whole tone
above the open string. (In this case the third symbol was abnormally derived from *c′,* though the note was actually produced by the *b* string, probably to avoid a chromatic interpretation.)

THE VOCAL NOTATION of the Greeks is built on the same principle: each note
of the diatonic scale is given three symbols. However, this second notation

[13] Curt Sachs, "Die Griechische Instrumentalnotenschrift," *loc. cit.,* pp. 289–301.

is apparently much more recent: the archaic letters, with their flattened and reversed positions, have disappeared. Instead, the classic alphabet— A B Γ Δ —runs through the groups of three, A B Γ serving the note f, Δ E Z serving the note e', and so on. And it runs the other way around, descending from A to Ω, as a vocal scale would be expected to do. Consequently, the third, not the first, symbol in each group of three represents the ground sign indicating the natural or open string, while the first and second signs indicate the sharps to be stopped:

The first sharp in each group of three (seemingly derived from a non-existent string but actually stopped on the next lower string) was used when a whole tone followed below it, and the second sharp, when a semitone followed.[14] Thus, Seikilos wrote his Skolion with the letters Z I O C for the naturals, and with the two first-row sharps K and X for $c\sharp$ (before b) and $f\sharp$ (before e). In the Hymn to Helios, on the contrary, the composer wrote $b\flat$ or rather $a\sharp$ with the second-row sign P because it was at the distance of only a semitone from the following a. (Pl. 8, p. 177)

There is still one puzzle left: though in its downward trend the vocal notation was adapted to vocal needs, it preserved the groups of three, which were meaningless with vocal melodies. But this seeming contradiction is easily explained: the singers, used to accompanying themselves on lyres, required a tablature for their fingers rather than a tonal notation for their voices. A tablature of downward direction was the proper way out.

[14] Curt Sachs, "Die Griechische Gesangsnotenschrift," in *Zeitschrift für Musikwissenschaft* VII (1925), pp. 1–5.

3

THE GENERA

DIATONIC, CHROMATIC, ENHARMONIC, the three genera of Greek music, provide the supreme evidence that both notations were tablatures rather than pitch scripts.

The Greeks called *diatonic*—as we do—a scale composed of five whole tones and two semitones, that is, having two whole tones and a semitone in each tetrachord.

The *chromatic* genus—in Aristides Quintilianus' words "as *chrôma* ['color'] is wedged between white and black"—was the "sweetest" genus and the best for expressing grief.[15] It had a minor third and two semitones in each tetrachord.

An *enharmonic* tetrachord consisted of a major third and two microtones of, more or less, a quarter tone each.

Both the enharmonic and the chromatic genus were written with the same symbols; the *pyknon* or 'dense part' was denoted by the three signs of a group of three, meaning that the open string, the stopping forefinger, and the stopping middle finger were used in sequence, regardless whether the fingers were set closely enough to produce enharmonic quarter tones or far enough apart to yield chromatic semitones. Only a small dash through the first symbol of the three indicated the chromatic genus (and its juniority). This proves that the Greek notation meant fingering, not notes.

The Greek notations, being particularly adapted to the enharmonic genus, failed the diatonic genus in its particular needs. A simple scale, like the one in which Seikilos wrote his famous little Skolion, had to leap from the sixth to the ninth, tenth, fifteenth, eighteenth, and twenty-second letters of the alphabet.

Does this imply that the enharmonion was older not only than the chromatic but the diatonic genus as well? 'Plausibility,' the foe of science, could not readily accept such a hypothesis; for is not the diatonic much more "natural" and therefore necessarily earlier than the "sophisticated" enharmonion?

The earliest evidence of microtones, a fragment from Euripides' *Orestes*

[15] Bellermann's Second Anonymus.

(fifth century B.C.), is indeed relatively late. Still, Aristides Quintilianus enumerates the three genera in the order enharmonic-chromatic-diatonic; he and Plutarch call the enharmonic simply *harmonia,* 'structure,' the word otherwise given to all kinds of scales; and less than a thousand years later, the Mohammedan heirs of Greek music theory describe the enharmonion as the 'normal' genus.

Aristoxenos, more directly, asserts that while there are three genera, "the ancients still have dealt with only one of them in their treatises. My predecessors have discussed the enharmonic genus exclusively, neither the diatonic nor the chromatic genus." The strongest opinion, however, is presented by Plutarch 34: "Of the three genera into which the musical scale is divided, corresponding in the number and power of their respective systems, sounds, and tetrachords, one only was cultivated by the ancients. In their treatises we find no direction given on the use of the diatonic genus or the chromatic, but of the enharmonic alone."

Scholars of the nineteenth century were unable to understand how Greek singers could have caught and reproduced differences so tiny, and some of them suggested that the so-called quarter tones might merely have been symbols to indicate portamento.

This is untrue; for, unlike India, Greece tabooed portamento. Aristoxenos stresses the fact that the singers avoided sliding and tried to poise every note as much as possible. Perfect singing depended on precise and sustained intonation. And Ptolemy briefly states: "Sliding tones are the enemies of melody."

However, in Hellenistic times the microtones were abandoned. "Our contemporaries," writes Plutarch about 100 A.D., "have thoroughly neglected the finest genus, to which the ancients devoted all their eagerness. Most of them have lost the discernment of enharmonic intervals." And Gaudentios confirms, in the second century A.D., that diatonic was the only genus sung in his days.

❀ ❀ ❀

THE ORIGINAL ENHARMONION, however, was pentatonic; its tetrachords had a major third with one uncleft semitone below. The quarter tones were a later refinement and are certainly not referred to in those evidences that stress the previous importance or even exclusiveness of the enharmonion.

The earlier enharmonion did not entirely disappear after the semitone had been cleft. It continued to persist along with the other genera whenever a solemn, archaic style was wanted; and it might even have outlived its own quarter-tone offshoot. As late as the second century B.C. the two Delphic hymns, with their truly megalithic downward leaps of a major third, then a semitone, and again a major third and a semitone, give an impressive picture of Greek music eight hundred and more years before.

Ex. 63. FIRST DELPHIC HYMN

Players of the aulós clung to this archaic genus with particular tenacity; Plutarch recommends that whoever wants to know about the old enharmonion should listen to their performances: no piper would allow himself to subdivide the semitone. It was indeed a Phrygian piper, the legendary Olympos, whom Aristoxenos credited with the "invention" of the earlier enharmonion. Olympos, happening to skip the note g in some melody, was so fond of the open major third a–f that he transferred it to the Dorian scale.

This remark is certainly cryptic. But Hugo Riemann had a "plausible" explanation ready: Olympos, as a Phrygian, must needs have devised his new genus in the Phrygian mode; only later, he bowed to the Greek taste and adapted it to the Dorian mode.

Nothing speaks for, but everything speaks against, involving the Phrygian mode at so early a date. Olympos, or whoever the "inventor" was, must rather have started from the original heptad of two conjunct tetrachords which, as we shall see, was called Ionian, Iastian, or Aeolian, not Dorian, and later passed to the more recent octave of two similar, but disjunct, tetrachords, which indeed had the title Dorian. Or else, since Plutarch speaks only of one note omitted, Olympos might have started from a mere tetrachord and later have skipped the corresponding note in the higher tetrachord in order to transform the entire Dorian octave.

Whatever the truth was it has been confused by the later mistake of assuming that Olympos delighted in skipping an already existing g and at last discarded it from the scale. Such a childish explanation is contrary to necessity as well as to the elementary laws of evolution. And it ignores the fact, known to the reader of this book, that major-third pentatonics existed in Japan, the Malay Archipelago, and India, that is to say, in the east and the south of the continent in which Olympos himself is supposed to have spent his life. In other words: a West Asian contributed an Asiatic scale to Greek music.

※　※　※

ONCE AGAIN, our attention is focused on Asia, and particularly on Japan, which offers the clearest picture of ancient Asiatic music.

Comparisons are certainly dangerous. Parallels are at best useless when, seeing some common traits, we just compare isolated facts, regardless of the whole and the place they take in it. But we should, indeed we must, compare similar facts that exist in, and depend on, similar circumstances. And this is the case here. Both Greek and East Asiatic music are strictly established on a melodic basis and organized in genera, keys and modal systems; consonances are used as spices to a certain degree, without interfering with the exclusive orientation toward melody. Stringed instruments are pentatonically tuned in both these areas, while vocal melodies evolve to heptatonic forms. Both racial groups indulge in cosmological connotations and general ideas concerning the influence of music on man, politics, and education.

I need hardly emphasize that this does not mean deriving Greek from Japanese or Chinese music. Both reach down, rather, into one Asiatic mother civilization that may be several thousand years earlier than either area. Do not the Chinese claim that they got their music from the West, and did not the Greeks inversely boast of the Eastern origin of theirs?

This had to be said before recalling to the reader's mind that the national pentatonic scale of the Japanese, the tetrachords of which had a major third above and a semitone below, was the exact counterpart of the Hellenic enharmonion in its archaic structure. One of its modes, *kumoi*, is the form in which it appears in the Delphic Hymn just mentioned.

In a more recent form, *zoku-gaku*, the major third of the Japanese scale, has been cleft in two seconds: the tetrachord *A F E* has become *A g F E*. This shows that in a natural evolution major-third pentatonicism turns into the structure we know as Dorian.

The extraordinary significance of the enharmonion may throw some new light on the evolution of Greek lyre tunings. Paintings on early vases and also literary sources from the early ninth and eighth centuries give evidence of lyres with only three and four strings. This fact has not been given much attention; the few authors who extended their interest from readable to visible sources took this to be an artist's license; after all, vases were small, and the painters had not much space to spend. But Ludwig Deubner was finally able to prove the existence of lyres with three or four strings.[16]

We even know their tuning: Plutarch's *Perì mousikês* indicates *d'-a-e* as the *accordatura* of three strings. This is convincing when we consider the stopping practice of Hellenic lyre players on the one hand and, on the other, the importance, if not exclusiveness, of the enharmonion in early centuries; the strings, far from providing a mere skeleton, made possible the playing of a complete enharmonic or chromatic heptad if the *pykna* were duly stopped on the *a* and *e* strings. They did not, however, suffice for any diatonic melody.

The tuning of four strings was, according to Nikomachos (c. 150 A.D.), *e' b a e*. Again, the four strings made possible both enharmonic and chromatic, but not diatonic, melodies, although having the range of an octave.

---

[16] Ludwig Deubner, "Die viersaitige Leier," in *Athenische Mitteilungen* LIV (1929), pp. 194–200.

4

THE SHADES

IT IS MISLEADING to speak simply of thirds, seconds, semitones, and quarter tones. So rough a classification is admissible in civilizations concerned with harmony and equal temperament; it was not compatible with the sensitivity of Greek musicians and the conscientiousness of the mathematicians interested in music.

The eternal wish to adapt the inexorable rigidity of codes and systems to the freedom of living, changing melody dissolved the three genera into an astonishing number of subgenera or 'shades' (*chroaí*) with differently balanced intervals.

Aristoxenos, for instance, indicated six shades (the ratios of which we translate from fractions into modern Cents):

Enharmónion:	400 + 50 + 50
Chrôma malakón:	366 + 67 + 67
Chrôma hemiólion:	350 + 75 + 75
Chrôma toniaîon:	300 + 100 + 100
Diátonon malakón:	250 + 150 + 100
Diátonon sýntonon:	200 + 200 + 100

The *diátonon malakón* is particularly interesting because in the pentatonic *accordatura* of the lyre (which skips the two smaller notes) it resulted in the series

$$
\begin{array}{ccccccc}
E & & D & & B & A & & G & & E \\
& 250 & & 250 & & & 250 & & 250 & \\
& & & & 200 & & & &
\end{array}
$$

which is, like certain Japanese singers' scales and Javanese *salendro* octaves, organized in halved tetrachords.

Only three of Aristoxenos' shades (the first, fourth, and sixth, respectively) answer our rash conception of enharmonic, chromatic, and diatonic tetrachords. The rest consist of awkward steps that have no place in our music: third, three-eighth, three-quarter, six-seventh, five-quarter tones, and neutral thirds of two sizes.

These are only a few typical cases, however; practically, Aristoxenos says, "one must understand that the number of *lichanoí* [notes second highest in the lower tetrachords] is unlimited; you can place a *lichanoíd* at any distance from the preceding note." Plutarch (39) indeed complains that singers invariably flatten the second-highest notes of all tetrachords, and Ptolemy's lyre scale, printed on page 213, evidences a lichanós, *g*, flattened by a third of a tone.

A tetrachord was considered softer than another if the distance between its two top notes was larger. Soft tetrachords were supposed to narrow and weaken the soul; hard tetrachords expanded and stimulated.

Arabian theorists later gave a somewhat different definition: a Greek tetrachord was soft if one of the three steps exceeded the sum of the two others. Soft forms were as a rule rejected, except for the characteristically Oriental tetrachord with the lessened minor third 7:6 (i.e., 267 Cents).

The so-called Aristoxenians, who like their master and his teacher Aristotle relied on man's senses rather than on mathematical subtleties, took an astonishing step to evaluate their shades; instead of representing *intervals* by ratios, they represented *distances* by dividing a fourth into sixty units of 8.3 Cents. Anticipating the latest achievement of modern musicology—distance measure instead of interval ratio—they reached a kind of equal temperament, with (supposed) equality of the two enharmonic quarter tones, the two chromatic semitones, and the two diatonic whole tones.

❋ ❋ ❋

PTOLEMY and his partisans, however, were passionately opposed to temperament; mathematically minded, they believed exclusively in the ratios their test monochord provided. They particularly insisted on dividing the whole tone into different semitones: (*a*) the *apotomé* or 'cut,' which is the difference between a perfect fourth and a major third ($4/3 : 5/4 = 16/15$ or 112 Cents); and (*b*) the *leimma* or 'remainder,' which makes it up to a whole tone ($9/8 : 16/15 = 135/128$ or 92 Cents).

Ptolemy's own shades, again translated into Cents, read:

Enharmonion:	$386 + 74 + 38$
Chrôma malakón:	$316 + 120 + 62$
Chrôma sýntonon:	$267 + 151 + 80$

Diátonon malakón: 233 + 182 + 83
Diátonon toniaîon: 204 + 233 + 62
Diátonon sýntonon: 182 + 204 + 112
Diátonon ditoniaîon: 204 + 204 + 90
Diátonon homalón: 182 + 165 + 151

The *diátonon ditoniaîon* was the normal scale that obeyed the up-and-down principle; the *diátonon homalón* was brought about by dividing a string into twelve equal parts (see page 75).

The digest of Greek theory in Arabian treatises might help us in comparing the systems of Aristoxenos and Ptolemy. A tetrachord, they say, was 'weak' when the two small distances were equal; it was 'energetic' when they were about two to one in size. Aristoxenos' tetrachords were 'weak,' and Ptolemy's 'energetic.'

The two systems held by no means undivided sway. Plato's friend, Archytas (fourth century B.C.), proposed an enharmonion of 386–50–62 Cents, while a century later Eratosthenes, librarian at Alexandria, preferred an enharmonion of 410–45–44 and a *chrôma* of 316–94–88 Cents; and many others had different suggestions.

Only one of these should be mentioned: another Alexandrian, the grammarian Didymos (first century A.D.), is credited with a *diátonon* of 204–182–112, in which—as in Ptolemy's *diátonon sýntonon*—a major whole tone 9:8 and a minor whole tone 10:9 differed by the ratio 81:80 or 22 Cents, named for Didymos the *Didymian comma*. Being the typical tetrachord of the divisive principle, it was well known in India and survived in the Islamic Orient and even in Europe until, after 1700, *equal temperament* was generally adopted.

In all, the Greeks had at least three major thirds, of 386, 400, and 411 Cents respectively; five minor thirds, ranging from 267 to 374 Cents; seven seconds, from 150 to 250 Cents; thirteen semitones, from 62 to 151 Cents; nine quarter tones, from 38 to 74 Cents. There was close touch between thirds and seconds, and even overlapping of seconds, semitones, and so-called quarter tones.

We have still not done with the complication of Greek shades.

Ptolemy relates that in his time players of the lyra favored two normal forms of intonation: a hard one, *stereón*, that is, the *diátonon toniaîon;* and a soft one, *malakón*, which was half *diátonon toniaîon* and half *chrôma sýntonon:*

	e′	d′	c	b	a	g	f	e
Hard:	204	231	63	204	204	231	63	
Soft:	204	231	63	204	267	151	81	

In both there is deviation of as much as a third of a tone from our modern scale.

These intonations were valid only for players of the lyra. Those who performed on the kithara preferred the two forms called *parhypátē*, which was half *diátonon toniaîon*, half *diátonon malakón*, and *lýdion* (half *diátonon toniaîon*, half *diátonon sýntonon*):

> *Parhypátē:* 204 231 63 204 231 182 84
> *Lýdion:*   182 204 112 204 204 231 63

And so with all these unwonted experiences, one more surprising fact must be taken in: the Greeks did not rest satisfied with scores of genera, modes, scales, shades, and keys; they even disregarded the symmetry of equal tetrachords and formed unbalanced octaves out of contrasting tetrachords, indeed, of contrasting genera. The two Delphic hymns are examples of mixed scales.

✳   ✳   ✳

MODERN MUSICIANS, spoiled by the ready-made distances on equal-tempered keyboards, could hardly be blamed for sneering at an overrefinement that to them meant decadence and snobbishness. Still, the Greeks would have stopped their ears had they heard our piano scales, just as, vice versa, modern music lovers unfamiliar with the different principles of Oriental scales would be utterly disgusted by Greek melodies.

For Greek melodies were indeed 'Oriental,' and their next of kin have lived in the Middle East to this day, not in the West. And the nearly one hundred scales of the Islamic Orient are not only the exact counterparts of the various Grecian Shades, but the great majority of them are actually 'mixed.' Two of the most popular Oriental scales, *Bayātī* and *Iṣfahān*, are composed of a *sýntonon* tetrachord and a *ditoniaîon* pentachord; and *Higāz*, the most "Oriental" scale of all, consists of a chromatic tetrachord and a diatonic pentachord. And this is not the music of decadents or snobs; both the Arabs and the Turks were young and unspoiled at the time their melodies were being classified.

The Oriental warning suggests a reconsideration of what norm and exception are. Is it really normal to construct an octave out of two similar tetrachords? On the contrary. The performer who starts with a whole octave in his mind creates a new configuration essentially different from the mere sum of its parts. Running up and down between the tonic, the confinalis, and the octave, his melody needs leading notes of different weight and measure and an equilibrium that totally ignores the boundaries of tetrachords and pentachords. The theorist, often at a loss to find the mathematical ratios under the comparatively simple conditions of a single tetrachord, has much greater difficulties in the complicated relations within a whole octave. Thus he helps himself from different kinds of tetrachords and pentachords in order to legalize by a combination of ratios what in itself is irrational and immeasurable.

The Shades, far from being hyperesthetic subtleties or mathematical sophistications, were serious, indeed vital, attempts to reach a norm that satisfies both nature and taste.

Despite all hairsplitting, no actual singing or even playing stands the test of measuring devices. Outstanding Egyptian virtuosos (whose musical position toward scales is well comparable) have been put to such tests with the first pentachord of a melody in the maqām *Nahawand*.[17] We print their distances under A and B and add the normal distances as indicated by Raouf Yekta Bey: [18]

$$(A) \quad 179\text{-}108\text{-}193\text{-}222 \text{ Cents}$$
$$(B) \quad 180\text{-}144\text{-}209\text{-}169 \text{ Cents}$$
$$(Y) \quad 204\ \text{-}90\text{-}204\text{-}204 \text{ Cents}$$

Such deviations seem to discredit both the players and the norm. This would be a wrong conclusion. Actually, it is the rigid law that allows melody to be so free and supple without sinking into anarchy.

---

[17] Alfred Berner, *Studien zur arabischen Musik*, Leipzig, 1937, p. 15.
[18] Raouf Yekta Bey, "La Musique Turque," in Lavignac, *Encyclopédie de la Musique* I v, pp. 2993, 3000.

5

EARLY MODES

THE TANGLE of Greek systems, scales, keys, and modes is unbelievable. The Greeks started this confusion themselves; they misunderstood their own terms and almost promiscuously used them where *tonos, tropos, eidos, harmonia, schema, tasis* should have been carefully distinguished. They spoke of Iastian, or Aeolian, or Locrian, without saying whether they had keys, modal octaves, or structures in mind; and Iastian, Aeolian, Locrian, such as Plato conceived them, had anyway nothing in common with the meaning of the same terms in Alypios' tables.

Disentangling, then, can start neither from terminology nor from the conceptions themselves. The third and last way would be chronological; but alas, the ancient authors continually referred to older sources the dates of which we do not know, and chronology is just as vague as terminology. And yet it is the relatively safest way. Only, it must be covered as by a dog: running to and fro, forward and back, anticipating and reverting.

At least, we shall try to separate the classical times from the postclassical period in which the so-called perfect system unified and leveled the old modes.

The word mode, applied to Greek music, evokes the familiar terms Dorian, Phrygian, Lydian and the notion of tetrachords with the semitone below, in the middle, or above.

The picture is correct; but the perspective is wrong.

Dorian was much more than just a mode; it was the standard form of the diatonic genus just as the similar arrangements with the small steps below were plainly *the* chromatic and enharmonic genera. Whenever an ancient author discusses *the* scale, it is the Dorian scale; his tetrachord is the Dorian tetrachord; his systems—that is, complete organisms with a center of melodic gravitation—are Dorian systems.

The smallest of these systems was the tetrachord *a g f e*. Two conjunct tetrachords formed the earliest complex system, the heptachord, or organism of seven notes, *d' c' b♭ a/a g f e*. The linking note *a* was called the 'middle' note or *mesē*, and a true center it was, equidistant from either end of the heptachord.

The second composite system was the octochord or octave, in which a tetrachord and a pentachord were linked. Such conjunction could be made in two ways: (*a*) the pentachord was placed above the tetrachord (*fifth-on-top*), as in the 'plagal' church tones; or (*b*) the pentachord was placed below the tetrachord (*fourth-on-top*), as in the 'authentic' church tones.

Octaves were given the well-known names Dorian, Phrygian, and Lydian. Dorian may be roughly represented on the white keys of our piano from *E* to *E;* Phrygian, from *D* to *D;* Lydian, from *C* to *C*. That is to say, the Greek names differed from the terminology of both the Middle Ages and our own counterpoint studies. And there was one more difference: whereas these names designated authentic scales in the Middle Ages, they denoted plagal scales in Greece. Indeed, even Islamic music, heir to Greek theory, called plagal the first form.

But it is important to know from the very beginning that the Greeks used authentic octaves as well and in later times even preferred them to the plagal octaves. In current terminology, the authentic octaves were later given the prefix *hypó:* Hypodorian, Hypophrygian, Hypolydian. There are, unfortunately, only two hypo melodies preserved, the hymn on the papyrus from Oxyrhynchos and the First Berlin Fragment.

It is not fully clear whether these scales evolved from one another or existed side by side from the very beginning. Nor is there any certainty as to whether the few evidences that we have refer only to the Dorian or also to other scales, or even to Dorian heptachords and to Phrygian and Lydian octaves. The latter possibility would explain the contradictory assertions in Nikomachos' *Enchiridion* (second century A.D.) that in pre-Orphic times the Greeks tuned their lyre in ground tones, fourth, fifth, and octave, and that in post-Orphic times, up to Terpander, they had heptads only, not octaves.

❁   ❁   ❁

TERPANDER, the greatest Greek musician of the seventh century B.C., has been credited with both the completion of the octave and the creation of the Mixolydian scale. This evolution, too, is mirrored in a feature of Japanese music: in the different arrangements of the *zoku-gaku* scale (which we write in the pitch of the Greek scales):

Hirajoshi: *e′ d′ c′ b a g f♯ e*

Kumoi: *e′ d′ c′ b a g f e*

Iwato: *e′ d′ c′ b♭ a g f e*

Exactly the same three arangements appeared in Greece and were later called Hypodorian, Dorian, and Hyperdorian or Mixolydian. The Greeks, like the Japanese, developed three different modes out of the Dorian tetrachord.

In the light of these simple statements, we at last understand the cryptic invective, ascribed to Herakleides Pontikos (fourth century B.C.), against the current triad Dorian, Phrygian, and Lydian. The two latter, he angrily says, must not be called *harmoniai;* the only *harmoniai* are Dorian, Aeolian, and Ionian.

Why? Were not *harmoniai* modes, and could anybody deny that Phrygian and Lydian were indeed modes? Hugo Riemann tried to solve the puzzle by saddling Herakleides with nationalism: Aeolian and Ionian took their names from truly Greek tribes, while Phrygian and Lydian were taken from foreign nations. But were the Greeks ever ashamed of the many foreign traits in their music?

We had better realize at once what Aeolian and Ionian were, and since we have reasons to postpone a detailed discussion of these two scales, it may here suffice to anticipate the result: Aeolian was similar to Hypodorian, and Ionian, or Iastian, to Mixolydian or Hyperdorian. All three of Herakleides' *harmoniai* were Dorian.

A puzzling limitation of the term *harmonia* had occurred before: it stood for the enharmonic genus. In the meantime, we have already found that the archaic enharmonion developed into Dorian; indeed, that both were the same scale, in its pentatonic and heptatonic forms. Consequently, the title *harmonia* seems to have belonged to this scale exclusively, in any stage and arrangement, before it was indiscriminately given to all kinds of modes; and if so, Herakleides, as one of the earliest writers, followed the older usage.

❀   ❀   ❀

THE FIRST DEVELOPMENT visible in Greek music is the construction of lyres with more than four strings: five strings appear on vases of the eighth century B.C., and seven strings on vases of the seventh century. Such instruments were rather antienharmonic, since they forced the performers to skip strings. Instead, they were perfectly convenient for melodies in minorthird pentatonics and even for diatonic melodies. In other words, the appearance of five strings in the eighth century certifies the arrival of minorthird scales with or without their heptatonic offshoots. This substitution is possibly, indeed probably, connected with a well-known substitution of names: the Homeric terms *phorminx* and *kitharis* yielded to the classical terms *kithara* and *lyra*.

Boethius relates that the fifth string was "invented" by a legendary musician, Torrhebos. We do not actually know who this man was; but he happens to be credited by Dionysius Iamblicus with another invention: the Lydian mode. Tradition, consequently, links the five-stringed lyre with the introduction of non-Dorian modes.

Lydian and Phrygian are generally understood to form a trio with Dorian, and it sounds convincing enough: Dorian tetrachords have the semitone below, Phrygian in the middle, Lydian above.

Still, a number of reasons indicate that Dorian, on the one hand, and both Phrygian and Lydian, on the other, had come from very different rootstocks before they seemingly converged.

It may hint at a pentatonic past of Greek music as a whole (and by no means only of Dorian) that neither the perfected lyre nor even the late notation ever abandoned their pentatonic arrangement. Moreover the tuning of all lyres with more than four strings indicates, by its minor thirds, a pentatonic past different from the Dorian pedigree.

Another symptom is, in Plutarch's words, "the custom among the ancients of omitting the note *trítē* in the Spondaean mode," that is, in the archaic melody sung on drink offerings before dinner. This omission of c' definitely created a pentatonic tetrachord ($e'\ d'\ b$). The corresponding f in the lower tetrachord was not omitted, however: Plutarch adds that the omitted *trítē* was unhesitatingly played on the kithara, in consonance with f, which consequently must have been sung. Thus, the tropos *spondeiakós* was certainly not pentatonic, but hexatonic—either as a direct remnant of older pentatonics, or as an indirect remnant suggested by the pentatonic tuning of the lyre.

Once more, our attention focuses on the clear picture of Japanese music, which has in actual life preserved the three things we are looking for: (*a*) stringed instruments tuned in minor-third pentatonics; (*b*) scales in minor-third pentatonics; (*c*) diatonic scales derived from minor-third pentatonics.

The Far East uses two entirely different forms of minor-third pentatonics, which, as stated in the East Asiatic section, go back to different roots and have existed side by side.

The first form, in Japanese *ritsu,* is *tetra*chordic with a fourth and a minor third: *E GAB DE* and corresponds exactly to the main *accordatura* of Greek lyres. In the Far East, it appears both in its original pentatonic form and in the heptatonic version $E \, f\sharp \, GAB \, c\sharp \, DE$.

This is the Phrygian scale of the Greeks.

The second form of minor-third pentatonics of the Far East, in Japanese *ryo*, is a *penta*chordic scale without a fourth: $FGA \, CD \, F$. It appears in East Asia both in its original pentatonic form and in the heptatonic version $FGA \, b \, CD \, e \, F$.

This is the Hypolydian scale of the Greeks.

❀   ❀   ❀

THESE PARALLELS provide the following tentative picture of early Greek music.

1) A strong pentatonic heritage may be inferred from the stubborn tenacity with which the Greeks clung to the pentatonic tuning of their two main instruments, the lyra and the kithara. Even in some vocal melodies, in Seikilos' Skolion (Ex. 79, end) and the Hymn to the Muse, for example, vestiges of pentatonic structures are easily found.

2) These pentatonic structures were of two kinds: with major thirds and semitones, and with minor thirds and whole tones.

3) The evolution from a pentatonic scale to a heptatonic *zoku-gaku* in Japan makes a similar evolution from the so-called Olympian enharmonion to Dorian almost certain. This development is emphasized by the fact that early Dorian scales were heptads of conjunct tetrachords, like original *zoku-gaku* scales.

4) Minor-third scales of the forms 124 and 134 begot the Phrygian octave.

5) Minor-third scales of the form 123 begot an octave, probably called Lydian at the beginning, and later Hypolydian. This would confirm the statement of Aristides Quintilianus: "Originally, there were only three scales, Dorian, Phrygian, and Lydian."

6) The intercalated notes that transform minor-third scales into heptatonic octaves are in Chinese called *pièn*, "becoming," with the name of the next higher note. Without question this means an ascending scale. It is probable that Phrygian and Lydian, too, were ascending.

7) The Japanese major-third scale, on the other hand, is considered a descending organism—so much so that it sometimes combines with an ascending minor-third scale. That Dorian, too, was descending is indicated by the epithets *arché* or "starter," and *teleuté* or "final" which the nineteenth pseudo-Aristotelian Problem gives to the highest and lowest notes

of the original tetrachord; it is confirmed by the name *tritē* which, in the
two higher tetrachords, is given to the third note *from above*.

8) As a result, there would be a definite contrast between Dorian, as a
descending heptad on the basis of an ancient major-third scale, and Phrygian and Lydian, as ascending octaves on the basis of ancient minor-third
scales. And this contrast at last would explain Aristotle's cryptic statement
in *Politics* 4:3 that "of harmonies there are said to be two kinds, the Dorian
and the Phrygian; the other arrangements of the scale are comprehended
under one of these two."

9) If Greek enharmonic scales derived from pentatonic major-third
scales, it is possible, or even probable, that Greek chromatic scales derived
from pentatonic minor-third scales.

10) The entire pedigree would be:

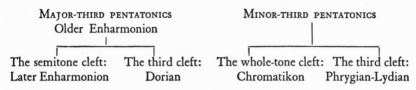

MAJOR-THIRD PENTATONICS		MINOR-THIRD PENTATONICS	
Older Enharmonion			
The semitone cleft:	The third cleft:	The whole-tone cleft:	The third cleft:
Later Enharmonion	Dorian	Chromatikon	Phrygian-Lydian

[6]

THE PERFECT SYSTEM

THE READER was and will be confronted with a large number of modes, each of which is referred to by one or more tribal names: Aeolian, Boeotian, Dorian, Iastian, Ionian, Locrian, Lydian, Phrygian, with or without distinguishing epithets; *aneimenē, chalará, hyper, hypó, mixo, sýntono,* in an ever changing and often contradictory terminology—the same uneasiness that he feels impelled the methodical spirit of Greek masters to organize the chaotic multiplicity of modes into one consistent system and eliminate those modes that were not adaptable.

This process was on its way in the fifth century and came to an end in the fourth century B.C., when the great mathematician Euclid first described the perfect system or *sýstema téleion.* As early as about 400, the kithara had progressed to eleven strings [19] which in some pentatonic sequence covered exactly two octaves and therewith had offered the possibility of representing the new system in its totality.

However, the perfect system was more than just a double octave; it was perfect as a unique attempt to organize the musical space from one center, *a.* The center stands in its original octave of Dorian structure, *e'–e,* which, by adding half an octave above and half an octave below, is extended to two octaves *a'–A.* This new unit could be shifted both up and down by half an octave either way and thus cover three octaves.

The notes added above and below the inner octave were named after the three extreme notes at either end of it: *nētē, paranētē, tritē* above; *lichanós, parhypatē, hypatē* below. Only the lowest note was given a name of its own: the 'added to' note, *proslambanómenos.*

The organization of the two octaves was rather strange. Subdivisions were neither octaves nor pentachords, but tetrachords throughout. This implied two kinds of junctions: conjunction at either end of the inner octave and disjunction or *diazeuxis* in the middle. Read downward, the arrangements resulted in the tetrachord *hyperbolaiōn,* 'of the exceeding' notes, conjunct with the tetrachord *diezeugmenōn,* which, as the name said, was 'disjunct' from the tetrachord *mesōn,* 'of the middle' notes; this, in

[19] Otto Gombosi, *op. cit.,* p. 77.

turn, was conjunct with the tetrachord *hypatōn,* 'of the low' (literally: 'high') notes. The *proslambanómenos* remained over.

The somewhat cryptic remark "literally high" refers to a strange inversion in Greek terminology: *nētē,* the highest note, meant 'low'; *hypatē,* the lowest note, actually meant 'high.' The current explanation is the inclined position of the kithara, in which the musically highest string became—or rather was supposed to become—low in space, and vice versa. But it is more convincing to relate the contradiction to the identical inversion in Oriental music discussed on pages 69–70.

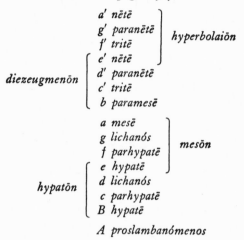

diezeugmenōn

a'	nētē
g'	paranētē
f'	tritē

hyperbolaiōn

e'	nētē
d'	paranētē
c'	tritē
b	paramesē

hypatōn

a	mesē
g	lichanós
f	parhypatē

mesōn

e	hypatē
d	lichanós
c	parhypatē
B	hypatē

A *proslambanómenos*

Similarly, the Greeks constructed a lesser perfect system or *sýstema téleion élatton* on the basis of the old heptad of two *conjunct* tetrachords. It comprised only an eleventh, from *d'* to *A.* The top tetrachord did not exist, and the disjunct tetrachord *diezeugmenōn* was replaced by a conjunct tetrachord *synemménōn:*

synemmenōn

d'	nētē
c'	paranētē
b♮	tritē

a	mesē
g	lichanós
f	parhypatē

mesōn

hypatōn

e	hypatē
d	lichanós
c	parhypatē
B	hypatē

A *proslambanómenos*

✳   ✳   ✳

SETS OF KEYS appear in the fourth century B.C. Aristoxenos indicates two of them. In one, the original (Dorian) scale was shifted upward three times by either a tone or a semitone, and again downward by one semitone. The resulting five Dorian keys were given well-known tribal names:

Mixolydian	d'
Lydian	$c\sharp'$
Phrygian	b
Dorian	a
Hypodorian	$g\sharp$

This means that the Dorian scales, called by these five tribal names, followed one another at the distance of a tone or semitone.

Aristoxenos' second key arrangement was awkward enough: Mixolydian, Phrygian, and Dorian were kept in place; Lydian and Hypodorian, on the contrary, were flattened by a quarter tone each, and an additional key, Hypophrygian, followed on $f\sharp$. These three-quarter tone distances were due to the peculiar hole arrangement of the pipes, Aristoxenos said.

The Hypodorian followed the Dorian key in both arrangements; indeed, it was the key later called Hypolydian. Such inconsistency cannot be surprising. The prefix *hypó* allowed for a certain vagueness, since in earlier times it was used in the meaning of 'approximate' rather than 'under': Herakleides Pontikos (fourth century B.C.) explicitly states that Hypodorian is "not entirely [*mè pány*] Dorian"—"just as we say what resembles white is rather white [*hypóleukon*]," adds Athenaios.

Later times provided transpositions of the Dorian scale in the range of a full octave (and even more). The two leading orders of transposition are called Aristoxenian and Ptolemean.

Ptolemy, who lived in the second century A.D., admitted seven keys, the centers of which ascended diatonically from e to d' in the sequence sol-la-si-do, do-re-mi-fa. We add the e' key, although Ptolemy expressly disapproved of it as being a mere repetition of the lowest key (which, as we shall see, was only a half truth). All eight Dorian double octaves were given tribal names; the term Dorian itself was left to the nontransposed scale with a as the center. (See page 225.)

The reader must be warned against authors who call the Dorian key A minor because the section from the mesē downward resembles a modern A-minor scale, and, for similar reasons, against thinking of Phrygian as B minor and of Mixolydian as D minor. Such terminology is inadmissible, both musically and logically. The term is musically inappropriate since

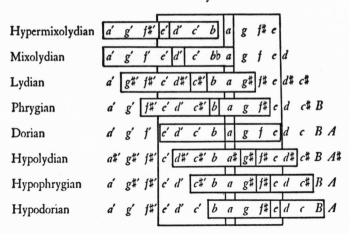

'minor' is a recent Occidental conception; it is logically unfit and contradictory in itself because 'minor' denotes a mode, not a key, while the writer who uses the word wishes to indicate a key, not a mode.

＊　＊　＊

THE TRIPARTITION is obvious: there is a higher group of *hyper* scales, a lower group of *hypo* scales, and a middle group without epithets. At first sight, all of them are similar Dorian keys; but the modal structures are fundamentally different in the three groups:

1) The middle scales, based on *disjunct* tetrachords, have the fifth on top and are plagal.

2) The *hyper* scales, based on *conjunct* tetrachords, with an additional note *above*, are likewise plagal

3) The *hypo* scales, based on *conjunct* tetrachords, with an additional note *below*, have the fourth on top, or rather, should have the fourth on top and be authentic:

$$\text{Hyperdorian} \quad E \ D \ C \ \overset{\frown}{B\flat \ A} \ G \ F \ E$$

$$\text{Dorian} \qquad\quad \overset{\frown}{E \ D \ C \ B} \ A \ G \ F \ E$$

$$\text{Hypodorian} \quad E \ D \ C \ B \ \underset{\smile}{A \ G \ F\sharp \ E}$$

But the perfect system ignored the authentic structure, obviously in order to keep *a* as the common center of all modal scales.

This was technically possible because hypo scales allowed for two structural forms each: in Hypodorian, for example, the same structure of tone, tone, semitone, tone, tone, semitone, tone could serve as TTs TTs T and as T TsT TsT.

Possibly, this fact solves the problem of the cryptic Aeolian scale. A strange passage in Athenaios 14:624 states that "since in certain songs the melody is Hypodorian, it naturally follows that Lasos [of Hermione, c. 500 B.C.] calls the *harmonia* Aeolian."

The passage is unintelligible, indeed nonsensical, unless Hypodorian in the perfect system was not exactly—Hypodorian. It becomes logical and momentous if we assume that both scales were A-modes and had the same notes and the same range, but differed in structure: one was rightfully 'authentic,' while the other had the plagal form that the perfect system forced upon all its scales:

Aeolian: e' d' c' b a g $f\sharp$ e

Hypodorian: e' d' c' b a g $f\sharp$ e

In other words, an Aeolian melody found itself in the perfect system misrepresented as Hypodorian.

Two passages confirm the Hypodorian character of Aeolian: Herakleides Pontikos calls Aeolian "Hypodorian," and Ptolemy, five hundred years later, calls it "Dorian conjunct." Hypodorian is indeed a conjunct Dorian. Moreover, the pseudo-Aristotelian Problems mention Aeolian as the main scale of kitharodists, and this matches perfectly well, since with only one sharp it must have been easy to play. And lastly: Herakleides calls Aeolian "low sounding," *barýbromos*. No scale, indeed, had a lower center of gravity than Hypodorian.

❋   ❋   ❋

THE EARLIER MIXOLYDIAN, too, can probably be restored.

Plutarch, in *Perì mousikês,* relates that at about 475 B.C. the Athenian Lamprokles, "perceiving that the disjunction of its tetrachords should be higher up in the scale than it was almost universally supposed to be, raised it to its true position; and determined its modal structure to correspond to the octave between *b* and *B.*"

Many explanations of this passage have been presented, but none of them is convincing.

The first conclusion should be: when a musician shifts the disjunction, he is changing a conjunct into a disjunct structure or vice versa. The perfect system is based on a mobile scale made of disjunct Dorian tetrachords. All difficulties vanish when we look for the earlier Mixolydian in the so-called lesser perfect system, which was based on a mobile scale made of conjunct Dorian tetrachords (cf. p. 223). (1) The earlier Mixolydian must be expected to derive from a conjunct heptad rather than from the later disjunct octave. (2) Such a scale did actually exist: the archaic Second Delphic Hymn shows continual modulation between Mixolydian conjunct and disjunct. (3) The two scales are

$$\overset{\text{!}}{}$$

disjunct (later) $\overbrace{A\ G\ F\ E}\ \ \underbrace{D\ C\ B\flat}\ \overbrace{A\ G\ F\ E}$

conjunct (earlier) $\overbrace{G\ F\ E\flat}\ \underbrace{D\ C\ B\flat}\ A\ \overbrace{G\ F\ E\flat}.$

$$\underset{\text{!}}{}$$

(4) In confirmation of Plutarch's words, the earlier Mixolydian (based on a conjunct Dorian key) was no so-called B-mode, and it had the disjunction lower in the octave: *a–g,* instead of *e–d.*

* * *

OTHER SCALES, too, were excluded from the perfect system, though they had been highly respected in earlier days: Boeotian, Iastian or Ionian, Locrian, Syntonolydian. Shall we once more attempt to determine their nature from the unsatisfactory descriptions the Greeks have left? I confess that after so much unconvincing guesswork in earlier books I feel little inclined to add new conjectures. Our hopes for solving the puzzles of ancient scales decline somewhat when we learn that not only Aeolian but also Locrian were similar to Hypodorian. The tetrachords within an octave can only be regrouped once; what, then, was the difference between Locrian and Aeolian?

But are there really no other possibilities? Have we not been all too much under the spell of neatly arranged white-key octaves, of tidy A-, B-, C-modes, and of our own equal temperament?

One glimpse at the Islamic world should warn us against so dangerous a bias. In the music of Turkey, which, as we shall see, is entirely ruled by Hellenic conceptions and laws, we face no less than six A-modes of the

Hypodorian-Aeolian kind. One of them, *Nahawand*, has the fourth on top (which we have claimed for Aeolian); all the others have the fifth on top. Of these, *Ḥuseini 'aŝīrān* and *Aradbār* have the 'divisive' structure with two sizes of whole tones and the major semitone (Greek: *sýntonos*) and three, *'Uŝŝāq, Bayātī,* and *Iṣfahān,* have both sizes of whole tones and both sizes of semitones (Greek: *sýntonon* mixed with *ditoniaîon*). The scales of these three *maqamât,* and again those of the two preceding *maqamât,* are indeed similar. Still, the *maqamât* themselves are essentially different for reasons that we discussed in the Indian section and shall once more go into in the Islamic section.

But then, certain facts in Greek music proper should caution against the prejudice that every tribal name necessarily meant a tidy diatonic octave of individual form.

Two of our terms, *sýntonon* and *lydion,* have been mentioned in the discussion on Shades with a meaning quite different from modal scales. Aristoxenos called *sýntonon* a certain shade of the diatonic Dorian tetrachord; Ptolemy's *sýntonon* was a shade of the diatonic Dorian tetrachord, too, though a different one; and also a shade of the chromatic tetrachord. *Lydion* was a special tuning of the kithara: an octave composed of two different shades of the diatonic Dorian tetrachord.

These are just shades, however; and the names themselves have slightly different endings.

With the usual endings and the meaning of modal scales (though not exactly in the later meaning) they were used by "the very oldest" musicians, according to Aristides Quintilianus:

Lydian	e^+	f	a	b	b^+	c'	e'	$e^{+\prime}$
Dorian	g	a	a^+	$b\flat$	d'	e'	$e^{+\prime}$	f'	a'
Phrygian	g	a	a^+	$b\flat$	d'	e'	$e^{+\prime}$	f'	g'
Iastian	e	e^+	f	a	c'	d'
Mixolydian	e	e^+	f	g	a	a^+	$b\flat$	e'
Syntonolydian	e	e^+	f	a	c'

All tetrachords in these six scales are enharmonic Dorian, either conjunct or disjunct, with open or filled major thirds. The seemingly abnormal Lydian structure is confirmed in a passage where Aristoxenos describes a certain arrangement of the enharmonic tetrachord with one quarter tone at the upper, and one at the lower end.

The essential features of these scales, however, are their ranges and omissions. They are not necessarily octaves: Dorian has the range of a ninth;

Iastian, of a seventh; Syntonolydian, of a sixth. And the two latter scales do not differ from each other save by the addition of *d'* in Iastian. Phrygian and Dorian are identical except for the highest note, which is *g'* in Phrygian and *a'* in Dorian. Iastian and Syntonolydian, again, have a minor third *A–C* close by the enharmonic major third *F–A*.

To sum up: the "very oldest" musicians gave the tribal names not to toptail inversions of the same basic octave, but to scales, chiefly established on the Dorian tetrachord and differing from one another in range and density.

This fact alone should suffice to caution us against the obsession that all cryptic names of scales belonged to diatonic octaves.

❊   ❊   ❊

THE LYRE, almost indispensable in Greek music both as a support to the singer's voice and as a solo instrument, was not prepared to meet the intricacies of such a network of keys—even within the simplification that the perfect system implied. With its pentatonic *accordatura*, it forced the player either to avoid certain notes or to produce them with the help of artificial devices difficult in technique and most probably unsatisfactory in timbre.

As a consequence, players were ready to vary their *accordatura* whenever such permutation granted more open strings for the melody to be performed. But even so, they never abandoned the pentatonic pattern of three seconds and two minor thirds in the octave.

One of these *accordaturas* was as natural as it was desirable. The player, we are told, started tuning from the central note *a;* jumping down to *e* by a fourth and back to *b* by a fifth, and, in the same way, upward to *d'* by a fourth and back to *g* by a fifth, he obtained:

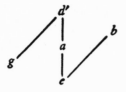

This was an excellent heptad of open strings for Phrygian melodies, but unusable for Dorian conjunct and Mixolydian, which, instead of *b,* needed *b♭*. Relaxing the *b* string would not have been possible: the semitone *b♭-a*

was against the anhemitonic principle. Thus the *b* string must have been replaced by a *c'* string (cf. page 204) even before the Dorian octave was created.

Censorinus (c. 230 A.D.) alludes to the introduction of this alternative *EDC accordatura* when he credits the Cretan Chrysothemis with adding the sixth string or *synemmenos*. Since *d'* and *a,* of the tetrachord synemmenon, had their strings already in the *EDB accordatura,* and *bb,* as we saw, could not be given a separate string, the note in question must indeed have been *c'*. Only, it was not a sixth string, because *c'* could not exist beside *b*. They alternated, and the lyre still was five-stringed. (In Greek terminology, 'string' and 'note' were synonymous.)

The actual sixth string was necessary when Terpander, according to tradition, added the high *e'* in order to transform the original heptad into an octave.

The seventh string, on *d* beyond low *e,* re-established the central position of *a* that had been sacrificed on the six-stringed lyre.

The double form of Greek tuning with the alternation of *b* and *c'* can easily be gathered from the notation of the melodies preserved: the ground signs clearly show the open strings required. These are the tunings that we find:

> *ED BAG E*   Seikilos' Skolion
>   Second Hymn to Apollo
>   Berlin Papyrus
>   Oxyrhynchos Papyrus
> *EDC AG E*   Hymn to the Muse
>   Hymn to the Sun
>   Hymn to Nemesis
>   Bellermann's instrumental piece.

             ❀   ❀
                 ❀

A THIRD ACCORDATURA for open strings, however, is disclosed by the ground signs: *E* has been sharpened to *F*. And to the list just given we have to add:

> *F DC AGF*   First Hymn to Apollo
>   Cairo Fragment

In connection with the *F* tuning, the entire perfect system with all its shifts underwent transposition by a semitone upward, which did not supplant the E series, but was alternately used when musical reasons made it preferable. The result (restricted to the central octave) was:

Hypermixolydian	f'	eb'	db'	c'	bb	ab	g	f
Mixolydian	f'	eb'	db'	cb'	bb	ab	gb	f
Lydian	f'	e'	d'	c'	bb	a	g	f
Phrygian	f'	eb'	d'	c'	bb	ab	g	f
Dorian	f'	eb'	db'	c'	bb	ab	gb	f
Hypolydian	f'	e'	d'	c'	b	a	g	f
Hypophrygian	f'	eb'	d'	c'	bb	a	g	f
Hypodorian	f'	eb'	db'	c'	bb	ab	g	f

❊   ❊   ❊

RECENT MUSIC HISTORIANS who have tried to explain the F series failed to see the point. This is what happened: Owing to developments unknown, the Dorian mode was driven from its once privileged position. Whatever the date of this change may have been, Bellermann's Anonymus, in post-Christian times, speaks "particularly of the Lydian trope"; Alypios claims that of the fifteen tropes "the first is Lydian"; and Boethius deals "of all keys" only with the Lydian.

Possible as a general shift of pitch might be—and especially a shift upward —all circumstances are against such an interpretation. When Bellermann's Anonymus speaks of the Lydian trope, he says that it has the Hyperlydian above and the Hypolydian below; no other trope is mentioned. Both Gaudentios and Alypios start from the Hypolydian, not from the Lydian. Thus the salient point is the structure common to the modes of the Lydian family, not the pitch of the Lydian key.

The inner reason for this change does not matter at the moment. It will be discussed presently. But the way it acted on the general system of keys can easily be seen.

1) At whatever time the change took place, it met with the *accordaturas EDC AG E* and *ED BAG E.*

2) Keeping the *E–E* octave meant four sharps for Lydian and five sharps for Hypolydian. Such complicated fingering might have been accepted at a time in which these scales played a minor role, but not with Lydian and Hypolydian to the fore.

3) The simplest expedient was to play Lydian on the *EDC* accordatura and Hypolydian on *ED B,* which allowed all strings to remain open provided that the higher *E* was taken for the paranete, and a new nete, *F,* was stopped on the *E* string.

4) The notation of Lydian and Hypolydian in the tables of all Greek theorists and among the melodies preserved confirms this statement: *E* was written with an open string symbol, and *F,* as *E♯.*

5) This first step toward an *F–F* octave had grave consequences. It shattered the ingenious consistency of Greek scales with their terminology and made any transposition anarchic.

6) To re-establish order and consistency, a general shift became unavoidable in order to adjust the remaining scales in the new *F–F* range of Lydian and Hypolydian. This, of course, altered all signatures: Phrygian got three flats, Dorian five flats, and Mixolydian as many as six flats.

7) Except for Lydian and Hypolydian, none of these *F–F* scales could be played on either *EDC* or *EDB* strings. Dorian, for instance, would have had one open string in *EDC* and not even one in *EDB,* and still both *G♭* and *F* had to be stopped on the same *E* string. Consequently, another tuning became imperative, with *F* as an open string.

8) Even then, Lydian and Hypolydian kept to the *E* accordaturas, which, on account of the semitone *F–E,* offered an easier fingering. Good examples are the instrumental piece in Bellermann's Anonymi and the papyrus from Oxyrhynchos (Exs. 76 and 82).

9) This might have been one reason for preserving the *E* accordatura and the *E* series of scales. But the mere fact that among the relics of Greek music all nine Mixolydian pieces require the *E* accordatura clearly shows that the ancients chose the easier fingering as far as possible and therefore kept the two accordaturas, just as the clarinettists of the nineteenth century carried instruments in *B♭* and in *A.*

❋   ❋   ❋

THE TWO SERIES of *harmoniai* that could be performed with three different *accordaturas* of a pentatonic lyre at last exculpate Plutarch who, quoting a snappish criticism of the poet Pherekrates, relates that the boldest 'modern' composer of the fourth century B.C., Phrynis, gave the lyre a turning device in order to play no less than twelve *harmoniai* on five strings.

Plutarch's editors were utterly at sea with so cryptic an assertion. And they did what embarrassed philologists do: they emended the text. Burette averred that five strings, being an obvious understatement, "seven" must have been meant; Ulrici outdid his guess by printing "nine"; and Théodore Reinach, still unsatisfied, translated "eleven."

Pherekrates and Plutarch, however, knew better than those who so profusely offered benevolent emendations: with two stopping devices, one for sharpening *E* to *F,* and another for sharpening *B* to *C,* twelve and more tonalities could easily be performed.

❁   ❁   ❁

THE TWO PITCH FORMS of the perfect system were finally dovetailed to form a dense double series of thirteen, or even fifteen, keys in chromatic sequence.

The names of the keys were either duplicated and, to avoid confusion, distinguished by the epithets 'lower' (*barýteros*) for the *E* scales and 'higher' (*oxýteros*) for the *F* scales, or else kept apart by reviving obsolete names, Iastian (Ionian) and Aeolian:

f	*eb'*	*d'*	*c'*	*bb*	*a*	*g*	*f*	Hyperlydian
	e'	*d'*	*c♯'*	*b'*	*a*	*g♯*	*f♯*	*e*	Hyperaeolian
[*f'*]	*eb'*	*db'*	*c'*	*bb*	*ab*	*g*	*f*	Hypermixolydian or Hyperphrygian
	[*e'*]	*d'*	*c'*	*b*	*a*	*g*	*f♯*	*e*	High Mixolydian or Hyperiastian
f	[*eb'*]	*db'*	*cb'*	*bb*	*ab*	*gb*	*f*	Low Mixolydian or Hyperdorian
f	*e'*	[*d'*]	*c'*	*bb*	*a*	*g*	*f*	High Lydian or Lydian
	e'	*d♯'*	[*c♯'*]	*b*	*a*	*g♯*	*f♯*	*e*	Low Lydian or Aeolian
f	*eb'*	*d'*	[*c'*]	*bb*	*ab*	*g*	*f*	High Phrygian or Phrygian
	e'	*d'*	*c♯'*	[*b*]	*a*	*g*	*f♯*	*e*	Low Phrygian or Iastian
f	*eb'*	*db'*	*c'*	[*bb*]	*ab*	*gb*	*f*	Dorian
f	*e'*	*d'*	*c'*	*b*	[*a*]	*g*	*f*	High Hypolydian or Hypolydian
	e'	*d♯'*	*c♯'*	*b*	*a♯*	[*g♯*]	*f♯*	*e*	Low Hypolydian or Hypoaeolian
f	*eb'*	*d'*	*c'*	*bb*	*a*	[*g*]	*f*	High Hypophrygian or Hypophrygian
	e'	*d'*	*c♯'*	*b*	*ȧ*	*g♯*	[*f♯*]	*e*	Low Hypophrygian or Hypoiastian
f	*eb'*	*db'*	*c'*	*bb*	*ab*	*g*	[*f*]	Hypodorian

❁   ❁   ❁

WERE WE MISTAKEN, after all, when we thought that Dorian, Phrygian, Lydian, and the rest of them were modes? Or had all the tribal names two meanings? But if so, how was such confusing ambiguity possible with a nation eminent in grammar, mathematics, and philosophy?

In trying to answer this question, I shall ignore the *F* series in order to simplify the argument. And I shall also avoid the calamitous term "transposition scales," which is so frequent in recent books on Greek music but only adds to the general confusion, since the reader rarely knows who transposes what, whence, whither.

The entire range of those seven, eight, thirteen, or even fifteen, double octaves would be three octaves and more, from Hypodorian *E* up to the two-lined octave. Neither singers nor instruments could be expected to cover so vast a range; Aristides Quintilianus expressly stated that voices did not span more than two octaves. For this reason, he adds, Dorian was the only key sung in its total range; the lower keys, from Hypolydian to Hypodorian, were cut off at the Dorian terminal *A,* and the higher keys, at the Dorian terminal *a'* (as indicated in our diagram on page 225). Indeed, far more restricted than even Aristides held, four out of the dozen melodies preserved are confined to the central octave: the Skolion runs from *e'* to *e,* and three other pieces, the Oxyrhynchos Papyrus, Bellermann's short instrumental piece, and the Hymn to the Sun, from *f'* to *f*.

Lyre players were no more able than singers to change through three octaves; no set of strings could at one blow be tuned now a fifth higher, for Hypermixolydian, now an octave lower, for Hypodorian. The player always started tuning from *a,* and from *a* proceeded to the outer strings. Thus he was confined to a normal medium accordatura whatever the key.

The consequences were strange—indeed unique. Musical space, vague and shapeless in our music, became a palpable reality in Greece. Each key had its own center, to be sure; but also musical space as a whole had its immovable center which, being the pitch tone, was never neglected. As a result, every melody had two foci; every note or group of notes gravitated toward two different centers at once, toward the center of the individual key and toward the center of the immovable perfect system. The first bearing was called *dýnamis* or 'mobile force,' and the second, *thésis* or 'stationary force.' A note changed its *dýnamis* according to the key; its *thésis* was immovable. The note *e',* for example, was in all melodies *nētē katà thésin* or highest stationary note, whatever the key; but in Mixolydian, it was also *mésē katà dýnamin* or 'mobile center,' and in Lydian *trité katà dýnamin* or 'mobile third' from above. The mobile and the stationary functions coincided only in Dorian.

Whoever looks at a Greek melody from the dynamic center—*b* in Phrygian or *d'* in Mixolydian—finds the modal structure that we call Dorian; descending, he steps through two whole tones and a concluding semitone to the (dynamic) *hypátē*. Things look different from the stationary center. The player, adjusting his *a* and tuning the outer strings to *e'* and *e* (the usual range of melodies), realized that each transposition of the (Dorian) scale altered the structure of his octave, since it shifted the semitones to places where previously whole tones had been. The central rectangle in the diagram on page 225 encases the resulting structures in all eight keys. The Phrygian key, by one tone higher than the normal Dorian, sharpened two notes of the central octave, *c'* and *f*; thus the two central tetrachords became *e' d' c♯' b* and *a g f♯ e*: the semitone moved to the middle of the tetrachord, and the originally Dorian octave changed to the Phrygian species. In the same way, the Lydian key sharpened *d', c', g, f* and shifted the semitones to the upper ends of the tetrachords that formed the central octave. Dorian as a key (*Dôrios tónos*) created a Dorian mode (*Doristì harmonía*) in the perfect system; a Dorian mode in the perfect system could only originate if the melody followed the Dorian key. And the same was true for Phrygian, Lydian, and the rest. Key and mode conditioned each other and rightly were given the same tribal names.

This explains the hopeless confusion of terms in Greek theory, which allowed Plutarch to speak, in *De anima,* of "the tones, tropes, or harmonies, or whatever you would call them."

✳   ✳   ✳

THE PUZZLE as to why the Greeks represented their modes as sections of Dorian keys finds a natural solution in the poverty of their musical terminology, which had no special words for sharps or flats. They actually contented themselves with a true and an approximate form of solmization.

The true solmization, designed for singers, symbolized the relative position of the notes regardless of their absolute pitches (which were nearly meaningless in singing). It called the (descending) Dorian tetrachord *te tô tê ta,* just as our own solmization would call it *mi re do si* or *la sol fa mi;* so that *tê-ta*—just as our *fa-mi*—indicated the semitone wherever it stood. The standard attribution was:

$$a'\ g'\ f'\ e'\ d'\ c'\ b\ a\ g\ f\ e\ d\ c\ B\ A$$
te tô tê ta tô tê ta te tô tê ta tô tê ta te
(te)   (te)

But with sharps or flats, the syllables had to be shifted accordingly

b' a' g' $f\sharp'$ etc.　　　　　　　g' f' $e\flat'$ d' etc.
te　tô　tê　ta　　　　　　　te　tô　tê　ta

in order to have the indicative pair *tê-ta* on the semitone. As a consequence, every octave of Phrygian structure, having the semitone in the middle of its tetrachords, would read *tô tê ta/tô tê ta/tô*, and every octave of Lydian structure, having the semitone above, *tê ta tô/tê ta tô/tê*. All modal octaves practically materialized in sections cut from the same standard *te-te* series. There was no other way to describe them by means of a solmization.

The official terminology of Greek music was no less a solmization, although instead of a standard (Dorian) tetrachord it covered a full stand-ard (Dorian) octave: *nētē, paranētē, tritē, paramesē, mesē, lichanós, par-hypatē, hypatē*. And since it had no special terms for sharpened or flattened notes either, it did not allow musicians to describe non-Dorian scales any better than the actual solmization: the tone words were made independent of absolute pitch and, without changing their sequence, moved up and down to bring the words *tritē-paramesē* and *parhypatē-hypatē* to wherever the semitones stood. While the Dorian tetrachord read *nētē, paranētē, tritē, paramesē*, the Phrygian tetrachord ran *paranētē, tritē, paramesē, mesē*, and the Lydian tetrachord, *tritē, paramesē, mesē, lichanós*.

The following table makes evident that as a consequence all modal scales within the same range appeared as differently shifted Dorian octaves. The central octave is in all cases represented by capitals; italicized small letters indicate extensions up and downward; parentheses illustrate the shifted Dorian octave; the letters themselves stand for the names of the tones given in the foregoing paragraph.

↓

Hypermixolydian	(*n*	*pn*	*t*	*pm*	M	L		PH	H)	L		PH	H	
Mixolydian	(*n*	*pn*	*t*	PM	M	L		PH	H)	L	PH	H		
Lydian	(*n*	*pn*	T	PM	M	L		PH	H)	L	PH	*h*		
Phrygian	(*n*	PN	T	PM	M	L		PH	H)	L	*ph*	*h*		
Dorian	N	PN	T	PM	M	L		PH	H	*l*	*ph*	*h*		
Hypolydian	T	(N	PN	T	PM	M	L		PH	*h*)	*l*	*ph*	*h*	
Hypophrygian	PN	T	(N	PN	T	PM	M	L		*ph*	*h*)	*l*	*ph*	*h*
Hypodorian	N	PN	T	(N	PN	T	PM	M	*l*	*ph*	*h*)	*l*	*ph*	*h*

↑

❋　　❋　　❋

Following the table downward along the vertical line that marks the upper limit of the modal scale, the reader seems to ascend the Dorian scale, though he actually never leaves the note *e'*. He starts from *mesē* and proceeds to *paramesē, tritē, paranētē, nētē;* going on, he would find *tritē, paranētē,* and *nētē* of the higher tetrachord.

This sounds familiar. We find similar statements in some later Greek treatises and until recently all books on the subject taught that the modal scales of the Greeks were toptail inversions, that is, so to speak, cut out of the series of white keys:

Hypodorian	*A G F E D C B A*	
Hypophrygian	*G F E D C B A G*	
Hypolydian	*F E D C B A G F*	
Dorian	*E D C B A G F E*	
Phrygian	*D C B A G F E D*	
Lydian	*C B A G F E D C*	
Mixolydian	*B A G F E D C B*	

The only exception to this confusion of absolute and relative pitches is an English thesis, written almost two hundred years ago, *Explanation of the Modes or Tones in the ancient Graecian Music* by Fr. Haskin Eyles Stiles.[20]

Dr. Otto J. Gombosi has finally proved that the Greeks did not say "Phrygian ran from *paranētē* to the lower *lichanós*" or *d'–d*, nor did they claim that "Lydian ran from *tritē* to the lower *parhypatē*," *c'–c*, but carefully intercalated the words *hoîon tó*, 'quasi.' [21]

Indeed, since the Greeks had no terms to denote black keys, so to speak, they were forced to shift their set of seven terms from *nētē* to *parhypatē* until it fitted the particular tone-and-semitone organization of the mode to be described.

Skeptics may look at the instruments. Athenaios gives the detailed description of a triple lyre in the form of a tripod that a certain Pythagoras of Zakynthos, at a time unknown, devised for playing in rapid change in the Dorian, the Phrygian, and the Lydian mode, each being given one of the three sides. With a white-key arrangement, it would scarcely have been necessary to construct a complicated triple instrument of this kind; one or two more strings would have sufficed to cut out the modal scale of each of the three *harmoniai*. The same is true with Athenaios' statement that "there were pipes peculiarly adapted to every *harmonia*, and every piper had pipes suited to every mode used in the public contests. But Pronomos of Thebes began the practice of playing all the harmonias on the

---

[20] *Philosophical Transactions* LI (1760) ii, pp. 695–773.

[21] Otto J. Gombosi, "Studien zur Tonartenlehre des frühen Mittelalters," in *Acta Musicologica* XI (1939), p. 85.

same pipes," that is, he obviously devised fingerholes in turnable rings to change the mobile notes between the immovable *hestotes*. Had the modes had white-key scales differently cut, two additional fingerholes would have sufficed.

The confusion outlined above also explains why the medieval monks misunderstood the system of the Greeks and transmitted to posterity (including our own counterpoint studies) a pseudo-Dorian between *D* and *D*, a pseudo-Phrygian between *E* and *E*, a pseudo-Lydian between *F* and *F*, and so on. Lost in the tangle of Greek terminology, they mixed two opposite facts: (*a*) that, defined in 'white key' terms, Hypodorian was an A-mode; (*b*) that in the perfect system Hypodorian was the lowest *key*. As a consequence, they established the following well-known system of eight church tones on Hypodorian as the lowest modal scale between *A* and *A*: [22]

Seventh tone or Mixolydian	*GABCDEFG*
Fifth tone or Lydian	*FGABCDEF*
Third tone or Phrygian	*EFGABCDE*
First and eighth tones or Dorian and Hypomixolydian	*DEFGABCD*
Sixth tone or Hypolydian	*CDEFGABC*
Second tone or Hypophrygian	*BCDEFGAB*
Second tone or Hypodorian	*ABCDEFGA*

[22] Cf. also Otto J. Gombosi, *ibid.,* pp. 128–35.

7

THE RELICS

THE INSEPARABLENESS, indeed oneness, of key and mode fully excludes twofold interpretation. To assert, as Hermann Abert did,[23] that the Oxyrhynchos hymn must be Hypolydian in key and Hypophrygian in mode was basically impossible and moreover an arbitrary diagnosis, based on entirely subjective impressions of what might be the characteristics of a mode.

But subjectivity can be eliminated for good and replaced by objective analysis on the ground of the following simple facts:

1) The two semitones of the Dorian octave, c'/b and f/e, are a fifth apart; e is simultaneously the lower end of the octave, while the third between c' and f is the mesē, a.

2) All keys preserve this (relative) structure, since they are merely shifted Dorian octaves.

3) To find the key of any melody in question, pick the fifth between the semitones out of your melody, and you will at once know the lower end and the mesē and therewith find the desired octave in the tables on pages 225 and 231.

4) The resulting name indicates *both* the key and the mode.

In two cases, however, analysis is less simple.

The first one is particularly momentous in view of an important part of the Greek relics: both Mixolydian in the E series and Lydian in the F series have one flat and the same dynamic mesē d'; and while generally the open-string symbols show perfectly well whether a piece belongs in the E or the F series, this does not come true in F Lydian which, as proved, was played and written in E tuning though it was an F key.

The best recipe in this dilemma is: look at the thetic mesē; E Mixolydian tends toward a, and F Lydian toward $b\flat$. In all the nine pieces that I am going to call Mixolydian, a is continually stressed, while $b\flat$ is at best a passing note or does not occur at all. The opposite is true in the only Lydian fragment, Bellermann's short instrumental piece.

---

[23] Hermann Abert, "Ein neu entdeckter frühchristlicher Hymnus mit antiken Musiknoten," in *Zeitschrift für Musikwissenschaft* IV (1922), p. 528.

In a similar way, it is somewhat difficult to keep *E* Dorian from *F* Hypolydian, both of which have scales without a signature. Here, too, the center decides: Dorian needs *a,* and Hypolydian, *c'* or *b♭* (cf. the following analysis of the Oxyrhynchos Papyrus).

The second difficulty results from modulation within the same piece. The Greeks knew two kinds of modulation: (*a*) the simple passage to a key higher or lower by some regular, diatonic interval (*metabolé*); (*b*) the awkward passage to a key higher or lower by some irregular, nondiatonic interval (*pathos*), as upward by three quarter tones (*spondeiasmós*), or downward by three quarter tones (*éklysis*), or upward by five quarter tones (*ekbolé*).[24]

The relics of Greek music show only *metabolé;* apparently it is always an alternation of disjunct and conjunct structures. In two melodies, the Cairo Fragment (Ex. 77) and Section A of the Second Delphic Hymn (Ex. 68), the upper of the two 'Dorian' tetrachords is lowered by a tone to form conjunction with the lower tetrachord; in other words, the melodies are built on both Dorian and Hypodorian structures. This might be a relapse into earlier heptadic organization rather than sophistication.

The archaic Second Delphic Hymn even has a triple modulation in its Section C: from pentatonic Mixolydian disjunct to conjunct; to disjunct with an enharmonic lower tetrachord; to Dorian with a pentatonic lower tetrachord.

The methodical use of these considerations leads to the following analyses of the musical relics.

❋　　❋　　❋

THE FIRST DELPHIC HYMN, Section B, is written in *FDC* tuning with four flats in the range *a♭'–a♭*. Dynamic mesē is *f'*, and the key and mode Hypermixolydian with modulation into the conjunct parallel.

Ex. 64. FIRST DELPHIC HYMN

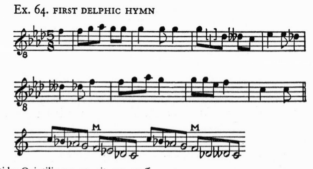

24 Aristides Quintilianus, *op. cit.,* pp. 25 ff.

The First Berlin Fragment is written in *EDB* tuning in the range *a'–g* with one sharp. Dynamic mesē is *e'*, and the key and mode Hypermixolydian. The melody has two centers of gravity, a stronger one on the dynamic mesē and its lower neighbor (forty quarter notes each), and a weaker one of the thetic mesē *a* (twenty-seven quarter notes), while the extreme ends of the range, *a'* and *g*, are only given six quarter notes each.

Ex. 65. FIRST BERLIN FRAGMENT

The Second Berlin Fragment, instrumental postlude, is written in *EDB* tuning with one sharp in the range *b'–c'*. Dynamic mesē is *e'*, and the key and mode Hypermixolydian. Hermann Abert's rhythmic interpretation as 4/4 is unsatisfactory; I tentatively propose the 5/4 time that the Greek musicians called *paiòn epíbatos*.

Ex. 66. SECOND BERLIN FRAGMENT

The Second Delphic Hymn, Section A, is written in *EDC* tuning with one flat in the range *g'–a*. Dynamic mesē is *d'*, and the key and mode Mixolydian pentatonic with modulation to the conjunct parallel.

Ex. 67. SECOND DELPHIC HYMN

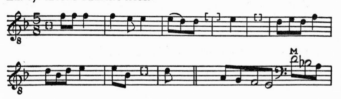

The Second Delphic Hymn, Section C, is written in *EDC* tuning with one flat in the range *a′–e*. It modulates from pentatonic Mixolydian disjunct (with *d′* as the dynamic mesē) to conjunct; to disjunct with an enharmonic lower tetrachord; to Dorian with a pentatonic lower tetrachord.

Ex. 68. SECOND DELPHIC HYMN

The Second Delphic Hymn, Section F, is written in *EDC* tuning with one flat in the range *e′–g*. Dynamic mesē is *d′*, and the key and mode Mixolydian enharmonic, modulating to the conjunct parallel.

Ex. 69. SECOND DELPHIC HYMN

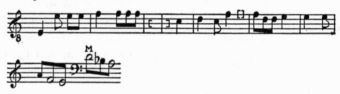

The Second Delphic Hymn, Section G, is written in *EDC* tuning with one flat in the range *b♭′–e*. Dynamic mesē is *d′* and the key and mode Mixolydian.

Ex. 70. SECOND DELPHIC HYMN

The Second Delphic Hymn, Section H, is written in *EDC* tuning with one flat in the range *g′–g*. Dynamic mesē is *d′*, and the key and mode Mixolydian.

Ex. 71. SECOND DELPHIC HYMN

The Hymn to Nemesis is written in *EDC* tuning with one flat in the range *g'–f*. Dynamic mesē is *d'*, and the key and mode Mixolydian. The third *e'–c'* is particularly stressed; outstanding tetrachords belong to the dynamic octave.

Ex. 72. HYMN TO NEMESIS

The Hymn to Helios is written in *EDC* tuning with one flat in the range *f'–f*. Dynamic mesē is *d'*, and the key and mode Mixolydian. Strong accents fall upon the three highest notes *e'–c'*; the thetic mesē, however, is used fourteen times as the starter, final, or repercussion, while the dynamic mesē serves only three times in these qualities.

Ex. 73. HYMN TO HELIOS

The Hymn to the Muse is written in *EDC* tuning with one flat in the range *f'–e*. Dynamic mesē is *d'*, and the key and mode Mixolydian. Here, *c'* and *a* are stressed; the tetrachords that occur are thetic, and the thetic mesē stands out seven times against one for the dynamic mesē.

Ex. 74. HYMN TO THE MUSE

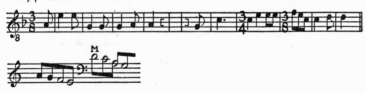

Euripides' Stasimon is written in *ED(C)* tuning with one flat in the range *f''–g*. Dynamic mesē is *d'*, and the key and mode Mixolydian enharmonic.

Ex. 75. EURIPIDES' STASIMON

Bellermann's instrumental piece is written in *EDC* tuning with one flat in the range *f'–f*. Dynamic mesē is *d'* and the key and mode Lydian. The dynamic center is stressed with ten out of thirty-six quarter notes and serves as the main finalis; the thetic center gets only seven quarter notes. Two outstanding tetrachords, both with the semitones above, confirm the Lydian interpretation.

Ex. 76. BELLERMANN'S INSTRUMENTAL PIECE

The Cairo Fragment is written in *FCD* tuning with three flats in the range *eb'–ab*. Dynamic mesē is *c'*, and the key and mode Phrygian. At the beginning of the short fragment, the piece has modulated to the conjunct parallel.

Ex. 77. CAIRO FRAGMENT

The First Delphic Hymn, Sections A and C, is written in *FDC* tuning with three flats in the range *ab'–eb*. Dynamic mesē is *c'*, and the key and mode Phrygian.

Ex. 78. FIRST DELPHIC HYMN

Seikilos' Skolion is written in *EDB* tuning with two sharps in the range *e'–e*. The dynamic mesē, *b*, is neglected—the melody is distinctly Phrygian without any dynamic bearings.

Ex. 79. SEIKILOS' SKOLION

The Second Berlin Fragment is written in *EDB* tuning with two sharps in the range *f♯'–a*. The key and mode are Phrygian; the dynamic mesē, *b*, is stronger than the thetic mesē.

Ex. 80. SECOND BERLIN FRAGMENT

The Second Delphic Hymn, Sections B, D, and F, are written in *EDB* tuning without signature in the range *f'–e*. Dynamic mesē is *a*, and the key and mode Dorian.

Ex. 81. SECOND DELPHIC HYMN

The Oxyrhynchos Papyrus is written in *EDC* tuning without signature in the range *f'–f*. The key and mode are Hypolydian. Notice the two conjunct tetrachords and the thetic mesē on *c'* instead of *b♭*, in accordance with the authentic structure that Hypolydian needs.

Ex. 82. OXYRHYNCHOS PAPYRUS

The First Berlin Fragment, instrumental postlude, is written in *EDB* tuning with one sharp in the range *a'–e*. The key and mode are Hypodorian, and the accent falls on the thetic mesē *a* rather than on the dynamic mesē *e*.

Ex. 83. FIRST BERLIN FRAGMENT, POSTLUDE

❋   ❋   ❋

THESE ANALYSES leave no doubt that key and mode were merely two different aspects of the same phenomenon. But they also reveal that the two aspects were not necessarily balanced. Some melodies gravitated toward the dynamic center rather than toward the thetic center; the opposite was true in other melodies. Indeed, prevalence of one gravitation might exclude the other: thesis is entirely neglected in the First Delphic Hymn; Seikilos' Skolion, on the contrary, avoids the dynamic center and is purely thetic.

Modal structure is more pregnant in melodies that gravitate toward the thetic center; it is nowhere more evident than in the Skolion, and nowhere more equivocal than in the First Delphic Hymn.

With this lack of balance between thesis and dynamis, between mode and key, we have at last an answer to the puzzling question why so many Greek theorists were entirely indifferent to mode. This paragraph must indeed end in the reluctant statement that the later period of antiquity disintegrated

the modes just as the sixteenth century disintegrated the church tones, and
the twentieth, major and minor. The predominance of the Dorian structure
was so strong that, when the perfect system was achieved, scales with signatures were considered rather as shifted normal scales than as scales in a
different mode. In earlier times, the smaller range of lyres had worked
against this conception; later, the increased number of strings weakened
the resistance on the part of instrumental music.

In the second century A.D., modal conception is so much overshadowed
by key relations that Athenaios scorns "those who cannot see specific differences"—he says *kat' eídos* or, literally, "according to the pattern"—"but
simply attend to the highness or lowness of tones and assume a Hypermixolydian *harmonia* and again another higher than that." [25]

What Athenaios means is simply this: Hypermixolydian, having one
sharp and merely duplicating Hypodorian in the higher octave, was, from
the standpoint of modal structure, entirely useless and testified to modal
disintegration. Athenaios' testimony is not the only one: Ptolemy, too,
opposed Hypermixolydian, and Plutarch related that in Argos the law
prohibited *paramixolydiázein*—a word that we must more clumsily circum-
scribe as "not to go beyond the Mixolydian key." These men had forgotten
that Hypermixolydian, which seemingly duplicated Hypodorian, was actually a plagal Phrygian mode, while Hypodorian was an authentic Dorian.

At the end of antiquity, Boethius' summary of Greek theory did not so
much as mention modes.

[25] *Deipnosophists* 14:625.

8

ETHOS

"A HARMONIA should have a shaped ethos or pathos," *eîdos éthous è pathous*. Thus Athenaios ends the passage quoted on page 247.

The famous term *ethos* denoted the emotional power of melodies according to their scales. Aristotle says in his *Metaphysics* 8:5 that "the musical scales differ essentially from one another, and those who hear them are differently affected by each. Some of them make men sad and grave, like the so-called Mixolydian, others enfeeble the mind, like the relaxed [*aneiménas*] harmonias, others, again, produce a moderate and settled temper, which appears to be the peculiar effect of the Dorian; the Phrygian inspires enthusiasm."

Exactly what gave a scale such emotional power? What made Dorian virile and bellicose; Hypodorian, majestic and stable; Mixolydian, pathetic and plaintive; Phrygian, agitated and Bacchic; Hypophrygian, active; Lydian, mournful; Hypolydian, dissolute and voluptuous?

The rationalistic authors of the nineteenth century were at sea with this problem. They looked upon Dorian, Phrygian, and Lydian as modal tetrachords and, as one easily understands, were unable to discover any relation between man's emotion and the arrangement of a semitone among whole tones. Had it not been for the great consideration the ethos was obviously given in Plato's and Aristotle's time, they would have laughed at it just as many a Greek critic had done in his own time.

Real progress was made when they took the absolute pitches into account rather than the modal arrangement.

Pitch was doubtless indispensable in creating an ethos. The pseudo-Aristotelian Problem 19:49 expressly calls a low note "soft and calm, and a high note, exciting." The most direct evidence of the emotional power of pitch is Ptolemy's statement that "the same melody has an activating effect in the higher keys, and a depressing one in the lower keys, because a high pitch stretches the soul, while a low pitch slackens it. Therefore the keys in the middle near the Dorian can be compared with well-ordered and stable states of the soul, the higher keys near the Mixolydian with the stirred and stimulated states, and the lower keys near the Hypodorian with the slack and feeble moods." [26]

Aristides Quintilianus obviously means this antithesis of low, middle, and high when, in the chapter on "The Art of Composing Melodies" (*melopoiía*), he opposes three kinds of melodies: *hypatoid, mesoid, netoid,* which, he says, coincide with the three *tropoi* or styles of melodies: tragic, dithyrambic, nomic. Dr. Schäfke, editor and commentator of Aristides, is certainly mistaken when he likens the three kinds to the hypo, middle, and hyper scales: melodies, not scales, are at stake. Notwithstanding their scales, they are netoid or mesoid or hypatoid when their prevalent zones are near the thetic *nētē* or *mesē* or *hypatē.*

Our analyses of the pieces preserved make this perfectly clear. Of the three hymns by Mesomedes, which are all Mixolydian, two have their stress on the notes between c' and e': since e' is the thetic *nētē,* they are doubtless netoid. The Hymn to the Muse, on the contrary, has the emphasis on c' and $a,$ which latter is the thetic *mesē;* it certainly is mesoid, although it belongs to the same key and mode as the two other hymns. Further netoid examples are: the Hypermixolydian Paean and Bellermann's Lydian piece; mesoid examples: Seikilos' Phrygian Skolion and Euripides' Mixolydian Stasimon. There are no hypatoid melodies among the relics.

❊   ❊
❊

THE THREE PITCH REGIONS, high, middle, low, and their ethical qualities were stressed in Islamic music as well, so we may be sure that this is the meaning of the passages quoted from the pseudo-Aristotelian Problems and from Ptolemy. However, pitch regions are not the only ethical qualities of Oriental melody patterns. There are also (a) the steps used— quarter tones, semitones, etc.; (b) their arrangement and sequence; (c) whether the scale appears in a medium altitude or transposed up or downward by a fourth or a fifth or an octave; (d) certain melodic turns; and (e) the tempo and mobility. As to the last trait, the maqām *Rāst* is always performed in a moderate tempo without small time values or graces. The maqām *Mahur,* the "trotter," which practically has the same scale as *Rāst,* is much faster.

The *rāgas* or melodic patterns of India are in a similar way characterized by their initial, final, and central notes, by their modal scales, and *by the notes omitted.*

[26] Ptolemy, *Harm.* 2:7:58 and 3:7:99.

This is remarkably reminiscent of the *petteía* or 'draughts' or 'checkers' of the Greeks, a branch of their Art of Composition which taught how to *avoid* and to play certain notes, how often each should be used, which one was to start, and which one to finish. And Aristides Quintilianus, who mentions this branch of learning,[27] adds: "This aids the ethos."

Here, at last, we gain a firm footing. The ethos of a melody depended on the co-operation of quite a number of qualities that Oriental musicians know as the characteristic traits of their *maqamât* and *rāgas*. No single feature makes up an ethos, neither modal structure nor pitch nor astrological connotation.[28] The problem of the Greek ethos is considerably more complex than previous authors realized. We may assume the question of pitch to have been more involved in Greek music, with its unique dualism of thesis and dynamis, than it was in Oriental music.

High and low in their simplest, absolute meaning seem to be irrelevant in view of the fact that all Greek scales, in spite of their theoretical ranges, were cut off at both ends to fit in the best register of voices and instruments: three of the pieces preserved run from *f′* to *f*: the Oxyrhynchos Papyrus, Bellermann's short instrumental melody, and the Hymn to the Sun; and yet one of them is Hypolydian, one Lydian, and the third Mixolydian.

'High' and 'low,' perceptible in the theoretical scales but imperceptible in actual melodies, must have meant something different from range, and probably something that the Greeks themselves found hard to grasp and describe—else they would have been more explicit.

The solution can certainly not be given out of our own experience of musical pitch, but rather from the two points that essentially distinguish the modern and the Greek co-ordinations of keys. Our Western music has (*a*) no definite borderline between high and low, and (*b*) the keys follow one another at equal distances without being organized in a consistent body. In Greece, on the contrary, the Dorian *mesē* immutably parted high from low, and in the relation of thesis and dynamis, this same note, immovable center of gravity whatever the key, linked the tonalities together in a perspective that made their characteristic distances apparent. Not the distances of range, however; but the distances from the thetic to the dynamic *mesē*, which gave Greek melodies their musical, and hence nervous, tension.

True, not all pieces preserved gravitate toward two centers: the Oxyrhynchos Papyrus has no thetic, and the Seikilos Skolion no dynamic, center.

[27] Aristides Quintilianus. M. p. 29, Sch. p. 207.
[28] Erich M. von Hornbostel, "Tonart und Ethos," in *Festschrift für Johannes Wolf*, Berlin, 1929, pp. 73–8.

Still, this is rather a confirmation than a contradiction. The ethos theory belongs in the classical period; it did not exist in preclassical times, and was derided in the centuries A.D. Similarly, keys as such, that is, dynamis, were not considered in preclassical times, and the modes, that is, thesis, disintegrated in the postclassical epoch. The two opposite forces coincided chronologically, and they probably also were in themselves connected. This would result in the presumption that ethos rested on the oneness of key and mode, of dynamis and thesis.

The two exceptional pieces represent styles in which this oneness was absent: the purely dynamic Oxyrhynchos Papyrus is known to be late, and the purely thetic Skolion might have been written in a much earlier spirit whatever its age, since popular songs follow styles given up by more sophisticated composers. The Oxyrhynchos Papyrus, an early Christian hymn, was certainly not "dissolute and voluptuous," in spite of its Hypolydian key and mode, and Seikilos' Skolion was rather melancholy than "agitated and Bacchic," as a Phrygian melody should be. These pieces, unifocal and therefore without the tension between two foci, defy the ethos theory. Thus they confirm our belief that ethos is a quality of bifocal melodies.

Just how the tension between two gravitations affected the Greek mind is beyond our understanding. But can we expect to comprehend the ethos in ancient Greek music any better than we grasp the definitions that Hindus and Arabs give of modern *rāgas* and *maqamât?*

In view of the perfect analogy of the Greek ethos and the specific qualities of both the Indian *rāgas* and the Arabian *maqamât*, the lack of any corresponding Hellenic term is extraordinary and questionable. But is it any less surprising that without discrimination the Greeks used three or four different terms for the scale, so that Plutarch could with a certain impatience speak of the "tones, tropes, or harmonies, or whatever you would call them"? After all, there is no such thing as absolute synonymity; terms, confused in a later stage, must originally have covered different notions.

If one of Plutarch's three terms had in earlier times the special meaning of a pattern in the Indian and Arabian sense, it must be *harmonia*, since this word, and never *tonos* or *tropos,* is connected with ethical qualities. Athenaios insists on the *ethos* and *pathos* that a true *harmonia* has, and Plutarch speaks of a "tearful," *threnodikê,* harmony.

This possibly sheds light on Plutarch's dark description of Olympos' composition *Nomos Athenâs,* in which the first movement is called *arché* or *anápeira,* and the main movement, *harmonia.* To Rudolph Westphal, this title was so incomprehensible that he assumed—once more—a scribe's mistake and in his translation rendered the word by noncommittal dots. To one familiar with Oriental music, on the contrary, the passage suggests the principle of form, preserved in Indian music to this day. On page 191 I explained the dual form in art music which carefully maintained the balance of freedom and law: "The first [arché] part, ālāpa, is an improvised introduction in which the singer rehearses the essential traits of the rāga in question, its scale, the notes particularly stressed, the appropriate ornaments—both for his own benefit and to facilitate the listener's comprehension." This is exactly what anápeira means: 'practice, test.' And the part following the ālāpa is simply called rāga, exactly as the part following the anápeira is simply called harmonia.

9

HEALTH AND EDUCATION

ARISTOTLE, in a long paragraph on music in his *Politics,* accepts the division of melodies according to their ethos, each class having its special *harmonia.* But, countering illiberals, he adds that one should not judge their value from preconceived standpoints; music ought to be studied with a view to (*a*) education, (*b*) purification, and (*c*) intellectual enjoyment, relaxation, and recreation.

"Some persons," he continues, "fall into a religious frenzy, whom we see disenthralled by the use of mystic melodies, which bring healing and purification to the soul."

Here, we are right in the middle of what the Greeks called *katharsis* or healing through purification. Aristotle states in *Politics* 8:1340 *b* 8 that if insanely overwrought ("enthusiastic") persons "listen to enthusiastic melodies that intoxicate their souls, they are brought back to themselves again, so that their catharsis takes place exactly like a medical treatment." Werner and Sonne are right in calling this a "treatment basically homoeopathic." [29]

Allopathic treatment, on the other hand, sought to soothe maniacs by impressing "upon their disorganized souls the magically numerical and cosmic order, attuning them, as it were, to the proportions of the universe." [30]

Treatment of bodily diseases is less frequently mentioned, though it was by no means unusual. Athenaios expressly states that "persons subject to sciatica would always be free from its attacks if one played the pipe in the Phrygian harmonia over the part affected." [31] Nor should we forget that the paeans were originally charms against sickness and death.

❊   ❊   ❊

INTOXICATION AND HEALING through music were among the numerous primeval remainders in the spiritual life of Greece. The twofold power

---

[29] Eric Werner and Isaiah Sonne, "The Philosophy and Theory of Music in Judaeo-Arabic Literature," *loc. cit.,* p. 274.
[30] *Ibid.*
[31] Athen. 14:624.

of music, both to soothe and to stir the mind, was in the classical stage of Hellenic civilization understood to affect the moral qualities of the nation. It strengthened or weakened the character, created the good and the evil, order and anarchy, peace and unrest. In the ninth century B.C., the musician Thaletas was appointed to assist Lykurgos, the Spartan lawgiver; during a civil war, the Delphic oracle advised calling the composer Terpander that he might pacify the town; and in Athens, Plato urged on the guardians of his ideal state to ground the republic on music.

These ideas were by no means Hellenic; they had existed in China and Egypt before they came to Greece. But it was a Greek trait (though Egyptian in its beginnings) to organize them in a pedagogical system. To Plato, the practice of music was simply education, *paideia*. Thus, musical training, both vocal and instrumental, should be obligatory. And it actually was obligatory to a great extent: every citizen of Arcadia was compelled to learn music from early youth to the age of thirty; music took precedence over grammar in Spartan schools; and as late a poet as Lucian still demanded that music should be the first subject in education, and arithmetic only the second.

For the idea of selecting music for educational purposes, Plato certainly depended on older authorities. In the fifth century B.C., Herodotos had related that Egyptian youths were not allowed to learn music at random; only good music was conceded, and it was the priests who decided what music was good. In the same order of thought, Greek boys started from the oldest hymns and eventually arrived at contemporary music; melodies of bad tonality were avoided, while those particularly appropriate to steeling the character took precedence. Aristotle gives in *Politics* 8:6 the clearest idea of the order of thought in his time:

And now we have to determine the question that has been already raised, whether children should be themselves taught to sing and play or not. Clearly there is a considerable difference made in the character by the actual practice of the art. It is difficult, if not impossible, for those who do not perform to be good judges of the performance of others. Besides, children should have something to do, and the rattle of Archytas, which people give to their children in order to amuse them and prevent them from breaking anything in the house, was a capital invention, for a young thing cannot be quiet. The rattle is a toy suited to the infant mind, and [musical] education is a rattle or toy for children of a larger growth. We conclude, then, that they should be taught music in such a way as to become not only critics but performers.

The question what is or is not suitable for different ages may be easily answered; nor is there any difficulty in meeting the objection of those who say that the study of music is vulgar. We reply (1) in the first place, that they who are to be judges must also be performers, and that they should begin to practice early, although when they are older they may be spared the execution; they must have learned to appreciate what is good and to delight in it, thanks to the knowledge that they acquire in their youth. As to (2) the vulgarizing effect that music is supposed to exercise, this is a question [of degree] which we shall have no difficulty in determining, when we have considered to what extent freemen who are being trained to political virtue should pursue the art, what melodies and what rhythms they should be allowed to use, and what instruments should be employed in teaching them to play, for even the instrument makes a difference. The answer to the objection turns upon these distinctions; for it is quite possible that certain methods of teaching and learning music do really have a degrading effect. It is evident, then, that the learning of music ought not to impede the business of riper years, or to degrade the body or render it unfit for civil or military duties, whether for the early practice or for the later study of them.

The right measure will be attained if students of music stop short of the arts that are practiced in professional contests, and do not seek to acquire those phantastic marvels of execution that are now the fashion in such contests and from these have passed into education. Let the young pursue their studies until they are able to feel delight in noble melodies and rhythms, and not merely in that common part of music in which every slave or child and even some animals find pleasure.

Painted vases give an idea of Greek music teaching, especially the beautiful bowl of Duris, excavated in Caere and preserved in the Museum at Berlin. The master is sitting on a stool: in front of him, the pupil watches his playing. In a singing lesson the boy is standing in a respectful attitude, while the teacher blows the tune on a pair of pipes: in a lyre lesson, the pupil is sitting and playing with the master, reading from the latter's hands in the way familiar to all Oriental and folk musicians who do not learn from written music. The master was expected to accompany in a simple unison; Plato thought that in a normal three years' course with a boy from nine to twelve years old, a contrapuntal accompaniment would be too sophisticated.

But—did counterpoint exist in ancient Greece?

10

COUNTERPOINT?

THE PROBLEM whether or not the Greeks had any kind of counterpoint or harmony has been so fiercely discussed—if discussion it is—that the reader occasionally wonders at the high spirits of both parties. Science is, after all, interested in finding the truth rather than in carrying some preconceived opinion through and defaming the opponent's character.[32]

The champions, for all that, fought blindfold, since they were not aware of the only comparable facts: the polyphonic forms of the primitives and of the ancient Orient. One cannot answer this difficult question with fugues and dominant chords in mind.

Even so, most evidences in Greek texts remain ambiguous. The only uncontested fact is negative: the Greeks had no vocal polyphony except those octave parallels forced upon singing by the co-operation of high- and low-pitched singers in choruses.[33]

Things were different in accompanied vocal pieces and purely instrumental music.

Preclassical accompaniment was simple, and all attempts to find evidence of harmony for that period in a certain passage of Aristoxenos[34] were failures. The only conclusion possible is that Olympos and Terpander, the legendary patriarchs of Greek music, played notes in the accompaniment that they omitted in the melody (which is also true of the Euripides fragment, Ex. 75). We do not know how closely the instrument followed the voice; but we know for certain that the strict unison that most modern authors have claimed for preclassical times is out of the question. Unison is neither usual nor even natural—nowhere in the primitive or Oriental world has such a practice existed. The role of instruments is often confined to just restriking the main note, to adding a short *ostinato* motif, or to playing 'heterophonically,' that is, in our own words, to interpreting the same melody according to the personal tastes and abilities of the players

[32] The earliest monographs: Fr.-Jos. Fétis, "Les Grecs et les Romains ont-ils connu l'harmonie simultanée des sons?" in *Mémoires de l'Académie Royale de Belgique*, 1859. A.-J.-H. Vincent, *Réponse à M. Fétis*, Lille, 1859. A. Wagener, *Mémoire sur la symphonie des Anciens*, 1863(?).

[33] Cf. Aristotle's *Problemata* 19:18.

[34] Plutarch, *Perì mousikês* ¶ 18.

and to the special conditions of their instruments without caring "for the consonant, or at least pregnant, character of their collisions."

The term *heterophony* has been borrowed from the Greeks themselves. But it unfortunately seems to have had a quite different meaning in Greece. Plato uses it in the *Laws:* a music teacher, he says, who trains boys from nine to twelve years old, should simply double on his own lyre the melody that the pupil's lyre plays; he had better refrain from *heterophony,* without answering closer by wider intervals, lower by higher notes, speed by slowness.

Some scholars, firmly determined to oppose the idea of Greek polyphony, have not been afraid to insist that, far from being an evidence of polyphony, this passage clearly testified to heterophonic paraphrase (in the meaning that modern terminology gives to this word). I do not share their belief. Whoever practices heterophony takes the two melodic lines for similar "without caring for the consonant or at least pregnant, character of their collisions." Plato, on the contrary, insists on their difference; the accompaniment he has in mind is willfully dissimilar in intervals, pitches, rhythms, and number of notes; and various intervals, 'symphonic' and 'antiphonic' (whatever these terms mean) are expressly indicated.[35] Several hundred years later, probably in the first century A.D., the pseudo-Aristotelian book *Perì kósmou* still clings to the same differences: "Music mixes high and low, short and long notes *in different voice parts [phonaís] to achieve one harmony."* [36] It would be scarcely possible to find a clearer description of what we call a mixed two-part counterpoint.

These counterpoints had not always the proper transparence. Athenaios 14:618 warns a piper: "Wherefore you and this girl shall go on with this piece . . . where you are to play together, or where you again play separately, there'll be no do together—no riddles—to make each part clear." [37]

❋　❋　❋

THE AUTHOR PSEUDO-LONGINUS asserts at about the same time that melody —the *kyrios phtongos* or 'regal voice'—is usually "sweetened" by the two 'paraphonic' intervals, the fifth and the fourth.[38] This is an unmistakable testimony to the frequent use, not of functional chords in a modern sense,

---

[35] Plato, *Laws* 7:812 D-E.
[36] J. Handschin, "Musikalische Miszellen," in *Philologus* 86 (1930), p. 57.
[37] οὖ τε κοινόν ἐστιν, οὖ χορὶς πάλιν, συννεύματ', οὖ προβλήμαθ', οἶς σεμαίνεται ἔκαστα.
[38] J. Handschin, *op. cit.,* p. 52.

to be sure, but of consonant notes, just as in East Asiatic, Babylonian, Egyptian, and medieval music.

Pseudo-Longinus, who probably wrote in the first century A.D., is a comparatively late witness. But we know from Plutarch that even those whom he called "the ancients" played *c′* in consonance with *f;* the higher *e′,* both in dissonance with *d′* and in consonance with *a;* and *d′,* in dissonance with *c′* and *b* and in consonance with *a* and *g.*

Such rudimentary harmony must have been the rule; for Plutarch relates that those musicians who opposed the enharmonic genus put it to "the incompatibility of quarter tones with consonance."

Only six intervals were called *symphonies* or consonances: the fourth, fifth, and octave and their higher octaves. Terminology, however, varied: Theo of Smyrna, an author of the second century A.D., called the octave and the double octave *antiphonies,* and the fourth and the fifth, *paraphonies;* maybe half a hundred years later, Gaudentios understood paraphony to be an interval neither consonant nor dissonant, such as the tritone and the major third,[39] while Aristides Quintilianus defined the octave as *homophony.*

The ancient definition of consonance had a remarkably modern flavor. "If symphonic notes sound *together* on stringed or wind instruments," Gaudentios said, "the lower one, in relation to the higher, and the higher, in relation to the lower one, form a unit. We call them symphonic, as the two notes melt into oneness." Bacchius found a more concise wording for the same idea: consonance is the combination of two notes in which neither seems to be higher or lower than the other. Boethius, however, gave the best definition: in a dissonance, each note is expected to go its own way, that is to say—to quote Grove's nice definition of the term *discord*—dissonance is "a combination of notes which produces a certain restless craving in the mind for some further combination."

Consonances, Boethius says, are "pleasant," and the pseudo-Aristotelian Problem 19:13 states that "any consonance is sweeter than a single note." And are we supposed to believe that the Greeks did not use them?

---

[39] Gaudentios, "Eisagoge," in Carolus Janus, *Musici Scriptores Graeci,* 1895, p. 17.

11

ACCENTS AND RHYTHM

GREEK VERSES have two kinds of accents, which may be distinguished as melic and metric:

Melic   *Chi-o-no-ble-phá-rou pát-er a-oûs*
Metric   ⏑ ⏑ ⏤ ⏑ ⏑ ⏤ ⏑ ⏑ ⏤ ⏤

This initial verse of the Hymn to the Sun clearly shows the dualism of accents: the two acutes and the circumflex, inseparable from the words themselves, and the longae, stressed by the specific meter of the verse in which they gather.

At first sight, the second accent seems to kill the first; modern readers would indeed, in reciting the verse, obey the poetic meter and entirely neglect the natural accents of the words. But they would be wrong. Ancient recitation, whether sung or spoken, did justice to both accents; the poetic meter shaped its rhythm, the word accents affected its pitches.

The three accents—acute, grave, and circumflex—were indeed symbols of tonal inflections which, as in Sanskrit and Chinese, were essential qualities of the ancient Greek language. They helped to indicate high, medium, low and rising, falling, level pitch.

These tonal inflections were respected unless they interfered with purely melodic conditions. The acute was often rendered by a higher note: in the first lines of the Hymn to the Sun, for instance, twelve out of sixteen acutes are marked by ascending steps. Exceptions are easily explained; in the same hymn, the accented syllable of the word *agallómenos* is lower, instead of higher, because the composer wished to assimilate this portion of the melody into the previous *íchnessi diókeis*.

Ex. 84. HYMN TO HELIOS

pta - noîs hyp'íh-nes-si di - o - keis,chry-

-séai - sin a - gal - ló - me - nos kó-mais

In the Skolion of Seikilos, the circumflex accent is—with one exception—answered by the ligature of a falling third, which recalls the *svarita* in the Vedic chant.

There are pieces, however, in which the melic accent of speech is more or less neglected. Greek music, too, knew the eternal difference of logogenic and melogenic music, of melody submitting to natural speech and melody disregarding its text.

Wherever at least the acute accent is respected, the Western musician is tempted to give it a downbeat. But it often falls on an upbeat or the short note after a dot, which are unstressed or even secondary in our music. But in Greece, the note rendered an actual accent and could not be secondary. As a consequence, such melodies must have had a delicate flexibility of rhythm that complied with both the melic and the metric accents.

*   *   *

THE METRIC ACCENTS in both poetry and melody followed the so-called quantitative principle; they materialized as long syllables or notes among short ones, not as strong among light beats.

The short note or *brevis*—that we render by an eighth note in modern notation—was the time unit or *chrónos prôtos*. The Greeks defined this 'first time' as an ultimate atom, which could not be divided by either a syllable or a note or a gesture. The *longa* measured two breves, or a quarter note, except at the end of a verse, where it required the length of an entire foot.

The feet were considered to have two (equal or unequal) phases each—not time units—and were classified in four groups according to whether the ratio of length of the two phases was 1:1, 2:1, 3:2, or 4:3. The Greeks realized very well that the rhythmic ratios coincided with the harmonic ratios of the unison, octave, fifth, and fourth; indeed, Dionysios of Halikarnassos (first century B.C.) expressly stated that rhythm and harmony were essentially one.

The four groups were:

A. *Isa* 'equals' or dactylic feet—our even-beat measures:

   1) *Prokeleusmatikos* or *Pyrrhichios*   ♫   2/8

   2) *Prokeleusmatikos,* double   ♫ ♫   4/8

   3) *Anapaistos* (our dactyl)   ♩ ♫   2/4

4) *Anapaistos*   ♫ ♩   2/4

5) *Spondeios*   ♩ ♩   2/4

6) *Spondeios*, double   𝅗𝅥 𝅗𝅥   2/2

B. *Diplasia*, 'doubles' or iambic feet, in which one part of the measure was double the other, that is, 2 + 1 or 1 + 2, corresponding to our three-beat measures:

1) *Iambos*   ♪ ♩   3/8

2) *Trochaios*   ♩ ♪   3/8

3) *Orthios*   𝅗𝅥 𝅝   3/2

4) *Trochaios Semantos*   𝅝 𝅗𝅥   3/2

C. *Hemiolia*, 'by one and a half' or paeonic feet, in which the two beats were three to two, corresponding to our five-beat measures:

1) *Paiòn diágyros* or 'bent paion'   = ♩. ♩   5/8
2) *Paiòn epíbatos* or 'climbing paion'   = 𝅗𝅥 𝅗𝅥.   5/4

D. *Epítrita*, 'by four thirds,' in which one part of the measure was to the other as four to three, corresponding to our seven-beat measures. These rhythms, however, were very rare.

The two beats of all these feet were called *arsis* and (by Aristoxenos) *basis* or (later) *thesis*. The term *arsis* means the lifting, and *basis* or *thesis* the dropping of the time-regulating hand or foot; in our terms: upbeat and downbeat. In groups (B) to (D), the shorter beat is up; in dactyls and anapaests, the two shorts are up; in proceleusmatics and spondees, the first is usually a downbeat.

All kinds of feet could be combined. There were two-foot units or *dipodies*, as, for example,

$$♩ \quad ♫♩. \quad ♩ \quad (\tfrac{4+5}{8});$$

or the *bakchios*, which consisted either of an iamb and a trochee or, vice versa, of a trochee and an iamb:

$$♪♩ \quad ♩ \quad ♪ \quad (\tfrac{3+3}{8})$$

or

$$\text{♩ ♪♪♩} \left(\frac{3+3}{8}\right).$$

Such dipody was assigned two beats as well: arsis-thesis in the two first examples, and thesis-arsis in the last.

Tripodies were combinations of three different feet, as a pyrric plus an iamb plus a trochee:

$$\text{♫♪♩ ♩ ♪} \quad \frac{(2+3+3)}{8};$$

tetrapodies were combinations of four feet, as iamb plus pyrric plus iamb plus trochee:

$$\text{♪♩ ♫♪♩ ♩ ♪} \frac{(3+2+3+3)}{8}.$$

The tripody and tetrapody just described were *prosodiakoí* or marching rhythms for solemn processions, which in our civilization are reduced to poor 4/4 beats—left, right, left, right. Nothing could better illustrate the richness of Greek rhythm.

Such wealth was possible only in a country where *mousiké* included poetry and the dance and took its inspiration, not from lifeless beats but from the spirited word and the expressive gesture of well-trained limbs.

❀   ❀   ❀

DACTYLIC, IAMBIC, PAEONIC rhythms are represented among the relics of Greek music.

The anapaests of the Hymns to Helios and to Nemesis and both the Cairo and the Berlin fragments are dactylic. Bellermann was certainly wrong when he transcribed the first two hymns in a hopping six-eight time; anapaests require two- or four-beat measures.

The Hymn to the Muse is iambic and has correctly been rendered in three-eight time.

The strange paeonic rhythm is recorded in the two Delphic hymns:

Ké-klyth' He-li-kó-na ba-thý-den-dron haì lá-che-te

Unfortunately, most students have known the two hymns in the unforgivable transcription of Hugo Riemann, who was foolish enough to 'drop' the five-beat time in order to make the melody "considerably simpler and more convincing." The reader should forget this clumsy offense against the genius of Hellenic music and re-establish the admirable nimbleness of the floating five beats.

Meter was important enough to provide the names even of wordless forms like the instrumental *nomos*. One was called *nomos trochaios,* and another, *nomos orthios*. And as a rule, meter was not changed during a piece. It is expressly said Sakadas' Pythian *nomos* had an iambic, a dactylic, a spondaic, and a cretic, that is, paeonic, movement, and that the *nomos Athenâs* had a strong effect on the audience because from the initial *paiòn epíbatos* it modulated into the trochaic meter. So these must have been exceptions.

❋ ❋ ❋

OVER AGAINST QUANTITATIVE METER stood 'qualitative' *time* with the rhythmic alternation of strong and weak beats and their free subdivision. It was the natural form of instrumental rhythm: Cicero speaks of beats as the characteristic rhythm of pipers' music.

Whether vocal practice, on the other hand, was ever able or willing to ignore time in its meters is more than doubtful. Even in poetry the metrical unit was called a verse *foot,* which like all metaphors must originally have been a reality: the Greek, accustomed to conceive poetry, melody, and the dance in its widest sense as one *mousiké,* cannot have forbidden his body and its time rhythm to interfere with meter.

So it happened that choir leaders used the foot to beat time. Indeed, on the stage they increased the downbeat by a thick wooden sandal, *kroúpalon,* in which two boards with castanets between were linked at the heel and clapped together with a sharp cracking sound.

The contrast between the noisy downbeat or *thesis* and the noiseless *arsis* or lifting was so strong—even without the clapping sandal—that a 'qualitative' discrimination was inevitable.

But this was not the essential issue. Above all, any beat rhythm leads straightway to conceiving the beat itself as the time unit or *chronos prôtos;* to uniting two, three, or more of these units in groups of measures; and to subdividing these measures in entire freedom, without sticking to poetic meters, by simply following those ratios that man's ear accepted as rhythmical.

A series of ten beats, the Greeks said, could not be rhythmically divided into one plus nine, or two plus eight, or three plus seven beats. Four plus six, on the contrary, would be admissible as *hemiolia* in the ratio 2:3, and also five plus five, as *isa* in the ratio 1:1. Three plus seven beats were acceptable by cleaving the seven into three and four, so that the ten beats could be organized into three plus three plus four in all permutations. Not only permutation was conceded; two or more beats could be drawn together in order to form longer notes.

Actually, this is nothing but the Indian *tāla*, the asymmetrical combination of meter and time. A period of three and two and two is exactly the tāla *Tripuṭa*.

Time beating, too, might have been similar. The orator Fabius Quintilianus' description of time beating with both the feet and the fingers—not the hands—recalls the complicated gesticulation of the various fingers that the ancient Hindu singers used; and the Hindu *dhruva*, the snapping thumb, reappears in Horace's Fourth Ode, which invites the maidens and youths to obey the Lesbian meter and the snapping of his thumb.

* * *

Two examples illustrate the difference between meter and time in Greek rhythm. The Hymn to Helios is strictly anapaestic: short-short-long, short-short-long; it is typically metric in rhythm (Ex. 73).

Seikilos' Skolion, on the contrary, is antimetric (Ex. 79). It has four verses, but of a very irregular form. The first has five, the second seven, the third eight, and the fourth nine syllables. But the composer, preferring a regular musical pattern, subordinated the metrical feet to the melody he had in mind. Each verse was given twelve beats, which allowed even the longest verse to stretch out the last two syllables, and while this latter was syllabic, the other, shorter, verses needed ligatures to house all twelve beats. Meter itself was destroyed: of the first three words—*hóson zês phaínou* —the metrically short syllable *phai-* is given three units, and the metrically long syllable *ho-* only one. The Hindus would call such a rhythm *tāla*, in fact, tāla *Rūpaka*.

Singers and players could not be expected to guess the antimetrical intention of the composer. He therefore added certain signs, which would have been unnecessary when he followed poetic meters: a horizontal dash above the note indicated two units, that is, an ordinary *longa,* an angle ⌐, three, ⌐⌐ , four, and ⊔⊔ , five units.

A small upright angle denoted a rest. It corresponded, when single, to the unit of time; longer rests needed the proper symbols among those just named. The angular rest $\wedge$ stood for the Greek letter *lambda*, the initial of *leimma*, 'left over.' It was sometimes replaced by an arc $\cap$. (Pl. 8, p. 177)

The importance of signs for rests can hardly be overrated. There were no rests in poetry or verse-ruled melody. A verse might have a caesura; but it was a mere breath to emphasize the incision. A relaxing silence might separate the verses; but the disconnection was irrational and not counted in: meter ran from the first to the last syllable of a verse; the following vacuum was ametric, indeed, antimetric. A musical rest, on the contrary, was rational and counted in as a part of the measure; though inaudible, it was felt to obey a beat and to hold the listener's attention.

✿   ✿   ✿

THE TEMPO unavoidably varied, since to a certain degree it was inseparable from the temperament of the performer, from the particular mood of the piece, and from the circumstances. But it was not vital, as it is in our music, and therefore not properly considered. Changes of speed were rather opposed: a fast tempo was too nervous, and a slow tempo too effeminate and passive. The *chronos prôtos* was expected to be given a steady moderate tempo, and the necessary variations in tempo merely consisted in choosing metric feet of an adequate number of time units: a double spondee was in itself twice as slow as a single spondee, and an *orthios* lasted four times longer than the reduced form called iamb.[40]

There is no wonder, then, that Plutarch does not mention tempo when he enumerates the "three impressions rapidly made on the ear at the same time; one, by the sound uttered, as it is acute or grave; another by the quantity of the same sound, as long or short; and a third, by the syllable or letter enunciated." [41]

One other means of expression, so essential in our modern music, is not mentioned either by Plutarch or by any other authority: the contrast of loud and soft. In all probability, the Greeks did not consciously use the various degrees of loudness beyond the physiological implications of high and low, of vigor and fatigue.

[40] Cf. Aristides Quintilianus, M. 42, Sch. 226, and M. 100, Sch. 294.
[41] Plutarch 35.

12

FORM

THE FORMS of Greek music elude defining and description. The relics, to a great extent fragmentary, do not allow of structural analysis, and literary sources indicate either mere names or at the best a few characteristic features without giving a clear picture.

Besides, musical forms could not have remained untouched by the change of taste and circumstances from the Dorian migration to the decay of the Roman Empire. Otherwise Plato would not have lamented in the *Laws* that in the good old days when musical forms were classified and fixed "it was forbidden to set one kind of words to a different class of tune . . . but later on, with the progress of time, there arose as leaders of unmusical illegality poets who, though by nature poetical, were ignorant of what was just and lawful in music; and they, being frenzied and unduly possessed by a spirit of pleasure, mixed dirges with hymns and paeans with dithyrambs . . . and blended every kind of music with every other."

We may add: "And they did well." After all, the evolution of musical forms is a history of creative blending and mixing. Without such continual regrouping we would not have Monteverdi's operas, or Bach's passions, or Beethoven's quartets. And the hymns and paeans that Plato, the incurable reactionary, wished to protect from contamination would not have existed either.

* * *

CHORAL SINGING, the most striking trait in Greek music, was not aboriginal in Hellas. The invading Dorians had found it in the ancient civilization of Crete, which they overran, and appropriated it. We do not know to what extent they maintained the Cretan association of choral singing and dancing; the *Hyporchémata,* at the least, were pieces in which, according to Athenaios' definition, "the singing chorus danced." But we do not know the exact range of this term, and in any case the definition implies that there were also choruses that did not dance.

The democratic esteem for choral singing spread from Sparta all over

Greece. Men and women joined in choral societies, and the famous Alkman (c. 650 B.C.) is said to have introduced special *partheniai* or 'maidens' songs' for choruses of girls. Official celebrations of all kinds, processions, sacrifices, and missions to interrogate oracles abroad were accompanied by choirs, and rivaling townships made boast of sending as many singers as possible. There were six hundred on one of these occasions. Such choirs may have sung the two Delphic hymns and the hymns to the Sun, the Muse, and Nemesis we have discussed so many times. Choral singing had, from the sixth century on, formed the concluding section of the musical contests at the great *agōnes:* the Pythian games in honor of Apollo, the Panathenaean and Dionysian games in Athens, and the Karnaean games in Sparta. There still stands in Athens a lonely monument from 335 B.C., destined to commemorate such an event: a graceful circular structure with, on top, a bronze tripod, the prize at the Festival of Dionysos, and, in front, the inscription "Lysikrates, son of Lysitheiedes of Kikyuna, was the dance leader when the boys' chorus of the Phylé Akamantis won the prize. Theon was the piper, Lysiades of Athens had trained the chorus. Enaenetos was *archōn* [mayor of Athens]."

Choral singing entered even private life: Athenaios 4:130 mentions a nuptial choir of one hundred men. He does not say what form of choral melody they performed; but we know that at least one of the wedding forms was the paean.

Paean meant 'healer'; it originally was a medicine dance and later, more generally, a chorus dance in honor of Apollo, the healing God. As early a source as the Iliad describes a paean to ban the plague, and several centuries later, when the plague raged in Sparta, the governing board appointed the Cretan musician, Thaletas, to organize paeans.

The only example preserved, from the second century A.D., is the first fragment on the Berlin Papyrus, *Paiàn ô paián*. It is Hypermixolydian in the range *g–a'*; the meter cannot be stated beyond doubt.

❋ ❋ ❋

THE DITHÝRAMBOS, second choral form in importance, had come from Phrygia, not from Crete. It was a strophic melody sung by ecstatic worshippers of Dionysos, but raised to the level of a choral art form as early as about 600 B.C. by Arion of Methymna, who founded the first dithyrambic choir of fifty boys and men performing in a circle around the piper.

This kind of dithyramb underwent a bifurcation at the end of the sixth century b.c. As a choral song, it developed into the tragedy and on the stage slowly blended into the *nomos*. Outside the drama, its enthusiastic character and melodic features merged in the intricate solo songs of professional virtuosi and were even admitted to the highest honor in this field: Lasos of Hermione, probably the discoverer of sound waves, prevailed upon the authorities to admit the dithyramb to musical contests.

The only thing we know about dithyrambic music is the fact that of the three styles of Greek music—the nomic, the dithyrambic, and the tragic —the dithyrambic melody was 'mesoid,' that is, its prevalent zone was near the thetic center *a* right in the middle of the musical space.

The dithyrambs seem to have been dramatic from the very first, as I pointed out in my *World History of the Dance:* the dance leader in the middle was the god Dionysos who lived, suffered, sickened, and died with the vegetation of the earth and at a given moment wakened anew like Osiris in Egypt and Attis-Adonis in Asia Minor; and, circling around him, fifty dancing singers shared his fate, interpreting, suffering and rejoicing with him. It was from these dance plays that in the sixth century b.c. the Greek drama originated, which, leaving the worship of Dionysos, took from mythology whatever subject aroused both awe and compassion.

Dramas were not singly presented, but always in tetralogies: three tragedies and, as a relaxing epilogue, a comedy. Strangely enough, the *tragodia* or 'goat song' had its name from the disguised satyrs and silenes of the Dionysian dithyrambs; the comedy preserved the paraphernalia themselves, the beards and tails and phalli for its chorus, though its name was no more reminiscent of the older dance plays.

The transition from a religious to a spectacular choir necessarily disrupted the circular formation. The tragic chorus acted and sang in a semicircle in front of the stage. It consisted of twelve singers, and later, of fifteen; the comic chorus had fifty, and later, sixty singers.[42]

Dramas to be performed were selected from the scripts of competing masters who were supposed to be poets and composers, and also conductors and stage directors. Some wealthy citizen paid for a choir of amateurs, while the state provided the actors. The accompaniment consisted of one or two pipers, and occasionally a lyre player to support the actor-singers.

At first the Greek stage had only one actor—the former leader of the Dionysian dance choir. Aischylos introduced a second, and Sophocles, a

[42] Edith Hamilton, "The Greek Chorus, Fifteen or Fifty?" in *Theatre Arts Monthly* XVII (1933), p. 459.

third. The dialogue was spoken, but once in a while interrupted by songs entirely soloistic or else alternating with the chorus.

The chorus, singing, dancing, and acting as an ideal spectator, played the main role up to the time of Sophocles (fifth century B.C.). It entered the stage with the *párodos* and left it with the *éxodos;* singing the *strophe,* it turned to the right to picture the orbit of the stars, so Michael Psellos, the Byzantine, said; in the *antistrophe,* it turned in the opposite direction. The songs between these two marchlike movements, sung in place, were called *stásima* or 'stationary' (which Psellos called the steady harmony of the earth). The fragment of a *stásimon* from Euripides' *Orestes,* has been preserved (Ex. 75); its enharmonic melody proves that the choral parts of the Greek drama were by no means simple or amateurish.

While the older tragedy dwelt upon lyric episodes and contemplation, the tragedy of classical times became more and more dramatic. This meant a momentous repression of the chorus, which by nature was better able to play a part in stylized tragedies of a meditative lyrico-epic type than in rapid action and counteraction and in refined psychology.

❋ ❋ ❋

SOLOISTIC MUSIC may, in this survey, be mentioned in only two of its most characteristic forms: the amateurish skolion and the professional nomos.

The *skolion* was a drinking song. It was sung in banquets over the brimming cups, says Clemens Alexandrinus, "after the manner of the Hebrew psalms, all together raising the paean with the voice, and sometimes also taking turns in the song while they drank healths round; while those that were more musical than the rest sang to the lyre." [43] Everybody in Greece was expected to know such songs; one general who refused to sing because he did not know any was unfavorably criticized.

The name meant 'zigzag': the guests lay crosswise at either side of the table so that the lyre was passed zigzag from the singer just finishing to the next one at the opposite side.

Seikilos' immortal skolion gives an excellent idea of the mellow and subjective character of this art form which, though certainly belonging to the highest lyrical style, still was popular in text and tune.

The *nomos* or 'law,' main art form for professional soloists and para-

---

[43] Clemens Alexandrinus, *Opera,* ed. Otto Stählin, Leipzig, 1905, I, p. 184. "Clement of Alexandria," eds. Roberts and Donaldson, Edinburgh, 1867, I, 218 (*Paedagogus* 2:4).

mount music in agonistic contests, has already been discussed on pages 251 and 263. Here, we state in a general way that it was a cyclic monody without strophic repetitions in three, five, or seven movements. In the older *nomos,* performers were not allowed to change the *harmonia;* later *nomoi* were written in different modes and meters. Aristides Quintilianus calls 'nomic' the so-called netoid style, which had its prevalent zone near the thetic nētē *e'*.[44] If this holds true for a normal *nomos,* it means that an agonistic singer was expected to have a tenor voice. We indeed learn from Suidas (tenth century A.D.) that two well-known nomoi, *Nomos Trochaios* and *Nomos Orthios,* were high in pitch and euphonious. But the pseudo-Aristotelian Problems (the date of which we do not know) stigmatize these two *nomoi* as particularly difficult. Both the discrimination and the express mention of two high *nomoi* caution us not to generalize from Aristides' classification.

There also was an instrumental nomos, best known from the description of a concert piece that the piper Sakadas performed in 586 B.C. at Delphi, at the Pythian games. On his double oboe, he represented the contest between Apollo and the dragon in five movements: a prelude, the first onset, the contest itself, the triumph following victory, and the death of the dragon, with a sharp harmonic when the monster hissed out its last breath.[45]

Readers familiar with European music history will be reminded of the similar program Johann Kuhnau gave his sonata on the combat between David and Goliath (1700).

It was no little surprise when, as a much closer parallel, Robert Lachmann found a very similar *nomos* among the Cabyles of Tunisia.[46] The oboe had become a flute, Apollo, a Bedouin, and the dragon a lion. But even the division into five movements had been kept. The Bedouin Dr. Lachmann saw added pantomime to music; crouching, he acted the horse shying when the lion neared, and he managed to free one hand to illustrate a girl grinding barley and donning her coiffure and belt. All evidences hint to a similar pantomimic illustration of the Greek *nomos.*

❋   ❋   ❋

SPORTIVE COMPETITION, not entirely unknown in modern music history, so dominated Greek musical life that even mythology saw music in the

---

[44] Aristides Quintilianus, M. 30, Sch., p. 207.
[45] Strabo, *Geographica* 9:3, 10; Julius Pollux, *Onomastikon* 4:84; E. Hiller, "Sakadas der Aulet," in *Rheinisches Museum für Philologie,* N. F. XLIV (1876).
[46] Robert Lachmann, "Die Weise vom Löwen und der pythische Nomos," in *Festschrift für Johannes Wolf,* Berlin, 1929, pp. 97–106.

form of challenge and duel. The Thracian Thamyris invited the muses to compete with him and was blinded for his insolence; and the Phrygian Marsyas, beaten in a contest by Apollo, lost his skin while King Midas, who had acted as the umpire, was given ass's ears.

With gods and muses, with blinding and skinning, myth mirrored the Greek conception of musical performance. Music was an essential part of the great tournaments that played so important a role in Greek civilization. The Pythian games, probably the oldest, celebrated at Delphi in honor of Apollo, were at first exclusively dedicated to poetry and music; the participation of wrestlers and charioteers came at a later time. These *agones* must have been a marvelous experience. No snobbish audience made *acte de présence;* the people as a whole, as it does in our games (and nearly does in our recent mass concerts in stadiums), listened to the *kitharodós;* and had they not kept quiet, the plucked strings of a single lyre would not have been heard in the gigantic open space. No citizen was absent; some Persian general made the census of conquered Greek towns simply by counting the listeners when a noted *kitharodós* performed in the arena.

Later, especially in Rome, the singer lost his hieratic dignity and became a virtuoso, who in his caprices, professional jealousy, phantastic fees, and hired claque was the equal of his brethren in the nineteenth century. Nor was he less spoiled by the fashionable ladies who would snatch from him the plectron with which he had touched the strings, much as the *afficionados* fight for the trophies when the matador has killed the bull.

13

ROME

NO ROMAN MUSIC has been preserved, nor have we much information about the musical habits of Rome. There is one fact, however: ancient
Rome did not recognize any instrument except pipes, either for her ceremonies or even at banquets; tolerance was frustrated by a special law
promulgated in the year 639 B.C. Livius and Virgil called the Roman pipers
Etruscans, and it is quite possible that Etruria was responsible for the
privileged position of pipes in Rome.

Matters were changed when, at an unknown time B.C., the so-called Sibyl-
line Books fostered the *Ritus Graecus,* which resulted in the admission of
the lyre and other instruments of the Greeks even to solemn sacrifices and
also in the creation of a *Societas Cantorum Graecorum* in the City.[47]

From this time on, Roman music cannot be separated from Greek music.
No source gives evidence of ancient folk music in Italy; its quality and
plenty can be gathered only from its present state. In art music, Greek style
and theory, Greek instruments and musicians were in authority. In accepting this fact, we too readily forget that Sicily and the south of Italy up
to the gates of Rome were *Magna Graecia,* 'Greater Greece.'

The only references to specifically Roman developments are poetic satires
against the nuisance and impropriety of music. Seneca, who lived at the
beginning of the first century A.D., complains that orchestras and choruses
grew to gigantic proportions, so that there were often more singers and
players in the theater than spectators; and five hundred years later, Mar-
cianus Cappella describes lyres as large as sedan chairs. Private teachers
and conservatories train the daughters of the bourgeoisie to strum on the
lyre; day and night, the slaves of the wealthy reduce the neighbors to
despair with their singing voices and instruments; at table, nobody can
talk for music; and an intolerable host of virtuosi, capricious, insolent,
intriguing, strut the stage.

This is the picture Roman poets trace.

Music had certainly lost the "austere sweetness" Cicero had found in

---

[47] Cf. R. Paribeni, "Cantores graeci nell' ultimo secolo della reppublica in Roma," in *Aegyptus, Serie scientifica* III (1925), pp. 287–92.

the older music of the Roman theater. In its present state, he said, it could give us some childish pleasure, but was practically useless since it led to no happiness.

Many Roman thinkers regretted with Cicero the degeneration of music, its sensuality, effeminacy, and lack of dignity. It is hard to subscribe to this judgment, however, which we hear throughout the history of music whenever a style abandons academic standards. It is still harder to accept a permanent state of decadence supposed to have lasted more than five hundred years.

Thus we prefer to draw the curtain over this section of music history.

Section Six

THE GREEK HERITAGE
IN THE MUSIC OF ISLAM

THE HERITAGE of Greek music was enormous. Or, rather, the heritage of Greek music theory. Rome, Byzantium, and Alexander's conquests from North Africa to India boasted of being heirs to the great Hellenic tradition; medieval music in Europe appealed to Boethius as the supreme judge; and the Persians, Arabs, and Turks underpinned their musical systems with the solid structure of Grecian scales, modes, and genera.

Its influence on Islamic music is more fascinating than any other the Greeks exerted, since, in opposition to the Westerners, the Arabs understood and applied classical theory without committing the mistakes of the West. Thus, any research in Greek music is incomplete without a glance at the practice and theory of Islamic music.

Arabian music in its proper sense is the music of the Bedouins in the desert and the oases—emotional songs of a limited range in free rhythm, thoroughly heptatonic and mostly what I have called 'positive,' starting from a low note, curving upward, and returning.

Ex. 85. SOUTH ARABIAN BEDOUINS   *after Helfritz*

The musical style we colloquially call Arabian comprises much more than the music of Arabia proper, or even of the Arabic-speaking nations. Its province reaches from Morocco in the west along the African borderland of the Mediterranean through Syria, Iraq, and Turkey, to Persia and even to the northern part of India. No racial or national tie links these heterogeneous peoples; their only bond is the Mohammedan religion. Hence this is an Islamic rather than an Arabian section.

The international character of Islamic, and even of pre-Islamic, music in the Orient appears from an ample stock of evidence. The young Persian king, Bahram Ghur (430–438), was sent to the Mesopotamian town of Al-Hira to study Arabian music. But Arabian music did not exclusively feed on Arabian sources. Hassan ibn-Thābit, a visitor to the court of an Arabian monarch two hundred years later, "saw ten singing girls, five of them Byzantines, singing the songs of their country to the accompaniment of the *barbat,* and five others from Al-Hira, who had been given to King Jabala by Iyas ibn-Qabisa, singing the songs of their country." Bilal ibn-Riyah, allegedly the earliest muezzin (d. 641), was the son of an Abyssinian slave girl, and it was Abyssinian women who used to sing. An English author, Lyall, even went so far as to say that Arabian singing girls "were all foreigners, either Persians or Greeks from Syria," and an ancient Arabian writer claimed that the origin and source of music were to be traced to the slaves in the market towns of the Arabs.[1]

The instruments, at least, were kept apart in this conflux of musical styles: in the tale of King Omar bin al-Nu'uhman, in *The Arabian Nights,* the princess had her slave girl bring some instruments, and the maid "returned in the twinkling of an eye with a Damascus lute, a Persian harp, a Tatar pipe, and an Egyptian dulcimer."

Music itself could not avoid an ever growing fusion into one Islamic style.

It would have been hard, however, actually to blend all the innumerable and heterogeneous melodies from countries between the Mediterranean, the Black Sea, and the Indian Ocean without the help of Greek theory, which provided a thorough system and an easily adaptable terminology.

The Persians called the Greek Pythagoras the patriarch of all scholarly music. They had been under a strong Hellenistic influence until the dynasty of the Seleucides (226–641) brought a nationalistic, anti-Greek reaction. Toward the end of the first thousand years A.D., however, the Orient underwent a second, decisive Hellenization of its scientific life, and its music, together with mathematics, medicine, and philosophy, took possession of Greek theory. The masters of Islamic musicology, the Arab Al-Kindī (d. c. 874), the Turk Al-Fārābī (c. 870–950), and the Bukharan Ibn-Sīnā (980–1037), better known under his latinized name Avicenna, shaped their doctrines to a great extent upon Greek patterns.

---

[1] Henry George Farmer, *A History of Arabian Music*, London, 1929, ch. I ¶ i.

SCALES AND MODES

THE HELLENIC TREND was strongest in the theory of scales. The conceptions, indeed the very terms of the Greeks, reappear in Turkish, Persian, and Arabian works: tetrachord, diapason, the shades and genders, *leimma* and *apotomé,* and many others.

Greek classification helped, above all, in legalizing, adapting, and merging the heterogeneous intervals that the motley mass of Mohammedan tribes had brought into the common stock of music. The irrefragable rule was that a scale had seven steps in the octave, no less, no more, as Al-Fārābī expressly states (tenth century A.D.); pentatonism or hexatonism existed just as little as microtonic scales. The standard shade was what Ptolemy had called *diátonon ditoniaîon:* the scale based on the *up-and-down principle* and consisting of major whole tones of 204 Cents and minor semitones of 90 Cents, that is, *leimmas.*

Symbol of this scale built on the cycle of fourths was the short-necked Persian lute *'ūd,* ancestor of the European lute and typical instrument of Islamic theory. It had four strings or double strings a fourth apart; the fingers stopped a tetrachord on each, and the stopped notes were expected not to disagree with the open strings.

This principle led to an arrangement that has haunted so many books on music like a troublesome hobgoblin: the alleged Arabian scale of seventeen thirds of tones. The number seventeen is correct; but there are no thirds of tones; nor do the seventeen steps constitute a scale. The earliest discussion, in Al-Fārābī's treatise, is unmistakable. It occurs in the description of a long-necked lute with only two strings (of which but one was used for the melody) called the *ṭanbūr* of Hurāsān, a province in the northeast of Persia. There were five fixed frets for the skeleton intervals, the fourth, the second, the fifth, the octave, and the ninth. In addition, there were mobile frets which, together with these frets, divided the octave into seventeen sections. Far from being of the same size, the sections followed the sequence of one *leimma* of 90 Cents (l), another of the same size (l), and a Pythagorean comma of 24 Cents (c), repeated five times and supplemented by two *leimmas* (llc llc llc llc llc ll). This arrangement allowed the player to perform in all three tetrachordal structures, by placing the mobile frets accordingly:

Semitone above ....

1lc	1lc	1
204	204	90

Semitone in the middle ....

1lc	1	1cl
204	90	204

Semitone below ....

1	1cl	1cl
90	204	204

It is obvious, then, that the seventeen steps formed a set of elements, not a scale.

The *divisive principle,* of outstanding importance in later times, first appears in Al-Fārābī's work, among many other shades and genders, as the Second Species of the Strong Conjunct Genus. Its scale is similar to Ptolemy's *diátonon sýntonon* and to the Hindu *ma-grāma.* And like the *grāma* of India, it has been presented by later authors mostly in the mistaken form of a set of elements: the Pythagorean comma of 24 Cents, *leimmas* of 90 Cents, *apotomés* of 114 Cents, minor whole tones of 204 Cents. Like their counterparts, the Indian *śrutis,* these elements allow of an easy and correct permutation of the seven steps of the octave and therewith are the fundament of modal changes.

❁   ❁   ❁

MODES are first indicated in ʿAlī al-Iṣfahānī's tenth-century collection of poems, the *Kitāb al-aghānī:* each of its songs is accompanied by a short note indicating which tonality and rhythm are required.

The complicated terms with which the poet described the eight occurring tonalities had been incomprehensible until the *Journal Asiatique* published an acceptable interpretation by the Reverend Father Collangettes in 1906. But the scales in which his ingenious deduction resulted were hardly quite correct, in either material or orthography, particularly since they had different thirds on the upper string, which was neither musically convincing nor in keeping with the terms 'ring finger' and 'middle finger' that the Arabs used for the major and the minor third. The Arabic descriptions may be broadly translated as: (1) and (2) starting on the open string of the '*ūd* and having respectively the minor and the major third; (3) and (4) starting on the first fret and having respectively the minor and the major second; (5) and (6) starting respectively on the third frets of (1) and (2); (7) and (8) starting on the fourth fret and having respectively the minor and the major third. If this translation is correct, the eight modes (if we start from *D*) were:

1)   *D E F G A B♭ C*   or Phrygian conjunct

2)   *D E F♯ G A B C*   or Lydian conjunct

3)   *E F G A B♭ C D*   or Dorian conjunct

4)   *E F♯ G A B C D*   or Phrygian conjunct

5)   *F G A B♭ C D E F*   or Lydian disjunct

6)   *F♯ G A B C D E*   or Dorian conjunct

7)   *G A B♭ C D E F G* or Phrygian disjunct

8)   *G A B C D E F♯ G* or Lydian disjunct

With the countless possibilities of permutation and combination, so dear to Oriental scholars, an incredible number of modal scales was brought about. Interchanging the places of semitones and of major and minor whole tones; putting a tetrachord on top of a pentachord, or oftener vice versa; coupling 'divisive' and 'up-and-down' groups—all these operations provided scores and scores of scales which the Near and Middle East—notwithstanding the individual languages of its various countries—has known under common names such as '*Aǧam, or Nahawand, or Awāǧ*.

It would be a mistake, however, to imagine that the intellectual processes of combining, permutating, and coupling were actually responsible for the motley diversity of Mohammedan music; in other words, that lifeless theory created living melody. If the anatomic structures give such an impression, one look at the physiology of these scales proves the contrary: the note next in importance to the tonic—the *confinalis,* is now the fifth, now the octave, now the fourth, now even the third of the tonic. This clearly emphasizes the self-evident fact that things happened the other way around: melodies of very different equilibrium and structure, sung in Arabic-, Turkish-, and Persian-speaking countries long, long before the scholars constructed their theories, were pressed into a system of apparent consistency that singers and players had never followed before and were never to follow afterward.

At first sight, these nearly one hundred scales seem chaotic in the confusing swarm of thirds, major and minor whole tones, three-quarter tones, and major and minor semitones. But detached from their Oriental order and rearranged according to their structures, they easily fall into line.

A first group, following the up-and-down principle, is made of equal major whole tones of 204 Cents and minor semitones of 90 Cents. Such are 'Aǧam 'ašīrān—a true Lydian on F—and Nahawand—a true Hypodorian on G.

A second group, following the divisive principle, is made of two sizes of whole tones (204 and 182 Cents) and of major semitones (112 Cents). Such are:

> Rāst, a Lydian scale on G
> Nawā, a Phrygian scale on A
> Yakā, a Hypophrygian scale on D
> Ḥuseinī 'ašīrān, a Hyperphrygian scale on E
> 'Arad, a Hyperphrygian scale on A
> Awaǧ, a Mixolydian scale on F

A third group combines both principles in the same octave: 'Uššāq, Bayātī, and Iṣfahān have a divisive tetrachord below and an up-and-down pentachord above; the structure of Buslīq is the other way around.

A fourth group includes the typically "Oriental" interval 7:6 or 267 Cents, that is, the augmented second, like, for instance, the most popular of all Arabian scales:

$$\text{Ḥiǧāz:} \quad 119 \quad 267 \quad 112 \quad 204 \quad 90 \quad 204 \quad 204$$
$$G \quad A\flat \quad B \quad C \quad D \quad E\flat \quad F \quad G$$

This classification is confirmed by an interesting statement of Islamic writers: with all possibilities of permutating the Greek shades, they finally concede that only four were really accepted: (1) 204–204–90 Cents, (2) 204–182–112 Cents, (3) 119–267–112 Cents, (4) 151–267–80 Cents.

We know three of them: the first is Eratosthenes' diátonon; the second, Ptolemy's divisive diátonon sýntonon; the fourth, Ptolemy's "Gypsy scale" chrôma sýntonon. The two chromatic scales (3) and (4) are—again as in Greece—combined with diatonic tetrachords in order to form complete octaves.

One remarkable fact should not be passed over: majorlike scales with major thirds and sevenths are Persian, not Arabian. *Rāst,* "though generally known in musical circles, yet lives as a Persian art *maqām* only; the [Arabian] people just does not sing it." [2] In the same way, the Do-modes *Mahur, Mahurani, Sasgar,* and *Gihārkā* are Persian. The case of the Sol-mode *Nawā* is doubtful.

❋ ❋ ❋

THEORY AND PRACTICE HAVE SELDOM AGREED, despite all attempts of the former to catch and legalize the vagaries of singers and players. Performers have never been able or willing to reproduce the rigid norm even of simple systems with the faithfulness of acoustical devices. How can the Persian, Turkish, Egyptian singers be expected to have stood the clash of two opposed systems and to have carefully distinguished between two different whole tones and two different semitones with all their combinations? Less than other countries could the province of Islam escape the common destiny of all scales: temperament.

The earliest temperament appears in the practice of Eastern lutanists. Just as the Greeks generally violated the law in playing the lichanos, second-highest note in the tetrachord, Mohammedan players had their own ways with this very note. Both "the Persians" and Zalzal, famous lutanist of Bagdad (d. 791), tried to enlarge the semitone at the cost of the neighboring whole tone and assimilated them by taking a quarter tone from the whole tone and adding it to the semitone: 204–90–204 became 204–147–147 Cents.

The Reverend Father Dechevrens thought that this temperament was a compromise to facilitate the transition from conjunct to disjunct tetrachords. This may be correct (cf. page 130). But not all three-quarter tone scales can be thus explained, neither the *diátonon homalón,* described six hundred years earlier by Ptolemy, nor the many modern Islamic scales of this kind.

The critical point seems to have been the proper size of the minor whole tone. Differing from the major whole tone by only a ninth of a tone, it was exposed to being reduced in size until its difference was sufficiently obvious. But the complementing semitone increased at the same rate and drew so close in size to the lessened whole tone that assimilation became unavoidable.

[2] A. Z. Idelsohn, "Die Maqamen der arabischen Musik," in *Sammelbände der Internationalen Musikgesellschaft* XV (1913), p. 17.

The three-quarter tone has since conquered large parts of the Mohammedan world, but only as far as scales of the divisive type are concerned. The two scales *Aǵam* and *Nahawand,* on the contrary, both derived from the up-and-down principle and, having merely one size of whole tone, have not been subject to this temperament.

The final step in achieving three-quarter tones was taken at the end of the nineteenth century by the Syrian, Michael Meshāqa, and the Egyptian, Kamel el-Kholey, who divided the octave into twenty-four quarter tones, allotting four of them to the major whole tone, three to the three-quarter tone, and two to the (minor) semitone.

This modern system allows for smooth transition from scale to scale, but it is more or less a theoretical fiction. Equal temperament has been inevitable in a musical world established on harmony and on the fixed keyboards of organs and pianos; in purely melodic styles it is a mistake. Neither singers nor players have ever sacrificed the vital freedom of melody to any rigid system, be it quarter tones or three-quarter tones or even the simple ratios of natural scales.

2

MAQĀM

MAQĀM, originally the name of the stage on which the singers performed before the caliph, is the exact counterpart of the Indian *rāga:* a pattern of melody, based (though with a certain freedom) on one of the modal scales, and characterized by stereotype turns, by its mood, and even by its pitch—middle, high, low—which is reminiscent of the Greek classification of mesoid, netoid, and hypatoid melodies. The initial note, too, is important: maqām *Rāst* starts from the tonic and *Mahur,* from the fifth; *Rāst* is dignified in carriage and tempo and avoids grace notes, while *Mahur* is faster; *Bayāt* stresses the fourth, and *Sīkāh* the third below the tonic.

Again, the classification of these patterns has at least one trait common with the classification of *rāgas:* the twelve main and inter-Islamic maqamât are called 'fathers,' and the thirteen secondary, rather local, maqamât, 'sons.' *Rāst,* for example, is a father, and *Mahur,* starting on its fifth, his son.

Maqām is, like *rāga* in India, the essential quality of a melody; a piece not in keeping with the traditional and obligatory traits of its maqām is not considered 'musical.' So important is maqām that every *diwān,* or collection of poems, is arranged according to the maqamât in which they are to be composed and sung; first, the *Rāst* poems, then those in *Mahur,* and after them the others in various arrangements.[3]

❀   ❀   ❀

ETHOS was among the qualities of maqamât as it pertained to *rāgas* and *harmoniai,* though perhaps to a lesser degree. The maqamât evoked, said Al-Fārābī, "such emotions as satisfaction, ire, clemency, cruelty, fear, sadness, regret, and other passions."

It should be remembered that the Islamic Orient has always known musical styles in which attributions of this kind were not merely systematic connotations of a philosophical order, but actual physiological effects. We think above all of those persistent, monotonous melodies used to create

[3] Cf. *ibid.,* pp. 14, 15.

ecstasy and trance in the gatherings of dervishes and other religious fraternities, which are related to primeval shamanic rituals of Central Asia rather than to the practice of modern Islam.

No wonder that the maqâmât, as the official, systematized patterns of Islamic melody, were also believed to have healing force, though in a less refined spirit than they had had in Greece. *Rāst* healed the eyes; *'Irāq*, palpitation of the heart and dementia; *Iṣfahān*, colds; *Rahāwī*, headache; *Buzurk*, colic; *Zangūla*, heart diseases.

On the other hand, the Arabs—like the Hindus—have connected certain maqâmât with the hours of the day and the signs of the zodiac:

Maqām	Sign of the Zodiac	Time of the Day
Rāst	Ram	sunrise
Iṣfahān	Bull	
'Irāq	Twins	nine o'clock
Kūček (Zīr-efkend)	Crab	
Buzurk	Lion	
Hiǵāz	Virgin	midnight
Bū-silīk	Balance	afternoon
'Uššāq	Scorpion	sunset
Huseinī	Archer	night end
Zangūla	Capricorn	
Nawā	Water carrier	before night prayer
Rahāwī	Fishes	morning

As early a theoretician as Ibn-Sīnā (980–1037 A.D.) protests, however, in a quite modern spirit against "comparing musical ratios with the stars or with mental states, since this is the habit of those who do not keep the various sciences apart nor know what they directly or indirectly include."

[3]

RHYTHM

ISLAMIC RHYTHM stems from the meters of poetry. These meters had feet of three, four, or five syllables and—with a long syllable equaling two short ones—either five units of time, or even seven, as

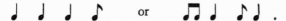

I am not going to bother the reader with the involved Arabian classification of meters light, light-heavy, heavy-light, heavy, conjunct, disjunct, equal and unequal, fast and slow, first and second. Only a few details are worth mentioning in this context.

The two main divisions of this classification are 'conjunct' and 'disjunct.' Conjunct meters, called *hazağ,* are uninterrupted series of equal beats without accents or any other grouping into superior units of two, three, or four beats; or series of actual feet, like iambs, trochees or otherwise. Such meter could easily be mistaken for our $\frac{3}{8}$ time; but it is definitely—as in India—a two-beat meter.

'Disjunct' meters, on the contrary, had an adequate rest before repetition set in, such as ♫ ↱ ♫ ↱ .
These, again, were subdivided into meters with equal and meters with unequal beats. All this was lifeless. It took to pieces the undecomposable rhythms of Islamic music in their fanciful and almost irrational configurations; it retied to verse meters instrumental rhythms that had broken loose from the despotism of poetry.

The antipoetic patterns, which the Arabs call *īqāʿāt,* are said to have been introduced into Arabian music in the seventh century A.D. by the first male professional musician in Islam, Ṭuwais. His lifetime coincided with the end of the Persian dynasty of the Seleucides, to which Persian tradition has attributed the elaboration of rhythm.[4] Persia might well have given the new principle to Arabia; but it is an open question how much she herself in turn was under Indian influence.

❊   ❊   ❊

[4] Cl. Huart, "La Musique persane," in *Lavignac, Encyclopédie de la Musique* I v 5, p. 3065.

THE RHYTHMIC PATTERNS appear in all melodies, whether vocal or instrumental, but particularly in the drum parts, which are almost as obligatory in Islamic music as they are in Indian music.

Accents are given in timbre rather than in force. The Islamic drummer knows muffled beats, called *dum,* and clear beats, *tak;* less muffled beats, *dim,* and less clear beats, *tīk.* When two little kettledrums are used, the *dum* skin is wetted, and the *tak* skin, heated; with one frame drum, *dum* is struck on the skin, and *tak,* on the hoop. If the player has no drum, he strikes *dum* with the closed hand on the right knee, and *tak,* with the open hand on the left knee. The clear timbre is often reserved for the actual beats of a pattern, and the muffled timbre for intercalated beats that decompose longer beats into their units. The simple pattern short-long, for example, would be rendered by two clear beats and one muffled beat to subdivide the long member.

The Arabian and the Indian patterns are doubtless related. They share one vital quality: the combining of meter and time; and both materialize essentially on drums.

But there are also differences. Arabian patterns are simpler. They scarcely exceed four units per member, and members which by exception have seven units are said to belong to "very old" and "Indian" patterns. In India, a certain piece is composed to a certain *tāla,* which the accompaniment keeps just as strictly as the melody does. Arabian practice is much freer. The drummer would accompany in a quite different pattern with counteraccents; indeed, he would with two or three independent drums act against the melody in the intricate openwork of an actual polyrhythm.

POLYPHONY

POLYPHONY is not essential in Islamic music. It exists, however, in the three forms of heterophony, drone, and occasional consonance.

Heterophony was less developed than in East Asia and in India. But it has been unavoidable in those small ensembles that we somewhat grandiloquently call orchestras: a singer, a flute, a plucked zither, a lute, a drum, and sometimes a fiddle.

Drones are mostly used in the *taqsīm*, the improvised prelude of solo instruments before the ensemble sets in. The zither *qānūn* frequently supports the *taqsīm* of the flute or the fiddle with the rapid, mandolinlike to and fro of the plectron on one string. In bands, the larger oboe plays a pedal while the smaller oboe performs its improvisation; or the player of the double clarinet *arghūl* accompanies himself on its dronepipe.

Ostinato basses spring up when the persistent drone dissolves into the so-called *waḥda:* a series of eight quarter beats which, to mark the beginning of a period, start with a silent eighth and subsequently syncopate. Lute and zither players often play such a *waḥda* on several notes instead of one drone note and thus perform obstinate ground basses.[5]

Consonances have a definite, though modest, place in the classical theory. Ibn-Sīnā (980–1037) defines a certain Arabic term, *tarkīb,* as "an ornament in which two consonant notes mingle in the same stroke. The noblest consonances are large intervals, and among these, the octave and the fourth are the best." This description appears in the section on ornaments: to Ibn-Sīnā, and probably to the Islamic world in general, consonance was not a harmonic function in the Western sense, but a simultaneous *appoggiatura.*

---

[5] Alfred Berner, *Studien zur arabischen Musik,* Leipzig, 1937, pp. 43–50.

FORM

STRUCTURES, in Islamic music, are of two kinds: simple folk melodies and elaborate art forms. Folk melodies have a small range and consist either of symmetrical periods in plain two-beat rhythms or of simple, endlessly repeated phrases of a declamatory and often richly ornamented character.

All art forms, on the contrary, rest on the contrast of free and strict movements. Most pieces, both vocal and instrumental, begin with a kind of cadenza, called *taqsīm* in Egypt. This is a free introduction, without a definite rhythm and, when sung, without words, in which the performers after one another improvise on the melodic pattern of the maqām and display to the best of their ability the peculiarities of their instruments and of their personal skill and inspiration, while the zither or the lute unobtrusively accompany with a drone or a short *ostinato*. Then the other instruments join in to start the strict movement which would have one of a number of similar forms as, for example, an instrumental prelude, a vocal strophe of eight lines, an instrumental strophe, and again a vocal strophe, all of exactly the same structure and in the same maqām and rhythm.

Instrumental ensembles without voices have a form of their own, the Turkish *peşrev,* which is also preceded by a *taqsīm* of every melodic instrument and itself consists of from two to six movements, each followed by a ritornello of the same structure.

I suggested in my *History of Musical Instruments* that the typically Oriental contrast of *taqsīm* and *peşrev* may already be alluded to in the strange description of King Nebuchadrezzar's orchestra in the Book of Daniel: "O peoples, nations, and languages, that at what time ye hear the sound of the horn, the pipe, the lyre, the horizontal and the vertical harp, and [then] the playing together [not bagpipe] of all kinds of instruments, ye fall down and worship the golden image that Nebuchadrezzar the king hath set up; and whoso falleth not down and worshippeth shall the same hour be cast into the midst of a burning fiery furnace." [6]

❊   ❊   ❊

[6] Dan. 3:5, 7, 10, 15. Curt Sachs, *The History of Musical Instruments, op. cit.,* pp. 83–5.

THE NŪBA is the largest cyclic form in Oriental music. The name appears for the first time in the tenth century A.D. to denote a company of musicians [7] and later is transferred to the particular form of composition developed in medieval Granada while it was under Mohammedan rule. There, it was abandoned after the Christian reconquest; but it has been preserved in Morocco and Algeria.

The *nūba* may best be described as a cantata in nine parts of the same tonality. The first, *dāïra* or "circle," presents a singer's prelude without percussion instruments, comparable to the *taqsīm* and the Indian *ālāp;* it is vocalized on a text now incomprehensible. The second movement is an instrumental prelude; the third, an instrumental symphony; the movements four, five, and six are three sets of songs, each set following a different form; after another instrumental symphony, the eighth movement is again a set of songs, and a single song, as the ninth movement, ends the cantata.

Under the fresh impression of one of the eleven *nūbas* still performed in Morocco, the author once wrote:

I still see them sitting on the floor in a long row with one or two players seated at right angles at either end: the ten or twelve men, slender, thoroughbred, with aquiline noses and short black beards, in white burnuses and white turbans and before them, taken off, the yellow slippers. I still hear the cracking sound of lute strings under the beat of the quill plectron, the trenchant melody that the short bows drew from tiny fiddles, and the boyish falsetto of the rapt old singer in the corner. How different was the incorporeal limpidity of this ensemble from the viscid sound of Western orchestras!

Why does this music captivate us so much more than any other Oriental style? Things foreign can touch us only if under the unwonted surface we sense familiar traits. Do we recognize the melody, the powerful impetus of the Magnificat which over and over again appears throughout the endless work? There is more than that. The longer we listen, the more distinctly we feel that this is the last living witness of that great music which half a millennium ago was played in Andalusia. The seven or eight hundred years of Moorish domination in Spain do not only mean the acme of Islamic civilization, which could not fail to set its seal on the medieval culture of Europe. The fateful war and interbreeding of the races also shaped the Mohammedan world, and not least its music. If we did not know it before, the singers and players of the Moroccan sultan, with their music so different from other Arabian music, have impressively taught us this fact. Future music history will find a remunerative task in examining this intersection. For to our stock of medieval notations, dead, incomplete, and difficult to interpret, the Moroccans contribute actual sound and unlost tradition. [8]

[7] Henry George Farmer, *A History of Arabian Music, op. cit.,* p. 153.
[8] Free translation from Curt Sachs, "Die Marokkaner," in *Zeitschrift für Vergleichende Musikwissenschaft* I (1933), pp. 17–18.

EUROPE AND THE ROAD
TO MAJOR AND MINOR

ROMAN EAR WITNESSES were not exactly appreciative of the musical achievements in barbarian countries—not even Tacitus, who for pedagogical reasons liked to stress the bright side of everything German. His book *Germania* did not mention music at all, excepting the *barritus* or battle song, in which, he said, the raucous sound was increased by singing against the shields and the harmony of gallant hearts mattered more than the harmony of voices.

Three hundred years after Tacitus, Ammianus Marcellinus (d. c. 400 A.D.) described the same *barritus* in his History of Rome 16:12; it began with a soft hum and grew stronger and stronger until at last it thundered like waves that broke on the rocks.

Other Germanic songs reminded Emperor Julian the Apostate of the shrieks of birds; as late as about 600 A.D. Bishop Venantius Fortunatus disparagingly asserted that the Burgundians and the Franconians were not able to tell the cackling of geese from swan song; and another two hundred years later, in Charlemagne's time, Roman church singers protested against the "bestial" song of the Franconians who with an artless, barbaric voice crushed the melodies in their throats (*naturali voce barbarica frangentes in gutture voces*).[1]

A deep gulf separated Greco-Roman and Oriental from extraclassical music in Europe.

❋   ❋   ❋

How DEEP this gulf was has been brought out in the author's recent paper on *The Road to Major*,[2] of which—with the editor's kind permission—the following section (with its musical examples) is an abridgment.

Ancient Europe was illiterate and thus unable to leave any musical document. When in the later Middle Ages it had achieved literacy, the evidence dealt exclusively with ecclesiastic music. The old jugglers and minstrels did not care about notating melodies. They saw no point in divulging what they knew; on the contrary, they would not have been willing to make available to everyone the repertoire by which they got their living. The monks, on the other hand, knew how to write and loved to handle the

---

[1] "Vita Caroli Magni per Monachum Egolismensem," in Du Chesne, *SS. Hist. Franc.* II, 75.
[2] Curt Sachs, "The Road to Major," in *The Musical Quarterly* XXIX (1943).

quill. Eagerly bent on devising adequate means of notation, they did their best to keep alive the music sung *in gloriam Dei*. But they were no more interested than the jugglers in preserving secular music.

Music historians, therefore, have entered Europe by the church door. They have received their information from monks and learned to use, and abuse, Greek conceptions in analyzing the melodies of the Western Church.

As a fatal consequence, they have tested all archaic melodies with a modal gauge, whether folk tunes still in use or 'art music' written down in the Middle Ages. Icelandic *tvisöngvar* and Corsican *voceri,* Provençal *cansos* and Spanish *cantigas* have indiscriminately been called Dorian or Phrygian or Lydian and thus likened to Gregorian melodies.

But as early an authority as Johannes de Grocheo (c. 1300) had warned his readers against looking for church modes in secular music: *"Non enim per tonum cognoscimus cantum vulgarem."* Most serious scholars have indeed had misgivings and have conceded that many melodies cannot be properly classified.

Still, a correct classification is possible if only we get rid of our modal obsession and realize that a division into a tetrachord and a pentachord is not the only melodic pattern in the world.

Aware of the motley diversity of musical styles that comparative musicology conveys to its students, the author has tried to look at medieval music with an unbiased mind. As a result, he has found that—regardless of race and region—there has been an all-embracing European style, neither modal nor pentatonic, but very primitive, though ready in due time to procreate the marvels of Western music.

This style, utterly different from Oriental styles, ignores the interval of the fourth, indeed the octave itself. Its melodies, rather, fall into patterns of thirds, as do many melodies of North American Indians, Melanesians, and Africans, especially African Pygmies and their Asiatic cousins. From Iceland to the Balkan States, from Sweden to Spain, they consist of single thirds, but mostly they jump to another third and yet another; there are melodies of no less than five such thirds of alternately major and minor size, each two of which form a perfect fifth. These thirds are sometimes open, sometimes filled by a note of minor importance. A few examples follow:

Ex. 86: one third, $b\flat$-g

Ex. 87: two thirds, *d-b♭-g*

Ex. 88: three thirds, *f♯-d-b-g*

Ex. 89. SWEDEN: four thirds, *f♯-d-b-g-e*

Ex. 90: five thirds, *d-b-g-e-c-a*

The thirds, above all the triple third, indicate the structure of an overwhelmingly great number of those medieval melodies which, in Heinrich Besseler's words, show that "strange tonal vagueness that admits an interpretation both as either Dorian or Lydian and as a melodic major."

Vagueness disappears once these melodies are gauged by their own standard.

The thirds also explain the famous cadence by the minor third (instead of the semitone) below the final that music history has erroneously called after the Italian master Francesco Landini, the blind organist at the cathedral in Florence.

❋   ❋
❋

GREGORIAN CHANT, the traditional music of the Roman Catholic Church, which again and again provides examples of third melodies, has had a somewhat contradictory position in music history. Most books suggest, though with reserve if not reluctance, that the national styles of Europe might have helped in shaping the melodies of the Church. Still, these hints are rare and vague, and the general impression that the reader is expected to form is rather that inversely the Gregorian chant has left its imprint on most national styles. How could they have reasoned the other way around, with all the authority of church music, with its elaborate theory and apparent unity of style, as against the seemingly illiterate and motley, indeed amorphous, mass of secular music?

The question should be re-examined in the light of our new knowledge of the European thirds.

After all, the composers of so-called Gregorian melodies were not born in church. They had passed at least their early childhood in secular homes and had been brought up on the songs of their mothers, of playmates, of street singers. They had been English, French, German boys before they entered Catholic monasteries; and even cloistering did not separate them from the musical world outside. A strict borderline between ecclesiastic and secular music is possible only where an old, traditional stock of melodies is kept alive without contemporary additions; and this was not the case with Gregorian chant.

The Orient doubtless contributed the first melodies. It imposed the general mood and also the performing style. But melodic invention itself has been free—and Western.

The 'Oriental style,' supposed to be at the basis of Gregorian chant, is the style of Oriental-Jewish, of Syrian-Christian, of Coptic-Egyptian cantillation. Definitely diatonic, it has almost exclusively the fourth as its structural interval; it is tetrachordal. Two examples might suffice, one from the Babylonian Synagogue and one from the Coptic Church:

Ex. 91

Ex. 92

And it often has the subsemitone, or leading note, that the earlier Gregorian chant, allegedly Oriental, so carefully avoided.

Ex. 93

While the Gregorian chant has very little connection with the Orient, it easily provides examples for all phases of medieval evolution in the West. Our survey has referred to melodies of the church just as it has referred to folk and written secular songs.

The so-called church modes should not deceive our judgment. In their classical form, order, and terminology, the system of eight dovetailed octaves, four of them (the odd-numbered ones) authentic and four (the even-numbered ones) plagal, they certainly depend on Greek and Oriental prototypes:

AUTHENTIC	PLAGAL	
First		DEFGA/ABCD
	Second	ABCD/DEFGA
Third		EFGAB/BCDE
	Fourth	BCDE/EFGAB
Fifth		FGABC/CDEF
	Sixth	CDEF/FGABC
Seventh		GABCD/DEFG
	Eighth	DEFG/GABCD

But this system was established as late as the tenth century—four hundred years after St. Gregory's redaction of the church music. Moreover, it is sometimes very hard to find these fifth-fourth structures in the melodies themselves. The fifths of the authentic modes are obvious enough, to be sure. But the fourths of the plagal modes and also the fourths on top of the authentic modes are not so clear; about half of the melodies ascribed to the Second Mode do not even reach the finalis *D*. Many attributions to one of the eight modes are so hard to comprehend that a real connection *via naturae* seems more than doubtful. Why, for instance, is the hymn *Immense Caeli Conditor* classified under the First Mode? Is not the simple melody a clear-cut *F* major with *F* as the tonic and *C* as the dominant?

Ex. 94

Other systems of a different cast contradicted and partly antedated the array of eight church modes. Monks had, as early as the ninth century, devised a notation in which the letters of the alphabet from *A* to *G* represented a *C*-major scale.[3] It was only later that it was shifted in order to start from the modern note *A*, which was the lowest note of the lowest Church mode. In the eleventh century, Guido d'Arezzo based melody—every melody, including those of the Gregorian chant—on three hexachords, starting from three different notes, *C, F,* and *G*. All of these had the same structure T T s T T—that is, tone, tone, semitone, tone, tone—and Guido adopted the same set of names for the six notes of the hexachord, regardless of the particular hexachord—*ut re mi fa sol la*. These three basic scales were definitely majorlike and averse to most Gregorian chants which actually demanded a continual veering from hexachord to hexachord, a so-called mutation.

Guido d'Arezzo, the greatest theoretician of the eleventh century, has been credited also with devising the perfect staff notation that we have used to this day, though we have added a fifth line. The original four lines and the three spaces in between them housed seven consecutive notes of the diatonic scale: the first, third, fifth, and seventh notes were privileged with places on the lines, while the second, fourth, and sixth were squeezed into the intermediate spaces. The abnormal consequence—so hard to grasp when you try to learn music—is that, of two notes an octave apart, which carry the same name, one is allowed to perch on a line, and the other is not. And the same is true of two notes a fourth apart.

The European staff notation is definitely in favor of chains of thirds: according to the key prescribed, it reads either *D e F g A b C* or *F g A b C d E* or *A b C d E f G*.

Is this not a true mirror of the medieval conception of music?

❋   ❋   ❋

A SINGLE CHAIN as the exclusive element of structure is tolerable in the fluent, 'endless' melody of true Gregorian cantillation. It is an ideal trellis to support the smoothly creeping compound neumes and keep them from lawlessness.

It is a lifeless principle, on the contrary, where syllabic and symmetrical melodies depend on a continual pendulating between tension and relaxation—not only from syllable to syllable, but also from phrase to phrase.

[3] Cf. Gustave Reese, *op. cit.,* p. 135 f.

In such symmetrical forms, the infixes, by nature unstressed and rather transitional, exchange parts with the structural thirds in all phases of relaxation: they take the stress and degrade the structural thirds. In doing this, they form a chain of thirds in their own right, indeed a counterchain.

Almost all melodies outside the church, and many inside it, actually consist of a chain and counterchain dovetailed. In the following dance of the thirteenth century, the two chains fitted together are $\begin{smallmatrix} F & A & C: \\ C & E & G \end{smallmatrix}$

Ex. 95

Dance, 13ª c. (after Johannes Wolf)

Dovetailed chains of thirds were certainly richer than single chains, since they allowed for pendulating between tension and relaxation. Nevertheless, they were far from being perfect organisms; the two chains existed side by side rather than as functional parts of one greater unit.

From the time of our earliest evidence, however, that is, from the tenth century on, the unpremeditated piling up of thirds has been questioned. A strong trend toward actual integration acted upon the chains and slowly succeeded in transforming them. The result was what we call major and minor today.

❊   ❊   ❊

A NATIONAL CLAIM to major for the Germanic race was made by Oskar Fleischer at the end of the last century. Referring to him, the Dane, Angul Hammerich, emphasized that Icelandic folksongs represented the *urtypus* of that primeval major scale "which has been stated to be the national scale of the Germano-Gothic peoples." His particular example is poor and far from being major. The other Icelandic songs printed in Hammerich's paper are even less to the point; he himself calls them Dorian or Phrygian or Lydian.

National and racial claims in general have, in our day, the advantage that few students care about verifying them. Since it is equally comfortable to pride oneself on the alleged deeds of one's forefathers, and dangerous to question them, most music historians, otherwise ready to fight indefatigably for a single sharp or flat in some manuscript or print, have bowed to the slogan and let it pass without examination—and without proof.

The origin of major cannot be established through noisy slogans, but only through sober analysis. The earliest melodies with all or most of the features of major must be parsed and tested.

These features include a skeleton consisting of an octave made up of a perfect fifth and a perfect fourth; the other intervals, reckoned from the tonic, are major; and a seventh degree acts as a leading note.

Melodies with most of the features of major first occur in the tenth century. The earliest evidence, an Italian (probably) love song in Latin, needs only the subsemitone and the octave to be a perfect major melody:

Ex. 96

But official theory rejected the subsemitone, and although it praised the subfinal as *emmelés* or 'well-sounding' as long as it was a whole tone from the final, it avoided the lower neighboring note in the Fifth Mode, where it would be a subsemitone: *E-F*.

Still, at least from the eleventh century on, even the church yielded to the growing tendency to raise the *tuba* (or note of recitation) from *B* to *C*, which replaced the previous subtonal inflection *B-A* by the subsemitonal inflection *C-B*.

Ex. 97

Correspondingly, secular and semisecular melodies show the subsemitone as early as the eleventh century:

Ex. 98

This and similar melodies were created in the same century in which Guido d'Arezzo so violently opposed the subsemitone; it must have become dangerous.

Singers abandoned the consistent perfection of the fifth in the counter-chains and admitted tritones several centuries before the monastic theorists eventually took cognizance of the procedure in the thirteenth century. The supercilious names given the new style—*musica ficta* and *musica falsa* —show how reluctant this cognizance was. The theorists could not foresee that a hundred years later the Frenchman, Philippe de Vitri, would disown them by professing that actually the music they had called "false" was the only true music.

The seventh, so important in triple and quadruple chains of thirds, had to yield to the octave: all over the world the octave has imposed its supremacy on more rudimentary scales when music has evolved to a certain stage—in the Far East as well as in ancient Greece.

In medieval music, the conflict is often obvious; the seventh has kept its accent, but the octave follows immediately. The rondeau from the *Roman de la Rose* may serve as an illustration:

Ex. 99

England (after Bukofzer)

Further examples are given in my paper in the *Musical Quarterly* mentioned earlier.

The final preference given to the octave changed the skeleton *CEGB* into *CEGC*, and the counterchain shifted to *DGB*, since the subsemitone had become obligatory: the dominant *G* became the 'joint' of the two sets.

In an analogous development, *DFAC* became *DFAD*, with *B* and *C♯* in ascending, and *B♭* and *C* in descending—in strict accordance with *musica ficta*. The ambiguous scale resulting was what today is called minor.

The power of the octave worked downward also. The *A* below *C* in the Landini sixth, lying below the octave, could not avoid the influence of the dominant *G* and became a *G* itself.

❀   ❀   ❀

THE GROWTH of major and minor seems to have been indigenous: the basic principle of chains of thirds, also known from other continents, was all-

European, regardless of race and region, and the development of chains of thirds into major and minor patterns was just as all-European. A German or Germanic origin is out of the question, since the earliest examples are French.

Indeed, just the opposite is true: Germany accepted the major and minor scales comparatively late and with reluctance. She found the subsemitone and leading notes in general so little to her liking that German versions of the Gregorian chant substituted a leap of a minor third for progressions of a whole or semitone in the Roman original.

The logical development from all-European principles makes the hypothesis of an Asiatic descent for major and minor almost superfluous. It is nevertheless important to state that Asia, too, shows evolution toward major and majorlike scales.

It may be useful in this connection to give some attention to the so-called Ugro-Finnish peoples. Anthropologically, they are Mongolian; linguistically, they are related to Hungarians and Finns. Scattered in small remnants over parts of Eastern Russia and Western Siberia, they live in a rather primitive state of civilization.

Owing to A. O. Väisänen's magnificent publication, we know the music of the Voguls and the Ostyaks better than any other Ugro-Finnish music. These two peoples, about twenty-five thousand individuals, live in Northwestern Siberia on the Ob and the Irtysh and make their living as fishermen and hunters.

The Voguls, like the Europeans, build most of their melodies on thirds or chains of thirds. Some mythological songs have kept the original single third, notwithstanding occasional deviations. Examples are in my paper. The leading note appears at a very early stage, in simple three-tone melodies.

Other Ugro-Finnish peoples show similar tendencies. The five thousand Votyaks in the northeast of European Russia often sing in single and double thirds, but never use the leading note. The Syrianes, their northern neighbors (not the Syrians), start from single thirds and achieve major pentachords and even full major octaves. The Mordwins have pentatonic scales of five, six, or seven notes; but in a lower stratum, in "old-pagan" melodies of only three or four notes, they use the leading note:

Ex. 100

Mordwines (after Lach)

Some non-Ugro-Finnish peoples deserve special mention also. The Turko-Tataric Kirghizes, whose habitat extends all across Asia from European Russia to the borders of China, have a surprising number of melodies in major with all the characteristics required, including the leading note.

It is not yet possible to give a comprehensive survey of structures in thirds and major-minor patterns outside Europe. There are many thousands of square miles that have not yet been musically explored. But it is important to have found in West and Central Asia the nearest relatives of the European thirds, and thus to have indicated a possible link between Europe and the earliest Asiatic seats of the North American Indians, who share with Europe the third and chains of thirds as structural elements.

※　※　※

Major in a wider sense, however, has not necessarily depended upon structures of thirds. The pentatonic so-called Chinese scale *CDE GA* was given two *pièns, F♯* and *B*, that actually were double leading notes in the sense of European music in the fourteenth century—two thousand years later. And in the sixth century A.D., a true major scale without the tritone *C-F♯* was very much admired and to a certain extent introduced. Though by no means generally accepted, it represented the latest development in China.

Of the three Indian *grāmas*, only *sa-grāma* has survived, which from an original D-mode has been converted into a C-mode and practically coincides with the major scale.

In ancient Greece, the Dorian mode, outstanding in earlier antiquity, later yielded to the Lydian mode, which in its scale arrangement coincided with major.

A similar process is running its course in modern Morocco. The tritonic maqām *Ṣīkā,* which uses a *B* scale without signature, is more and more frequently given a perfect fifth by sharpening the note *F;* and the *F* maqām *Māya,* tritonic as well, is, by a more and more general flattening of its suggested fourth *B,* well on its way to *F* major.

The common development toward majorlike and minorlike melodies from systems as different as East Asiatic pentatonicism, Indo-Islamic and Greco-Roman modes, and European and Ugro-Finnish thirds, suggests that there may be some immanent force at work, a force embracing all mankind rather than merely a race or region.

The development had nothing to do with sentiment. And that missionary who once wrote that African Negroes had no songs in major, since only believers in the true God were blessed with its cheerfulness, was certainly well meaning but not exactly enlightening. The explanation lies elsewhere.

Most higher civilizations have tended to evolve, in all their arts, from a mere coexistence of parts to an actual integration, in which the elements are organically related to one another and to the whole. Such evolution has led to the sophisticated balance that the Greeks achieved in the dualism of thetic and dynamic centers, and the Hindus in the intricate relationship of starters, finals, tonics, dominants, and 'prevalent' notes that characterize their *rāgas*. In systems established on the third and the fifth, the classical stage of integration and perfect balance between static and dynamic forces is the major-minor tonality with its dominant function and the significance of the tonic to which the leading note inevitably leads.

The contrast between the tetrachordal patterns of Hindus and Greeks on the one hand and the third-fifth patterns of Europe on the other hand is at bottom the conflict between vocal and instrumental styles. An actually vocal style originates where emotion results in singing, where mirth and affliction, hope and longing burst into melody. Such melody organizes mostly in descending fourths; the singer, under an irresistible stress, begins at the top of his voice and range and comes down as his vocal chords slacken.

Players behave differently. A piper's scale is brought forth by opening the fingerholes hole by hole or by stopping a string fret by fret; it is ascending, and organized in fifths and thirds, indeed, in sevenths. It is certainly not accidental that such chains occur in those few archaic civilizations in which instruments have a normative role. There are excellent illustrations from the Solomon Islands (pieces for panpipes) or in the following (pentatonic, thirdless) composition for three large mouth organs from Laos:

Ex. 101

Laos (after Humbert-Lavergne)

The theories of Chinese and Indian music acknowledge the contrast in trend by juxtaposing descending scales for voices and ascending scales for instruments. In all Oriental civilizations, however, instrumental music has steadily gained, and since systems are after all much more meaningful in instrumental music with its inevitable interest in correct tuning than in the relative vagueness of vocal music, instrumental scales have gained the ascendancy over vocal scales.

This process has been abbreviated in countries in which emotion does not often result in singing. Such countries sing; but their melodies are born from words and either merely convey poetry or else intensify it, and, beautiful as they may be, they are basically different from those melodies that follow purely vocal impulses. This deficiency—from a singer's point of view—implies greater independence from vocal laws and less resistance to the normative power of instrumental music. As a consequence, the physiologically conditioned fourth and the downward trend scarcely ever appear.

Europe, with the exception of its Mediterranean region, has been a typical nonsingers' land.

A thousand bits of evidence confirm the leadership of its instruments. The ancient texts of Scandinavia never mention them as the source of a mere accompaniment; singing and playing existed side by side. Every well-bred Anglo-Saxon was expected to play and own a *hearp*. The instrument was his by an unrestrained right of possession, and not even a creditor was allowed to sequestrate it. All miraculous effects that in India, for example, were attributed to the singing of certain *maqamât*, emanated in the north from instruments. Pirates, an Irish legend tells us, had stolen the druid Daghda's *cruit*. Daghda hunted them up, found the instrument suspended from the wall, and called it back. It obeyed with such force that it killed nine men before reaching its rightful owner. Daghda then took it in his arms and played three melodies; the first made the women cry; when he played the second, men and women burst into laughter; but the last piece lulled them all to sleep, and he safely stole away.

The later history of European music confirms the innate and never abandoned preference given to instruments. The climax of this preference is seen in the evolution of an all-dominating orchestra since the middle of the eighteenth century and the role of this orchestra in the opera, so entirely un-Oriental and antivocal, in which often three or fourscore instruments drown the singer's voice.

Singing, in contrast, has had a minor position. It has, in the main, been a vehicle for words, and wherever melismatic effusions have been attempted

—as in the Gregorian Alleluia and in the *organa*—native reaction has rapidly solidified them into syllabic melodies with new texts. Singing in a narrower sense, as a self-sufficient art, has always been imported from the Mediterranean; *Frisia non cantat,* says a proverb, and Frederick the Great retracted his impatient remark that he preferred a neighing mare to a German singer only when he realized that Miss Schmeling sang "like an Italian."

The king's verdict is too reminiscent of ancient Roman judgments upon German and Frankish singing for us to overlook the eternal antithesis between the playing north and the singing south.

❊   ❊   ❊

THE CONTRAST between vocal and instrumental styles may well have been decisive in the fundamental contrast between the melodic and harmonic concepts. A survey of the music of ancient Greece and the Orient shows very distinctly that the need for harmony develops with instruments more easily than with voices. Everywhere, in China, Japan, India, the Middle East, and Hellas, attempts at chordal formations are bound up with instruments, whether in accompaniment or in purely instrumental music. Parallel singing in intervals of various kinds seems to be an exception. Actually, it confirms the rule, since it has never occurred in the singing of mature, truly vocal melodies. The delicate *rāgas* of the Hindus as well as the *maqamât* of the Middle East pulse with life in their sensitive and untrammeled lines and do not stand harmony any more than a perfect engraving would stand coloring. And just as, inversely, good painting is incompatible with self-sufficient drawing, polyphony subordinates the line of melody to its harmonic needs.

In Europe, which had no self-sufficient singing in the sense of Indian and Arabian melody, the chances for the development of harmony were good. Conditions were similar to the situation in the Far East. There, too, vocal melody was merely a vehicle for conveying words and never became autonomous; inversely, instrumental music has been to the fore and, just as in Europe, has resulted in colorful orchestras that have never played in unison.

There is certainly more than one reason, nevertheless, why the Far East did not, and Europe did, achieve actual harmony and counterpoint. There is the essential contrast of their musical genera. The static character of Far Eastern pentatonicism is definitely antiharmonic, though it favors consonance. Europe, on the contrary, had harmony latent in the triads of its chains; and the contrasting triads of its dovetailed double chains anticipate the functional oscillation on which real harmony is based. The final development of major and minor in their balance of statics and dynamics facilitated this oscillation, indeed made it inevitable.

Even in Europe, singing and harmony are inversely related. The instrumental center of the Continent has brought harmony to the peak of meaningful complication; the singing south gives it an accessory role and reduces it to a minimum of simplicity.

This is certainly not the whole truth. The secret forces far behind the musical scene are still invisible. But it may be more than a coincidence that, at exactly the same time as Europe attained the third dimension in music that harmony represents, its painters conquered the third dimension in space by means of perspective.

❋   ❋   ❋

EUROPEAN POLYPHONY AND HARMONY in their earlier phases I shall not describe or discuss. A voluminous monograph on this subject was recently published by Dr. Marius Schneider, and any rediscussion would endanger the balance of this book.[4]

Instead, we end this section with a short discussion of European rhythm. The problem is hard. Neither the neumes nor the plain-song notation of the Middle Ages indicates time values, and even the mensural notation of the twelfth and thirteenth centuries is by no means beyond doubt. Nor is folksong rhythmically reliable; the development of language and also the change in style of 'official' music must to a certain degree have influenced both beat and meter. Still, a few general conclusions may be reached by other means.

In antiquity, the Continent had no drums (except for the occasional use of Semitic frame drums in Greece and the Roman Empire). Medieval drums, imported from the Western Orient, were exclusively struck with sticks, never with the bare hands. Wherever such is the case, drumming consists in mere time beating without any leaning to metrical patterns. This holds true of modern practice, in both Europe and the Far East; but not even the earliest book in which percussion is written down, Thoinot Arbeau's treatise on the dance (*Orchésographie*, 1588), has the slightest trace of metrical conception beyond the simple dactyls in which a drummer likes to subdivide his quarter notes.

[4] Marius Schneider, *Geschichte der Mehrstimmigkeit*, 3 vols., Berlin, 1934.

Meter itself consisted in the contrast of accented and unaccented syllables; no European language, including later Latin, had the 'quantitative meter' based on the contrast of long and short syllables.

The antiquantitative disposition of European music is particularly evident when humanist circles of the fifteenth and sixteenth centuries make experiments—and nothing but experiments—in metrical writing. The most outstanding examples, the German *Melopoiae secundum naturam et tempora syllabarum et pedum* (Augsburg, 1507), a product of the learned society around Conrad Celtes, and the French *Pseaumes en vers mezvrez,* a posthumous work of Claude Lejeune inspired by Baif's *Académie de Poésie et de Musique,* show how artificial, indeed un-European, these experiments were.

One might object that the Middle Ages expressly established metrical *modi* to rule musical rhythm. First described in the treatise *Discantus positio vulgaris* (c. 1230-40), they appear as six meters: the first, trochee: long-short; the second, iamb: short-long; the third, dactyl: long-short-short; the fourth, anapaest: short-short-long. A fifth mode contracted all short values into lengths, and a sixth mode dissolved all long values into shorts.

No doubt, this means meter. But whoever knows actual poetico-musical meter in India and Greece must see that the *modi* are somehow different: instead of following the all-metrical distinction of two breves equaling one *longa,* they behave almost antimetrically: the dactyl takes the form three plus one plus two beats, and the anapaest, one plus two plus three; the long syllable is by no means twice as long as the short one, while there are two different shorts, one being twice as long as the other.

This complication was a consequence of a thirteenth-century trend to impose three-beat rhythms on the polyphonic music of the church. But triple time collided with the obvious duple time of dactyls and anapaests and needed special adaptation. Thus the *modi* were evidently a recipe to fit the main meters of poetry into an antimetrical principle.

Modern music historians have unduly exaggerated the binding force of these *modi* and extended it to practically all secular compositions (which in the Middle Ages were written down in plain-song notation without time values), whether the melodies had been composed in the fourteenth century or in the tenth—three hundred years before the *modi* made their first appearance, whether in their probable homeland France or in remote Denmark. Without discrimination, the briskest and straightest melodies were transcribed in a tedious, limping triple time.

This has been a violation of common sense in music and of scientific method. But it also has been a blind neglect of the only contemporary source at hand. For we have the unmistakable statement by the outstanding theorist around 1300, Johannes de Grocheo, that *musica mensurata* comprised exclusively the three polyphonic forms—motets, organa, and hoquets—but neither Gregorian chant *nor any monophonic secular music.*

Fortunately, a certain reaction against triple-time fanaticism has set in.

But would duple time be correct? There is not one allusion to duple time or triple time in Grocheo's long treatise, no reference to beat, no hint of accents. The only enlightening passage is a discussion as to whether non-modal music should be described as immeasurable or as not so precisely measurable, even when it was sung *totaliter ad libitum.*

Whatever exact translation we give the term *mensura,* there is hardly a doubt left that the medieval performer of secular melodies was rhythmically free. Rhythm was accessory just as the accompaniment was accessory. Played for a marching dance, a piece would assume duple time; for a fast-leaping dance, triple time. Its singer, independent from the dancers' needs, was no more interested in any consistent time pattern than the singer of Gregorian melodies. Such freedom, and nothing else, would account for the awkward fact that composers wrote all monophonic music in the vague signs of plain chant, although they possessed in the mensural notation a perfect means of expressing time in general as well as the length of each individual note.

The reason why we are so late in understanding essential features of the past is, once more, our education on the piano and the staff-lined music sheet. Once more, we have tried to squeeze into bars and staves what was created without keyboards and writing pens. Thus, the last section of this book ends as the first section begins: with the statement that music as a whole, in its overwhelming wealth and endlessness, is inaccessible unless we free ourselves from the limitations of our own restricted training.

EPILOGUE

THIS FIRST ATTEMPT at a musical archaeology has unveiled a motley picture of constancy and variation. In China and India, changes since antiquity appear to be insignificant. On the other hand, we have found Japanese scales in Java, Egypt, and Greece; Hellenic theory in Arabian countries and medieval Europe; Indian conceptions in Egypt and Morocco. Musical provinces stand out with satisfactory clearness: the Far Eastern district and the Indian district, overlapping in Southeast Asia; the Western Orient; Greece. But all of them, including Greece, belong to the vast Oriental commonwealth in which music was firmly established on a subtle art of melody, on conjunct or disjunct tetrachords and pentachords, on modal inversions, and on cosmological connotations.

Non-Mediterranean Europe, on the contrary, had no connection with the cultivated musical styles of the East. Until far into the Middle Ages, it remained in a primitive musical layer that we can trace to the northern parts of both Asia and America and, in the south, to Melanesia and Africa.

The European chains of thirds brought our Western music into other ways than those of the fourth-based music of the East. They barred the development of actual melody in the Oriental sense and led instead to the typical Western melody, which has essentially been harmony broken up and cemented with passing notes. They took the shape of major and minor and eventually found the way to simultaneous harmony and, as a consequence, to equal temperament.

The global trend of Western civilization has not spared music. European and American compositions have been exported wholesale; the Imperial Academy of Music in Tokyo teaches Beethoven and Chopin; Egyptian colleges have jazz bands; and even native music, in Turkey, China, Japan, has recently been influenced by Europe.

But the West, too, is questioning the validity of its latest heritage. The regular tension and relaxation in harmonic functions have been abandoned; consonance and dissonance are no longer what they were a generation ago; and most rules of harmony have been consigned to the rubbish pile. This revolution implies a renovation of our musical language, which has been modeled to fit the needs of harmony.

Some composers write solo pieces without any accompaniment, and others, tired of the ceaseless one-two-three-four that we take for rhythm, are developing a new sense of periodicity. Indeed, there is opposition against the very limitation to twelve semitones and the antimusical rigidity of our equal temperament; some composers have endeavored to write in quarter tones and to discuss the possibilities of other microtones.

In doing so, they mostly take Oriental music as a precedent. This is unjust; the East has never had such scales and is not responsible for these attempts any more than Greek tragedy should be held answerable for its would-be children, the opera of the Florentine *Camerata* and Richard Wagner's *Musikdrama*.

Yet this acknowledgment is one of many symptoms that the orbit of Western music has passed beyond the point furthest from Oriental music and in its cyclic course is again approaching regions we thought we had left for good. With the illusion of ever-flowing progress broken, our musicians have begun to realize that once more they themselves are engaged in the ceaseless battle for melody and rhythm that their ancestors fought for the rise of music in Asia and Europe, in the East and the West.

INDEX